2/06

Sandra Day O'Connor

FRONTISPIECE:

Supreme Court Associate Justice Sandra Day O'Connor.

Photographed by Richard Strauss, Smithsonian Institution.

Sandra Day O'Connor

JUSTICE IN THE BALANCE

Ann Carey McFeatters

UNIVERSITY OF NEW MEXICO PRESS | ALBUQUERQUE

Printed in the United States of America
10 09 08 07 06 05 1 2 3 4 5 6

LIBRARY OF CONGRESS CATALOGING-IN-PUBLICATION DATA

McFeatters, Ann Carey, 1944–
Sandra Day O'Connor : justice in the balance / Ann Carey McFeatters.
p. cm. — (Women's biography series)
Includes bibliographical references and index.
ISBN-13: 978-0-8263-3218-9 (pbk. : alk. paper)
ISBN-10: 0-8263-3218-8 (pbk. : alk. paper)
1. O'Connor, Sandra Day, 1930– 2. Women judges—United States—Biography.
3. Judges—United States—Biography. I. Title. II. Series.
KF8745.025(O'Connor...) M +
347.73'2634—dc22

2005024586

Design and layout: Melissa Tandysh

A volume in the WOMEN'S BIOGRAPHY series

Also available:

Pat Schroeder: A Woman of the House by Joan A. Lowy

SERIES EDITORS: Krisitie Millier, Melanie S. Gustafson, and Pamela Reeves

To my wonderful parents, Norman and Mildred Carey,

Who taught their children what is best in life

Contents

CHAPTER ONE

The Right Woman at the Right Time

> We don't accomplish anything in this world alone . . . and whatever happens is the result of the whole tapestry of one's life and all the weavings of individual threads from one to another that creates something.
>
> —Sandra Day O'Connor

When fifty-one-year-old Sandra Day O'Connor was summoned to a secret meeting in a Washington hotel on June 30, 1981, to meet with Attorney General William French Smith, White House counsel Fred Fielding, and White House aides Edwin Meese, James Baker, and Michael Deaver on a possible nomination to the Supreme Court, she went as much out of curiosity as from any sense that the meeting would change her life. She went because she was intrigued with Ronald Reagan, who was still recuperating from an assassination attempt by young John Hinckley, and with his plans to change the country. She had read that candidate Reagan had promised that if he were elected president, he vowed to put a woman on the highest court in the land. But even as she had heard that she was on the list, she did not think she had a serious shot at the job. And just thinking about it, she was washed in waves of conflicting emotions. Being considered to be the first woman in history nominated to the Supreme Court after 191 years and 101 male justices was daunting. Exciting, but daunting. She wasn't at all certain she wanted the job, even if it were offered.

As she flew to Washington, she grew more apprehensive. Was this what she really wanted? To have her life examined? To put her cherished family in the spotlight? To move away from her beloved Arizona to the strange city of Washington far away from everything she loved?

"I was very happy where I was," she said later, much later, in a speech to a group of students. "I had a very full life and a happy one. It wasn't something I aspired to. Everything was fine. Everything was good. I had a good life. [Being on the Supreme Court] is such a great responsibility. It's great to be the first, but you don't want to be the last. I thought if I didn't do it well, I wouldn't enhance the opportunities of others."

She quickly understood, on that long, anxious flight to Washington, that her most important meeting was with the attorney general. As she and Smith talked, during what she would later describe as a rambling discussion, she found herself relaxing, her natural confidence returning as her self-assurance reasserted itself. She thought at one point that the attorney general was asking her questions as if she was, in fact, a serious candidate. The next day he startled her by saying that the president wanted to meet with her and that she should go right away to the White House. She had a problem. She didn't know Washington, and she had never been to the White House. She didn't even know how to get to the White House. Smith said he would arrange for his secretary to pick her up in a green Chevrolet. "And I stood on the sidewalk, waiting to be driven to the White House. And we made our way to the White House. That was pretty exciting."

At 10 A.M. on July 1, Reagan's chief of staff, Jim Baker, ushered her into the Oval Office, and she stared around the imposing room with awe. It was, she thought, a beautiful room, and she especially loved the windows looking out to the gardens. She shook Reagan's hand, thinking that he seemed remarkably vibrant for a man who had almost been killed mere weeks before. They sat in the wing chairs in front of the fireplace where presidents traditionally greet heads of state. Then they walked around the Rose Garden. It was, she quickly realized, the most important interview of her life. She was awed at being in the White House and at first felt shy. Reagan seemed as physically muscular and forceful as ever, with that legendary telegenic charm that, in person, came across as hesitancy, even his own form of shyness. The two westerners gradually warmed up to each other and in the space of forty-five minutes, O'Connor and Reagan discovered they had a lot in common because of their love of horses and ranch life. She reminded him that they had met when he was governor of California ten years before he became president and that they had talked about ways he was considering to rein in state spending. Mainly, O'Connor and Reagan chatted about the West and people they knew in common. "We talked about ranching and fence-mending and cattle. He was a westerner, and I think he was sort of intrigued with the fact that that was my background. We didn't really have much of a discussion about issues. I think he knew his advisers had read my opinions," she recalled years later.

Perhaps surprisingly, since this would be one of the most important appointments he would make in office—he called it the president's most "awesome" appointment power—Reagan asked her almost no tough questions. He had left the details to others—whom did she feel closest to philosophically on the Court? How did she feel about the exclusionary rule (it says evidence that is obtained unconstitutionally is inadmissible in court)? And should the Court take into consideration practical implications of its decisions? Reagan's aides told the president they felt she had answered those key questions satisfactorily although they didn't reveal what she said. Reagan's image guru, Michael Deaver, later said that Reagan had an instinctive feeling that O'Connor was right for the job even though he had not discussed the issues with her. "It's like buying a car," Deaver said. In a few minutes, the "short list" of potential nominees went from twenty-five to one. O'Connor's support from Arizona's two conservative senators, Barry Goldwater, a Republican, and Dennis DeConcini, a Democrat, was also helpful.

Reagan knew that she wouldn't be meeting with him unless his aides had decided she shared his overall judicial philosophy of restraint and deference to the legislative branch in making law. In short, she wouldn't be what he loathed: an activist judge. Having been assured of that, Reagan was satisfied to get her measure as another human being. He did ask her for her personal opinion about abortion. She assured him that it was "personally repugnant" to her. That satisfied the president, who knew he would take a beating from his anti-abortion supporters if she seemed to be at all sympathetic to abortion. Ultimately, Reagan wanted to size her up to decide whether he would be comfortable defending her nomination. And she charmed him. Humble yet confident, funny and warm, she came across to him as a real person, a westerner who made him feel she could accomplish whatever she set out to do. And, as a rancher himself—who would spend almost a year of his presidency riding horses and cutting brush on his place in California—he was intrigued that she had grown up on the Lazy B, a 250-square-mile ranch straddling the Arizona–New Mexico border, and, like him, knew how to handle a branding iron.

On the airplane back to Arizona that afternoon, O'Connor recalled later looking out the plane window and thinking, "what a remarkable visit it had been and how amazing it had been to be in the White House. And I said to myself, 'thank goodness, I don't have to do that job,'" being president and setting policy for the entire United States.

Clearly delighted with his choice, Reagan telephoned O'Connor in her Phoenix court chambers on July 6, 1981, and said, "Sandra, I'd like to announce your nomination to the Court tomorrow. Is that all right with you?" O'Connor, who was on the phone with an old friend—Chief Justice Warren Burger—had to put the justice on hold to take the call from the president. Her pulse pounding, she was wracked with concerns. "I didn't know if it was or not" all right with her, she later said. In a dazed state, she said, "Yes, Mr. President."

He told her he thought it would be a good idea to send someone out to help with the press. She wasn't certain that was necessary, but it proved vital. In the weeks ahead, she would be deluged with requests for interviews. She could go nowhere without eager journalists trying to waylay her and get a good quote. News footage at the time shows her driving out of her driveway and telling a phalanx of camera crews in her slow, deliberative way, "I don't think this is a very good time for an interview."

When Reagan introduced his nominee to the world, he said, "I had the pleasure of meeting with Mrs. O'Connor last week, and I can report to you that she not only has a long and brilliant record as a legislator and jurist, but she also impressed me as a thoughtful, capable woman whose judicial temperament is highly appropriate for the Court. After listening to her and examining her whole record in public life, I am fully satisfied that her appointment is consistent with the principles enunciated in our party platform this past year. Judge O'Connor, in my view, will bring new luster and new strength to the Supreme Court, and I feel certain that her term upon the bench will be one of the proudest legacies of my [presidency]."

Talking with Katie Couric of NBC's *Today Show* in January 2002, O'Connor admitted that she had been scared. To go down in history as the first woman in history to sit on the Supreme Court was unnerving. But she was less worried about being the first than she was about being competent and doing a good job. "I was concerned about whether I could do the job well enough to deserve saying yes," she told Couric, who later admitted she was awed by O'Connor and taken aback that a woman who would become perhaps the most influential woman in America wasn't sure she was up to the task.

In 2000, in an interview with Cardozo Law School constitutional law professor David Rudenstine, she said, "When I was nominated in 1981, and took the position, it was incredible to see doors opening for women around the world on courts and for other positions, too. And law schools became more open. More young women started attending law school. It's now half and half, at least, if not more. My concern was whether I could do the job of a justice well enough to convince the nation that my appointment was the right move. If I stumbled badly in doing the job, I think it would have made life more difficult for women. And that was a great concern of mine and still is."

O'Connor came to Reagan's attention as no political novice. She was unique among many judges for the route she had taken to the bench. She was a tough, seasoned Arizona legislator—the first woman majority leader of a U.S. state legislature. Before she was named as a judge in the Arizona State Court of Appeals, O'Connor had been through the internecine wars of state politics. She knew that her position on abortion would be debated incessantly for weeks, if not months. Even—if she got the job—for years. She knew that old enemies, including Carolyn Gerster, a doctor from Scottsdale, Arizona, and a vehement anti-abortion activist who considered O'Connor a closet abortion supporter, would try to discredit her. She knew that the fact that she was the first woman ever to be nominated for the highest court in the land would be both in her favor and held, albeit secretly, against her. She knew, above all, it could be a titanic battle, one that would take a lot of her energy to win, and that much of the battle would be not just about her judicial temperament and credentials but also about her often vague views on sensitive issues.

The men in the White House—all the top players in the first Reagan term were men—were aware of these facts as well as of potential problems that she could not yet expect. They knew that, even within the White House, there were forces at work against her, men who considered themselves politically savvy but weren't sure that the country was ready for a woman justice or that an obscure jurist from Arizona was the right woman to test the case. In 1978 O'Connor had said no to state Republican leaders who wanted her to run for governor against Bruce Babbitt, a Democrat who was a friend of hers. She had decided then that she wasn't ready for all-out political war. But now she would be fighting just as hard in a national arena. Some presidential aides were not convinced she was tough enough to be an associate justice on the Supreme Court, deciding cases about the death penalty, abortion, affirmative action, who lives and who dies.

The men in the White House knew that even though Reagan liked O'Connor personally and said after forty-five minutes with her that she was the right woman at the right time, there would be hell to pay from Reagan's right-of-center constituency. The Reverend Jerry Falwell's newly powerful Moral Majority would charge that Reagan had betrayed the movement in selecting someone they saw as a supporter of abortion and of the Equal Rights Amendment, both anathema to Falwell and his supporters. Even a personal appeal from Reagan would not keep Falwell from publicly criticizing the choice.

What tipped the scales in O'Connor's favor was not her relatively short tenure on the Arizona bench, meaning she did not have the paper trail of some more seasoned jurists, but her gender. Reagan's promise, made in Los Angeles in October 1980, when he was faltering in the polls and the election was less than a month away, that he would be the first president to nominate a woman to the Supreme Court, had excited many women. Jimmy Carter, president for just four years, never had the chance to nominate anyone to the Court. Republican Potter Stewart, who was considered the most likely to retire, wasn't willing to let himself be replaced by what surely would have been a more liberal justice if Carter had had his way. Carter in the campaign had suggested that if elected president, Reagan might run roughshod over the forces that had prevented war with the Soviet Union and get the country into full-scale war, possibly even a nuclear war. To soften his image, Reagan had courted the women's vote, where he was weak, by pledging to name the first woman to the Court.

It was an exciting prospect for many women. Eleanor Smeal, then president of the National Organization for Women, who held no brief for conservatives, said that a woman on the Supreme Court would be a significant victory for the women's movement. Feminists now recall that until the O'Connor nomination, Reagan had an abysmal record of appointing women—only 45 of the administration's top 450 positions were held by women in the first year of the Reagan presidency. A senior administration official told *Time* magazine that in political terms, the appointment of O'Connor was worth naming women as "25 assistant secretaries, maybe more." Iris Mitgang, then head of the National Women's Political Caucus, exulted, "This nomination will be a major step toward equal justice in our land."

But even then there was some concern in the White House about upsetting the careful balance on the Supreme Court. Would the men accept her? A key factor would be Stewart's opinion. When Stewart tipped the White House on April 21 that he intended to resign, Reagan reminded his staff of his promise to nominate a woman. The relief in the White House was palpable when O'Connor passed muster with Stewart, whose position she would be taking. He had spent twenty-three years on the Court, knowing it as well as anyone then sitting. Even though he had never met her, he had asked others about her—"many sources," he said. "Everything I know about Judge O'Connor is favorable—not only good, but very good." He added, "Her professional competence is of the highest quality, and her character is very, very good." Her acceptance by the all-male bench wouldn't be a problem, he predicted, because she "is truly qualified to be there." She would, however, have a difficult learning curve, as would any new justice. "For anyone coming onto the Supreme Court, it is not easy. She is intelligent, and the more intelligent you are, the harder you have to work when you get there."

Nevertheless, the most influential officials in the Reagan administration, including political advisor Lyn Nofziger, keeper-of-the-Reagan-image Michael Deaver, Attorney General William French Smith, and the powerful triumvirate—Jim Baker, Ed Meese, Don Regan—were concerned that O'Connor's relatively brief eighteen months as an Arizona appeals court judge didn't shed much light on her attitude about the big controversies looming before the Court. While she was thoughtful and careful to cite precedent, her twenty-nine published opinions never dealt with abortion, desegregation of schools, prayer in schools, the death penalty, or the constitutional rights of criminal defendants—all issues on which Reagan and his major conservative backers had strong opinions. And she steered clear of long, convoluted opinions that went up the mountain and down again. She wrote short opinions, and she wrote clearly.

Stuart Taylor Jr., a legal specialist writing in the *New York Times* at the time of O'Connor's nomination, observed, "It appears to be far too early to determine whether the ideologically divided Court will become more conservative or more liberal if Judge O'Connor fills the vacancy created by the retirement of Justice Potter Stewart, who has been viewed as a moderate leaning to the conservative side of the Court's delicate philosophical balance."

While a member of the Arizona Senate, O'Connor at first advocated passage of the Equal Rights Amendment and then supported a less sweeping provision. She opposed a measure that would have outlawed abortions in some state facilities. But to call her either a supporter or an opponent of the Equal Rights Amendment or abortion on the basis of those decisions would be unfair. The White House defended her position, saying there was no record of a claimed 1970 vote that could have been construed to favor legalizing abortion in certain circumstances and that a 1973 vote permitting Arizona state agencies to participate in family planning said nothing about abortion. Further, the White House said, O'Connor sponsored a 1973 bill that became law and gave hospitals and doctors the right not to participate in abortion procedures. She voted against a bill forbidding abortions at a university hospital, said the White House, because it was added to a measure that permitted the university to issue bonds to build sports facilities, and the Arizona Constitution forbids legislation dealing with unrelated topics. As for the proposed Equal Rights Amendment, which never passed the required number of states and thus never became part of the Constitution, White House aides off the record explained that Reagan himself had once supported it before changing his position. It was all vague enough, however, that feminist groups supported O'Connor's nomination, convinced she favored the proposed amendment.

Ultimately, O'Connor's appeal to the Reagan White House was exactly that she was not known as a doctrinaire conservative, "not an ideologue [but] a perfectionist rooted in the law," in the words of Alfredo Gutierrez, a Democrat who succeeded O'Connor as majority leader in the Arizona Senate. While she would cause raised eyebrows at both extremes of political opinion, she simply had not written enough to give either side the ammunition needed to shoot down her nomination. She was definitely from the conservative wing of the Arizona Republican Party, but nothing in her judicial opinions was controversial enough to derail her—or cause the White House embarrassment.

And, they found out, in law school she had briefly dated Justice William Rehnquist, a fellow Arizonian who would later become chief justice. Rehnquist, happy in a devoted marriage, was thrilled with Reagan's consideration of O'Connor. Repeatedly, he assured White House aides she would be a good choice, a fine justice. Rehnquist, chosen by Richard Nixon in 1971 to fill an associate justice seat on the Supreme Court, had been a little-known assistant attorney general when he was tapped, a last-minute substitute for controversial southerner Richard Poff, who pulled back his name because he didn't want his son to find out at that point that he was adopted.

Just before Rehnquist was nominated, the first White House to have debated seriously naming a woman was the Nixon White House. John Dean, counsel to Nixon, says that the woman under consideration was Mildred Lille, a conservative California appellate jurist who was touted by Ronald Reagan, then governor of California. The discussion, which went on for weeks, did not go well. Attorney General John Mitchell, Dean alleges, told Nixon, "If you feel [you need to] go with a woman, I've mixed emotions about that." Dean, in his 2002 book *The Rehnquist Choice*, quotes Nixon as saying, "I know. I know. Let me tell you so that we have a total understanding on this. I don't think a woman should be in any government job whatever. I mean, I really don't. The reason why I do is mainly because they are erratic. And emotional. Men are erratic and emotional too, but the point is, a woman is more likely to be."

Lille's name kept coming up and eventually Mitchell was pushing her even as Nixon and his aides dropped false hints, to mislead the press, that Senator Robert Byrd, a Democrat from West Virginia, was a contender for the Court vacancy. For one thing, Nixon and his aides liked Lille's personality and her conservative opinions even though she was a Democrat. She's not "one of these frigid bitches, you know," Mitchell said, according to Dean. Nixon also liked the idea of getting the "women's lib" vote, and Senator George McGovern, a Democrat from South Dakota, who was going to run against him, was pledging to put a woman on the Supreme Court. Finally, Nixon said, his wife, Pat, and two daughters, Tricia and Julie, were telling him to name a woman. Lille was gray-haired, funny, warm, articulate, hard-working, handsome, personable, tough, and fair-minded—a judge out of central casting. She also was Catholic, and her husband was a respected businessman, although the *New York Times* said he had been sued twenty-two times in ten years for nonpayment of debts. Rehnquist was asked to help "vet" her, checking her credentials and background for a possible Court nomination. When Rehnquist was asked by a friend if he might be nominated, Rehnquist said, off the record, that he would not be nominated because he wasn't from the South, wasn't a woman, and wasn't mediocre.

Lille's potential nomination was shot down by the American Bar Association's rejection of her as not qualified. Nixon ordered his staff to leak to the press the ABA committee's sexist reasoning that even though she was probably as good a woman judge as possible to be considered, she still was not qualified for the Supreme Court.

With Senator Howard Baker, a Tennessee Republican, not sure he wanted the job, Nixon's attention turned to Rehnquist—literally hours, says Dean, before Nixon made the announcement that Rehnquist, the president's lawyer's lawyer at the Justice Department, was his choice for a lifetime tenure on the Supreme Court. Dean recalls, "I'm confident that Rehnquist had no warning prior to October 21 that he was even under consideration." In effect, Rehnquist, who would later become chief justice, was never properly vetted for the job despite his obvious brilliance as a legal scholar.

Dean insists that Nixon had once dismissed Rehnquist as a "clown" but went with him because he was a "rock-solid" conservative (who would reflect Nixon's beliefs in Court decisions for thirty years). Dean also argues that Rehnquist was confirmed with little opposition only because the White House was able to have sealed unfavorable Justice Department documents indicating that Rehnquist supported snatching American drug dealers off foreign streets to bring them home for trial and showing an unsympathetic stand on other issues involving the rights of the accused. Rehnquist's tenure on the Supreme Court would become one of the most conservative in U.S. history. In 1986, Reagan, after briefly considering Sandra Day O'Connor for the job but deciding she had too little experience, would nominate Rehnquist as chief justice.

Rehnquist's selection by Nixon was a fateful choice for O'Connor. It is probably Rehnquist as much as anyone besides Reagan and her old friend Barry Goldwater who was responsible for O'Connor's nomination to the nation's highest court. After Reagan was elected in 1980, his transition team in charge of selecting officials to run the Department of Justice had considered O'Connor briefly as a possibility to run the civil division. An alumna of Stanford University, where she had been in the top ten, she had maintained strong ties with other graduates, including Rehnquist, then the Court's most conservative member and Stanford's most prestigious alumnus. The Department of Justice team checked her out with Arizona lawyers who almost to a person described her as clear, no-nonsense, brief, to the point, and meticulous about legal detail. When Stanford Law School dean Charles Meyers and Reagan's antitrust chief William Baxter joined Rehnquist in saying that she would be an excellent candidate for the highest bench in the land, her place on the list of twenty-five names as possible candidates was assured. On that initial list, according to Reagan aides, were about twelve women. Reagan's top staff wasn't particularly enthusiastic about any of them although they reluctantly agreed with the president that after promising to name a woman, he would be skewered if he picked a doctrinaire conservative male. According to top aides who later briefed reporters, one factor was future vacancies on the Court. The thinking was that with such liberals as Thurgood Marshall, then 73, and William Brennan, 75, becoming more interested in retiring if they could be assured Reagan wouldn't appoint knee-jerk conservatives to replace them, a solidly respected woman might convince them to go sooner rather than later. Indeed, the opponents of Reagan's choice of O'Connor knew that while they might not block her, Reagan would think seriously of their concerns the next time he had a vacancy to fill.

Less than a week before Reagan made his decision, three other women besides O'Connor were under consideration. They were later identified by the *New York Times*: Amalya Kearse, then forty-four, a widely respected black woman on the Second Circuit Court of Appeals in New York; Cornelia Kennedy, fifty-seven, who was on the Sixth Circuit Court of Appeals in Cincinnati, appointed by Carter; and Mary Coleman, sixty-six, who was chief justice of the Michigan Supreme Court. O'Connor was at the top of the "female" list. Department of Justice lawyers went to Phoenix, to O'Connor's sprawling Paradise Valley home, to interview her. One of those on the interview team was Kenneth Starr, who would become solicitor general and then the independent counsel who investigated President Bill Clinton in the case for impeachment. Starr reported back to the White House, according to the *New York Times*, that O'Connor was the right age, had the right philosophy, the right combination of experience, the right political affiliation, and the right backing. Besides, he said, he really liked her. After hours of talks about federal-state relations, she fixed everybody iced tea and a lunch of salmon salad.

When Reagan stepped into the White House briefing room on July 7, 1981, to announce his decision to nominate O'Connor, he said, "She is truly a person for all seasons, possessing those unique qualities of temperament, fairness, intellectual capacity and devotion to the public good which have characterized the 101 'brethren' who have preceded her." He did not name her because she is a woman, he insisted, because that would be unfair to everyone. He nominated her because of her competence, he said. He did not reveal that he was naming her in part because she was considered likely to shift the Court to the right and that it was his profound hope to shift it more solidly by future appointments. July 7, said Reagan, was "a happy day for me and, I hope, for my country."

He told Republicans at a fundraiser that night that O'Connor seemed to him to be a "thoughtful and capable woman whose judicial temperament is highly appropriate for the Court." And, he assured the group, her principles came right out of the Republican Party platform. Deaver, who viewed it as his job to keep the president in line with actions that would polish his image as an avuncular and irreproachable president, told reporters that Reagan most liked O'Connor's "moderate" approach and the fact that she wasn't an "activist" judge. Reagan, said Deaver, trusted his instincts about O'Connor. And Rehnquist's unqualified endorsement was significant. Rehnquist said in his 2001 book *The Supreme Court* (dedicated to his wife, Nan, after her death) that he was decidedly pleased with Reagan's choice. "Sandra and I were classmates in law school and my late wife, Nan, and Sandra's husband, John, were undergraduate classmates there. We go back a long time, and I was overjoyed at her appointment to the Supreme Court."

Stunningly, perhaps, the White House did not even ask the Federal Bureau of Investigation and the American Bar Association to vet O'Connor until after Reagan asked her to be the nominee and announced his decision. If the FBI or the ABA had found anything in her past to discredit her, it would have been an enormous embarrassment to the White House and ruinous to her. Attorney General Smith, who had looked at her background, told reporters that her record on the bench was "quite satisfactory," even though she had dealt with almost no constitutional issues, the life-or-death decisions that now would become her daily fare on the Court. Reagan simply trusted his instincts in naming her to leave large "footprints on the sands of time," as Reagan said, quoting Henry W. Longfellow.

The firestorm that hit the nation was enormous. As anticipated in the White House, the "left" loved O'Connor, despite her conservative, cloth-coat-Republican credentials. The "right" immediately tried to demonize her, despite those same conservative credentials (she cochaired the Arizona effort to reelect Richard Nixon in 1972) because of her murky and, to them, suspect opinions on abortion and the proposed Equal Rights Amendment. Dr. J. C. Willkie, then president of the two-million-member National Right to Life Committee, publicly asked Reagan to withdraw her nomination, insisting she was "pro-abortion." The White House logged 263 calls supporting O'Connor's nomination and 2,573 opposing her. "We've been betrayed," said one conservative after another on one talk show after another. Senator Jesse Helms, a right-wing Republican from North Carolina, called Reagan to tell him that opposition to O'Connor was coming from "people who have been down in the trenches for you since day one." A leading Democrat in Arizona told reporters who called, off the record, that O'Connor was being targeted by conservatives because "she's Junior League" and not "out of the knee-jerk mold." Her longtime friend Sharon Rockefeller, wife of then West Virginia Governor Jay Rockefeller, a Democrat, told the *New York Times*, "She has an open mind when it comes to her conservatism. I can't conceive of her closing off her mind to anything." Liberals touted her leadership on publicly opening meetings in Arizona, her commitment to better conditions in mental institutions, dedication to reforming probate court processes in the state, her work to promote selection of Superior Court judges on the basis of merit rather than politics, and her work getting the concept of no-fault divorce approved. In Arizona she was remembered as a painstakingly thorough craftsman when it came to drafting legislation. When called on to rate her job as an appellate court judge after a year on the job, 90 percent of the Arizona bar recommended she stay on. Senator Barry Goldwater, dean of conservatives in the Senate who had made an ill-fated bid for the presidency in 1964, became her most ardent defender. When Jerry Falwell, leader of the Moral Majority, continued to voice his opposition to O'Connor despite Reagan's appeal that he support her, Goldwater was quoted as saying that "every good Christian ought to kick Falwell right in the ass." Goldwater continued to boom out, "I don't like getting kicked around by people who call themselves conservatives on a non-conservative matter. It is a question of who is best for the Court. If there is going to be a fight in the Senate, you are going to find 'Old Goldy' fighting like hell."

The summer of 1981 was a long, difficult one for Sandra Day O'Connor, who knew that her entire life was about to change and would never be the same. The word had come down that she would go before the Senate Judiciary Committee for three days of confirmation hearings in September. That meant she had to sandwich in courtesy calls to members of Congress, particularly the eighteen members of the committee, between the August recess and a busy Hill schedule. She had to prepare to go on the Court for its session beginning the first Monday in October but she had to avoid looking overeager or assuming she would be confirmed. As a wife and mother of three sons, albeit grown, she also had to prepare for a physical move to Washington, but again, unostentatiously. And she had to study as intensively as she had in law school to be well briefed for what probably would be highly contentious confirmation hearings. Always assiduous about doing her homework, no matter what the situation, she had to come across as knowledgeable but not domineering, pleasant but tough enough, competent but friendly. And all during the summer was a drumbeat of opposition coming from the right-of-center Republicans. Three in particular, Senators Charles Grassley of Iowa, James East of North Carolina, and Jeremiah Denton of

Alabama, were making no secret of the fact that they intended to come down hard on O'Connor's positions on abortion and the Equal Rights Amendment. Anti-abortion groups such as the national Pro-Life Political Action Committee, the National Right to Life Committee, and the International Council of Christian Churches kept up a barrage of opposition. Conservative political activist Richard Viguerie began a publication called "The O'Connor Report" to chronicle and stir up unrest over her nomination.

But in her corner was courtly old Strom Thurmond, the senior Republican senator from South Carolina who was chairman of the Senate Judiciary Committee. This was the same senator who had once skewered Associate Justice Abe Fortas during confirmation hearings on Fortas's nomination to be chief justice when Fortas respectfully refused to comment definitively on cases before the Court. Now Thurmond deferentially advised O'Connor that she didn't have to answer his questions about pending or past cases if she was worried about prejudicing future decisions. It didn't hurt that Thurmond's wife, Nancy, a lawyer, planned to welcome O'Connor to Washington with an elaborate tea. Also backing her, in an important display of bipartisan approval, was Arizona's Democratic governor, Bruce Babbitt, who would give her a warm endorsement. House Speaker Tip O'Neill, the Democrat's Democrat, called O'Connor's selection the best decision Reagan had made as president. And Barbara Jordan, a Democrat and former congresswoman from Texas, gave her unqualified approval. "I congratulate the president," she said in her marvelously stentorian voice. "The Supreme Court was the last bastion of the male, a stale dark room that needed to be cracked open. I don't know the lady, but if she's a good lawyer and believes in the Constitution, she'll be all right."

O'Connor received another important vote of confidence from the American Bar Association committee reviewing her credentials. After turning down Mildred Lille just a decade before with the scurrilous implication that no woman was ready for the Court, the committee told the Senate Judiciary Committee on September 8 that O'Connor "has the professional qualifications required of an Associate Justice of the Supreme Court of the United States" even though she had not had much experience with constitutional issues. On judicial temperament and integrity, the ABA's Standing Committee on Federal Judiciary's fourteen members unanimously concluded that O'Connor "meets the highest standards." On a category called professional competence, the committee said that she didn't have as extensive or as challenging experience as other possible candidates. Her opinions to date, the committee said, usually did not deal with elaborate legal analysis or complex social issues found in Supreme Court decisions. But overall she passed muster for the committee, which said it particularly liked her competently written opinions and her "clear and logical" writing style.

When O'Connor was called to answer questions before the committee, she was quiet, calm, and confident but, as expected, refused to say how she would rule in abortion cases certain to confront her on the Court. Leaders of the anti-abortion movement said that her nomination should be rejected because she would not promise to vote to overrule the 1973 Supreme Court decision, *Roe v. Wade*, that legalized abortion. Senator Denton said that abortion was even more fundamental than the issue of slavery in the nineteenth century. In a rare break from his conservative colleagues, Thurmond admonished Denton, saying, "We're really not having a hearing on abortion. We're having a hearing on the fitness of the lady." As witness after witness testified in favor of O'Connor, including speakers for the American Bar Association, the National Bar Association, the National Women's Political Caucus, the National Organization for Women, and the National Association of Women Judges, anti-abortion witnesses complained that the hearing was "stacked" in O'Connor's favor. That appeared to be true when Thurmond abandoned all pretense of neutrality as he concluded the three days of hearings by telling her that she would make "an outstanding Associate Justice of the Supreme Court."

When the committee voted on O'Connor's nomination, the result was not surprising, given how well the hearings had gone for her and in the absence of any Senate lion such as Senator Jesse Helms willing to lead the opposition against her. Seventeen of the eighteen members of the committee voted for her; Jeremiah Denton voted "present" because of her refusal to commit herself on how she might vote on abortion cases, although he said O'Connor was "a fine lady" and "a distinguished jurist." Senators East and Grassley said they were displeased with her refusal to talk about abortion but had decided they liked her overall judicial approach. East gave Reagan the benefit of the doubt and said he supposed the president knew some things about O'Connor that he didn't. East said he had concluded, "This is a conservative woman of conservative instincts." That the issue of abortion had played such a role in her hearings dismayed liberal members of the committee, including Senators Howard Metzenbaum, an Ohio Democrat, and Patrick Leahy, a Vermont Democrat, who would one day become chairman of the committee. Leahy said, "An agreement to vote a certain way can never be the price to be paid for confirmation by the United States Senate." Such a movement would subvert the Constitution and destroy the independence and integrity of the federal court system, he said.

By the time the Senate voted in September 1981 to confirm O'Connor as the 102nd justice, the first woman ever to sit on the Supreme Court, a seat that would be hers for lifetime if she wanted it, there was little suspense. Ninety-nine members voted for her, a record for Supreme Court nominees. (Senator Max Baucus, a Democrat from Montana, was absent.) Afterward, she stood in triumph on the Capitol steps between her mentor, Senator Barry Goldwater, and Vice President George Bush. Twenty-three years later, asked why she thought she had been confirmed by a unanimous vote after a summer of controversy, she said, "I think they were all a little hesitant about voting 'no'" on the first woman nominated to the high court.

On September 25, 1981, more than four hundred people, including her parents, Harry and Ada Mae Day; her husband, John Jay O'Connor; and her three sons, Scott, Brian, and Jay, were wedged into the crowded, ornate courtroom as, at 2:04 P.M., the doors swung open and President Reagan and Sandra Day O'Connor entered from separate doors. Placing her hand on a family Bible, she was sworn in by Chief Justice Warren E. Burger, repeating the oath of her new office: "I, Sandra Day O'Connor, do solemnly swear that I will support and defend the Constitution of the United States against all enemies, foreign and domestic; that I will bear true faith and allegiance to the same; that

I take this obligation feely, without any mental reservation or purpose of evasion; and that I will well and faithfully discharge the duties of the office on which I am about to enter. So help me God." The fifty-one-year-old woman who twenty-nine years before had been refused a job at every law firm she applied to then put on the black judicial robe she had brought with her from her service on the Arizona appeals court and took her place on the bench, the seat reserved for the newest member, the first woman in history to sit there. The investiture had taken barely ten minutes, but it changed history. The Court would not convene for work until the first Monday in October, but that didn't matter. The whole nation was excited. At a session for photographers following the brief ceremony, Burger tried awkwardly to deal with the moment and quipped, "You've never seen me with a better-looking justice, have you?"

Legal scholars scrambled to figure out where to place her on the spectrum of conservatives, moderates, and liberals. Ultimately, most said, they weren't certain. They rated her a perfectionist, scholarly without being brilliant, dependable, clear, concise, dogged, a workaholic. But ultimately, they said, she would be pragmatic, not doctrinaire. Rehnquist, they said, should not count on her to be his philosophical clone. They would not, most scholars surmised, be the Arizona Twins as Justices Warren Burger and Harry Blackmun had once been called the Minnesota Twins, voting in tandem before Blackmun took a separate, more liberal path. Rehnquist, in *The Supreme Court*, said that geography, as a factor in naming justices, vitally important when the nation was young, was no longer a major issue. "This sort of geographic qualification in Supreme Court appointments has long since disappeared, the last logical reason for it having gone out with the repeal of the circuit-riding duties of the Supreme Court justices more than a century ago. Today it could be said that the Supreme Court has two justices from Arizona—Justice O'Connor and me—although my pedigree is doubtful; my commission as associate justice showed me as being from Arizona, but my commission as chief justice shows me as being from Virginia, where I have lived for the last thirty-two years."

O'Connor was joining a Court that had two solid liberals, Brennan and Thurgood Marshall; two staunch conservatives, Rehnquist and Chief

Justice Burger; and four members who were hard to predict: Blackmun, Lewis F. Powell Jr., John Paul Stevens, and Byron White. The Court was dignified, austere, and surprisingly liberal considering Richard Nixon had appointed four members and Gerald Ford had appointed one. It had rejected Nixon's claim of executive privilege for the secret tapes during the Watergate scandal, leading to his resignation. It had upheld school integration cases. It had insisted on the rights of the accused and the convicted. And now the eight justices would have a new distinction: the first woman to sit with them as an equal. Would she make a difference, as a woman and as a jurist? Would she be true to her conservative roots or, with the freedom of lifelong tenure, would she branch out? Would she become a woman that women of all political persuasions could relate to and admire or would she sink into the bland anonymity of the Court, bound by centuries of tradition to tamp down her own personality and become a faceless justice? Many thought that probably O'Connor herself didn't yet know where she would come down on some of the issues that would affect the daily lives of many Americans. Yale law professor Paul Gewirtz told *Time* magazine, "It's not only that we don't know what her views are on some issues. She probably doesn't know what her views are either. She hasn't been put to the test of figuring them out."

Ed Magnuson, writing in the *New York Times*, said at the time of her nomination, "America waits to see what place in legal history will be carved out by this daunting daughter of Arizona pioneers." A true daughter of the so-called Sagebrush Rebellion—the anger of many westerners that they wanted to be left alone by the federal government—O'Connor was going to be confronted head-on with challenges that would force her to choose between states' rights and federal laws. She would be ruling on abortion, school prayer, the death penalty, prison conditions, parental rights—a gamut of concerns that directly affect lives. To most Americans, she was a blank slate. They wondered how she would leave her mark. Thurgood Marshall, the first black American on the Court, was a powerful voice for civil rights. Louis Brandeis, the first Jew on the Court, became one of its legendary great minds. But as O'Connor prepared to take her seat for the presession conferences of the justices before October 5, 1981, nobody, certainly not O'Connor, could know what her impact would be. But less than one year later, before Americans could know how she would change the country, she was so popular that the *World Almanac* ranked her the most influential woman in America.

CHAPTER TWO

A Girl of the West

I don't know that there are any shortcuts to doing a good job.
—Sandra Day O'Connor

Sandra Day O'Connor was born March 26, 1930, in Hotel Dieu Hospital in El Paso, Texas, and spent her formative years on a vast ranch straddling Arizona and New Mexico where, for eight years, she was the only child, dependent on cowboys for company and much of her early education. The ranch had no electricity or running water until she was seven. Years later she and her brother Alan wrote a book about how wonderfully picturesque their lives were, noting that while the ranch with its impressive 2,000 head of cattle totaled 160,000 acres, all but 8,560 acres were leased from Arizona and federal agencies for grazing. But behind the romantic image of ranch life, it was a trying childhood in many ways. When O'Connor was inducted into the Cowgirl Hall of Fame in 2002, part of her message was that she had earned the honor and that growing up among taciturn, busy adults who expected her to be independent and help with chores prepared her for a career in law.

When the subject of her childhood comes up—as it does often, for growing up on a vast ranch on the Texas/New Mexico border seems an exotic, remote experience, especially on the East Coast where she has spent most of her time for the past quarter-century—Sandra Day O'Connor sometimes gets a momentary faraway look in her eyes. She is recalling not only the good times but the difficult parts as well. For as charming as her childhood is in retrospect, at the time much of it was drudgery.

"I grew up on a remote cattle ranch in the Southwest, where I learned to be independent," she told Dr. Sylvia Rimm, author of the book *How Jane Won: Fifty-five Successful Women Share How They Grew from Ordinary Girls to Extraordinary Women*. O'Connor went on, "We had to do everything ourselves. If something was broken, we couldn't call a repairman; we had to fix it. If we wanted something built, we had to build it. If we wanted something done, we had to do it. I was expected to do many things and do them well without complaint. That was probably a good thing for me to learn. Other people depended on me doing a good job."

In addition to her parents, her main companions were horses, ranch hands, and books. "There were no other children for me to play with," she recalled. "And I didn't have a brother and sister for about ten years and was an only child in a rather godforsaken place."

The remoteness of the ranch is still in O'Connor's psyche. In a speech in March 1998 at Scripps College, O'Connor said, "We were 35 miles from any town. A trip to town was a significant event and occurred only about once a week, to buy groceries and pick up the mail. My favorite author, Wallace Stegner, described the West best. He wrote, 'There is something about living in big empty space where people are few and distant under a great sky that is ultimately serene and furious, exposed to sun from four in the morning until nine at night and to a wind that never seems to rest. There is something about exposure to that big country that not only tells an individual how small he is but steadily tells him who he is.'"

She said that some of her sharpest memories are of driving around the ranch with her father, called D.A. by everyone, including his children, "hour after hour, bumping slowly along over rocky terrain to check on a windmill or a water pipe or a tank, to see if there was a salt block out for the cattle at a certain place or if a cow with sore eyes was doing all right or needed some medication."

She also recalls yearning for rain and speaks of it like a poet in *Lazy B*:

> We would watch the skies constantly hoping for rain. Rain was our life's blood. It produced the grass and the vegetation the cattle had to have to survive. Like all the arid Southwest, rain was the most essential element, the most treasured event, prayed for, hoped for, anticipated, savored when it came, treasured, celebrated and enjoyed, every drop. In summer when the big cumulus clouds would begin to form around noon, on the days when moisture was moving in from the Gulf, we would watch those clouds. When they produced rain, it was often in the late afternoon. The clouds would grow dark, almost black, and then there would be a strong wind, blowing dust, leaves and small bits of everything lying around. And then a sudden stillness, the earth silent and waiting for the momentous event. Then the crack of lightning touching something on earth with all the electric fury of the universe. Seconds later, the incredible sound of the thunder, the sound produced by the lightning bolt rolling through the clouds above. And then, wonder of wonders, the first big few wet drops of rain, forming muddy places on the dusty range. Then more and more until we would just stop the pickup truck and sit inside, unable to see the closest objects outside because the rain would come in rains and sheets. Joy. Wonder. Incredible gift from above.

Sandra's mother, Ada Mae Wilkey, was born in Mexico in 1904. Ada Mae's father, W. W. Wilkey, one of seven brothers who grew up in Texas, and her mother, Mamie Scott, married when Mamie was only sixteen. O'Connor, in *Lazy B*, described Mamie as a "vivacious, precocious, brown-eyed beauty." W.W., as the family always called him, as a young man took his entire savings of $100, got on the Southern Pacific Railroad, and rode it until his money ran out—in San Simon, Arizona. He found a local rancher who gave him a one-room shack to live in and about forty dollars a year in exchange for tending cattle on two hundred square miles of barren land. With nothing to spend his money on, W.W. saved everything he earned, including two twenty-dollar gold pieces two cowboys left him for putting them up for the night. He later found out they were train robbers and his windfall had probably come from a mining company payroll. He kept the money.

Eventually W.W. went into the cattle business for himself, fattening calves for resale to packinghouses. It was a hard life and there were times he lost money as cattle prices fluctuated, sometimes wildly. But he was a hard worker and naturally frugal and eventually had enough money to ask the only young woman he knew, neighbor Mamie Scott, to marry him. They were briefly living in Cananea, Mexico, when their first child—Ada Mae—was born. Soon after her birth, they moved back to Arizona, to a little town called Douglas. When the family numbered five—by then Ada Mae had a sister Evelyn and a brother Scott—the family moved to Duncan, Arizona. W.W. bought the general store and a house next to it. Mamie took care of her three children and ran the store while W.W. bought a ranch north of the Gila River and stocked it with cattle.

One day a young man named Harry Day, visiting from Pasadena, California, came into the store with his parents, H. C. Day and Alice Day, and three brothers and sisters. Family legend has it that Harry took little to no notice of Ada Mae but that she was immediately taken with the handsome young man, six years older than she.

When Ada Mae was in high school, her parents sold the general store and moved to El Paso, Texas, where W.W. bought a second ranch east of the bustling young town. Sandra and Alan Day recall hearing that their mother loved to play the piano and sing and was in a number of high school musical productions. They describe her as "very attractive" with "an outgoing personality." When Ada Mae graduated from high school, her parents were eager for her to go to college, unusual for women at the time, and she enrolled in the University of Arizona. After her graduation, she returned to El Paso and met and married a young dentist, but the marriage ended after a few months. O'Connor says she learned of her mother's first marriage when she was eleven and a school friend told her. "I was shocked and frightened. Had I been adopted? Is that why M.O. and D.A. sent me off to school in El Paso? I asked Grandmother Wilkey, 'Am I adopted? Was M.O. married to someone else?'"

Sandra says her grandmother told her that she was definitely not adopted and that, yes, her mother briefly had been married. "It didn't work out and that was soon over. We don't talk about that." It took weeks before young Sandra could summon up the courage to ask her mother about her first marriage. Her mother looked at her, and said shortly, "I never think about it. And D.A. is my husband and you are my daughter."

While Ada Mae Wilkey was returning to the social life of a young single woman in El Paso after her failed marriage, teaching school by day and partying at night, she met Harry Day again. This time he noticed her.

His father, Henry Clay Day, had left Vermont at the age of twenty-one, making his way to Wichita, Kansas, where he went into the lumber business, married Alice Edith Hilton, and talked her into going west to start a ranch. With the proceeds of his lumber business, he bought three hundred square miles in southeastern Arizona near the New Mexico border and built a four-room adobe house made of sun-dried clay bricks. The ranch was named the Lazy B because of the sloping B brand on cattle a previous owner had used. The couple had five children, and Henry built a small schoolroom where they could study. But, worried about the children's education—and Indians, who sometimes stole their horses—Henry and Alice decided to move to Pasadena, California, where their children could attend school. They left the ranch in the care of a foreman.

By the time Harry was old enough for high school, his family had decided to leave the Lazy B and Harry went to high school in Pasadena. He won a number of California swimming championships but never went to college. After his father died, he went back, reluctantly, to Arizona to the Lazy B, which had fallen on hard times. The foreman had nearly driven the ranch into bankruptcy, and the family was close to losing it. It would be up to young Harry Day to save it.

By the time Harry Day re-met Ada Mae, he was a rancher with the thought always uppermost that he would try to get the ranch out of debt and then move on to something else. He was buying bulls from W.W., who asked him to dinner. Sandra and her brother Alan would later write that "if there is such a thing as love at first sight, it happened" the night that W.W. invited Harry to dinner after they settled on a price for the bulls. Harry and Ada Mae talked late into the night. For the next three months they wrote back and forth. One passage the sister and brother quote from letters they found was from Harry, written not long after the fateful supper: "I love you more than anything in the world.... It seems I have loved you always, dear, and you have always been mine." They said that their mother replied, "I would have died, I do believe, if your precious letter had not come this morning." Ada Mae's mother strongly disapproved, especially when she learned the young couple planned to live on the Day family's Lazy B ranch, which was particularly primitive even by the standards of the early twentieth century. Because of her disapproval, Harry and Ada Mae eloped to New Mexico in 1927 and were married by a justice of the peace. They went on to the Lazy B Ranch, where they would live until they died, half a century later.

The ranch where Harry Day brought his new wife and where Sandra Day O'Connor would be brought home after her birth in El Paso had no plumbing and no electricity. Water had to be brought in buckets carried from an outdoor pump. Ada Mae, the pretty young schoolteacher who had captivated El Paso society, found herself cooking for rough-hewn cowboys, who slept a few feet away from the young couple in a screened-in porch. She heated water for baths in a portable tub dragged into the kitchen, and washed filthy clothes on an old washboard. When she had time for herself, her daughter Sandra says, she read or played on the upright piano her father had given her. Her daughter recalls, with admiration, that despite the rough life, Ada Mae never stopped trying to look good, never went outside without a hat and long sleeves to avoid tanning (unlike their father, who was always darkened by the sun), and took pride in wearing dresses. One of her indulgences was to travel to Lordsburg, 35 miles away, to have her nails done and her hair washed and set.

Sandra and Alan remember that she subscribed to newspapers and magazines, including *Vogue*, *New Yorker*, and *National Geographic*, stored in piles in closets and under beds. Ada Mae took special pride in teaching her three children to read. Sandra says that her mother was patient and loving and taught her to read at the age of four. One of the family's favorite evening pastimes was playing card games, from gin rummy to bridge to pinochle. And the children remember with great fondness their mother's banana cupcakes and homemade ice cream in the summer. They shot quail and doves for dinner, rode horses, took picnic lunches to out-of-the-way places on the ranch, had their cousin Flournoy, "like a loving older sister," stay over and listen to such radio programs as *Fibber McGee and Molly* and *The Shadow*.

From kindergarten through high school, O'Connor did not live on the ranch during the autumns or winters but was sent to school in El Paso to live with her grandparents. When Sandra's parents told her she had to go to El Paso to be with other children her age, Sandra said she was heartbroken. Even though she would spend every school year away from home through high school, she never stopped being homesick for the ranch and never tired of going home for the summer. "I was always homesick when away from the ranch. My grandmother was loving and caring, but the ranch was where I wanted to be." While she finally had friends, she remained, she says today, shy and often lonely, wondering what was going on at the ranch, occasionally angry that she had been sent away, often unhappy, even continuing to wonder if she was adopted. Asked now how she recalls feeling—a little girl who never saw her parents for months at a time, a ranch that had no telephone when there was no such thing as e-mail, she refuses to dwell on that time. All she says is, "I was homesick most of those years for the ranch and felt sad that I wasn't there."

El Paso was a major shock after her relatively sheltered young life. In some accounts, her early life in El Paso resembled that of Heidi, who yearned for the mountains and her grandfather when she went to the big city. Young Sandra didn't understand why she had to leave home, but her parents decided their smart little girl, who often had her nose in a book when it wasn't time for her chores or meals, would not get a good enough education if she stayed on the ranch. So she was sent to live with her grandmother in El Paso. She credits her grandmother with being the woman who most influenced her life. Mamie Scott Wilkey had not had an easy life, but she did not complain. In Sandra, perhaps, she saw the chance for opportunities she had never had. She loved her granddaughter and was determined that Sandra would learn there was nothing she could not do.

When she was away from the ranch, Sandra's days were ordered by her mother's mother, her grandmother, Mamie Scott Wilkey, about whom she always talked glowingly. It was her grandmother who told the little girl that she could do anything she wanted if she worked hard and had fun too. O'Connor talks with respectful admiration but a certain detachment about her mother, who, she has written, felt closest to Alan, born when Sandra was nine years old. In contrast to expectations that she would be competent and uncomplaining, her brother, she wrote in their book *Lazy B*, had grown up "in a very permissive environment and had his own way in most things." Yet the adult Sandra also remembers her mother, called M.O. by the three Day children (the name originated with the baby of the family, Sandra's only sister, Ann), as a loving, kind role model who "made a hard life look easy."

On the Lazy B, with a family to support, Harry Day, who had not wanted the life of a rancher, found he had a knack for business, for accounting, for mending broken things, for hiring good cowboys, and for handling animals. Sandra and Alan recall one occasion when their father found a cow whose uterus had come out of her vagina and was hanging beneath her tail. Harry pushed it back inside the cow, inserted an empty wine bottle to hold the uterus in place and stitched around it to keep the bottle in place. A few weeks later he removed the stitches and the wine bottle and returned the healthy cow to pasture.

Over the next half-century, through dint of sheer hard work and determination, Harry Day built the Lazy B into the biggest and one of the most profitable ranches in that part of the West. He expected to be obeyed and was a perfectionist at work. He knew cattle, did not like to be second-guessed, and demanded that everyone around him do their jobs to the best of their abilities. He could also be moody and depressed and hypercritical of his wife and Alan and even of Sandra, although less so. He was exceptionally frugal—sometimes to a fault, his family thought. Even as adults, his children would recall that their father owned only one suit, which he wore to weddings and funerals. He kept his 7X Stetson hat all his adult life.

Despite his yearning for California and a different, more predictable life than that of a careworn rancher, Harry Day had built a good life for his family. But even he couldn't deal with drought, and the early years of his marriage to Ada Mae were tough. Having paid off the $300 debt on the ranch when he took it over, he was determined never to go into debt again. There were times his friends thought he would never make it because he passed up so many opportunities to expand, fearing new debt. Sandra Day O'Connor's conservative Republicanism undoubtedly stems from her father, who, like many ranchers, loathed the New Deal. They were suspicious of most government programs, and Sandra remembers hearing her father sitting at the kitchen table voicing his distrust of Franklin D. Roosevelt. Like his wife, he was determined, even in remote Arizona, to know what was going on in Washington and read magazines and newspapers assiduously. Like many men of his generation, he insisted, both Sandra and Alan recall, on having the last word. "All three of us [children] picked up this trait, and we find ourselves as adults mirroring the same tendency," Alan and Sandra wrote, somewhat ruefully, in their book.

They can still quote verbatim one of their father's mantras: "Keep the grass healthy, keep adequate water reserves, take care of the land and it will take care of you."

Recalling her father, O'Connor said he was friendly, intelligent, self-reliant. "He had to build a house. He had to doctor the cattle. He even doctored cowboys on occasion when something went wrong."

One of her most vivid childhood memories is of being told by her father to paint a badly chipped screened door. "I undertook the job of trying to paint it and freshen it up a little bit. My father came along to inspect it. And he said it hadn't been done properly. He thought I should start over and sand it down and put masking tape on the hinges before repainting it. 'Because, Sandra, if you're going to do something, do it right.'" So she spent the rest of the day taking off the new paint, sanding the door down, and then repainting it. At dinner that night, she asked if he had seen her work. All he said was, "Yes." No thank you. No praise. Just an expectation that she would do the job well.

It is clear, listening to Sandra Day O'Connor talk about her father, that his perfectionism, his absolute insistence on doing things right—poring over his ledgers until he had them perfectly balanced, carefully managing the land to avoid overgrazing it, insisting that card games be played according to the rules, taking the extra steps to fix windmills correctly—rubbed off on her. She learned to fire and clean a rifle, could drive a car at seven and a tractor by the time she was ten. She learned to use tools and could help brand cattle without flinching. To this day, her law clerks talk almost reverently about how hard she works, her near zealotry in doing her homework, her penchant for crossing the *t*'s and dotting the *i*'s. But, they acknowledge, she still insists on having the last word.

One of Sandra Day O'Connor's best attributes, in the eyes of her friends, is her empathy with women who have not been fortunate in life. Some of them speculate this began when she was whisked off the desert ranch she loved to El Paso, where she felt out of place because it seemed so big, so sophisticated, and so unlike anything she had known. She was homesick for life on a ranch that was so vast, she has told many, that it was like having "your own country, almost." She missed the cowboys who patrolled desert land that ranged from 6,200 feet above sea level to 3,400 feet at the banks of the Gila River and who often took her along on their rides through cactus country for the day. She missed the low-slung ranch house, which, when she was a child, magically got electricity and running water and an inside bathroom and, to her mother's delight, a gas stove. She missed the after-dinner card games, especially pinochle. She missed the horses—Flaxy, Chico, and a large white horse with the improbable name of Swastika. Chico was her favorite. In her book about the ranch she recalled that Chico was an especially fine horse for children. He never ran away with a child on his back and he stopped in mid-stride if a child fell off. She learned to ride on Chico and so did her sons and some of their children. There is no other relationship like that between a horse and its rider, she often said from her vantage point in the hallowed halls of the Supreme Court, where relationships are often not nearly so secure and where the common thread through an endless parade of cases is human relationships that have failed.

Sandra's growing-up years would make her not only an independent, strong-minded woman, but an empathetic one with a keen awareness of the value of friends. When she went off to school in El Paso, her first thought was that she would have real friends her own age. In those days it was far safer for children to travel alone, even on trains, and after admonitions from her mother to the conductor, she rode by herself to Texas, where her grandmother would pick her up and keep her until it was time for Christmas, spring break or, best of all, summer vacation.

At the Radford School for Girls, Sandra was exposed for the first time in her life to what having money means. El Paso in those days was far more a western border town than it is today. Classes didn't mingle and money equaled social position. The little girl who had spent her life on the Lazy B never got over the feeling she was different from the other girls, some of whom had servants and lawn parties and what seemed to Sandra vast wardrobes. She learned that there were such people as gardeners who would work all day long trimming bushes and chauffeurs who would spend hours polishing long, glistening cars. Her father's pickup truck had never been washed since he bought it. No gardener was needed to heft the tumbleweed out of the way. And for a while she was lost and felt different. She didn't have a different dress for every day. She had never before seen a house that had more than one bathroom. In her autobiography about life on the ranch, Sandra recalled that seeing how some of the girls at the school lived made her "feel awkward and a bit uneasy."

But Sandra's curiosity and eagerness won people over and soon she had built her own circle, most of whom she still counts as friends. Every other year, says one of the friends who stays with the O'Connors when she goes to Washington, the old network gets together in a different part of the country to "have an adventure." This woman took the group rafting on the Middle Fork River in California. The woman says of Sandra, "She is a very loyal person. All of her accomplishments don't drape over her."

Perhaps O'Connor's intense loyalty to her friends stems from her first eight lonely years spent on the ranch with nobody her own age for twenty-five miles. In a "Dare to Dream" video profile done for young people, she said, "I grew up in different circumstances than probably most of you young people did. I grew up on a cattle ranch that was in Arizona and New Mexico, and I spent my childhood in a very remote place. We didn't have other children around. I did a lot of horseback riding, and the whole family had to get out and help on the ranch. We learned to be pretty independent that way, I think."

One of her fondest memories was when she persuaded her parents to let five of her friends from school spend spring break at the Lazy B. Preadolescent Sandra was both excited and worried, eager to have friends see her beloved ranch but also fearing they would be bored or, even worse, hate ranch life. But she needn't have worried. Her twelve-year-old friends were enthralled with riding horses, milking cows, playing with the animals, and finding eggs for breakfast. A picture of the girls shows the six friends sitting on a wall, their bare legs dangling as they squinted into the sunlight, a picture of the happiness and innocence of childhood. Perhaps, too, Sandra's competitive spirit might have been gratified that on that trip the friends from El Paso not only fell in love with her ranch life, they also envied her skills on horseback and at milking cows and her astuteness at after-dinner card games.

Most famous people have a teacher they remember with great fondness. In elementary school, Sandra's was Miss Fireovid, who taught dramatic arts at Radford School for Girls and forced the exceptionally shy Sandra to stand before the class and recite poetry, give speeches, and read aloud. It was agony at the time but now O'Connor is immensely grateful. "It is something that probably helped me the rest of my life," she says. Even more than for most children, public speaking was foreign to her. She had spent much of her time alone with her thoughts, whether on the range or riding the train to school. It was a time without telephones, and the Days were not big letter writers, having little spare time. Her mother was busy not only with ranch chores but with Alan and Ann, Sandra's younger brother and sister. The only time she had much of an audience was at supper, when she had to compete for attention with her strong-willed parents.

When Sandra was at school, she was thinking about home. She has never forgotten the homesickness that dogged her grade school days. She missed the card games with her competitive father. She missed the high calorie desserts her mother made for dinner. She missed sitting in the living room and talking about current events. She missed, maybe most of all, the family all going outside just before bed to look at the sky, gauging the weather for the next day and gazing in marvel at the stars. She began her chapter on her school days in *Lazy B* with a poem by S. M. Grannis, "Do they miss me at home? Do they miss me? 'T'would be an assurance most dear, to know that this moment some loved one, were saying, 'I wish (s)he were here.'"

In 1942, when Sandra was about to enter eighth grade, her parents relented and reluctantly let her return home, where she commuted long miles to school in Lordsburg every day. But there was no going back to her old life. By then Sandra had assimilated some of the ways of the city and was taken aback at the rough frontier life she had put such a sweet patina on.

One of her most vivid memories as a child was of a little, frightened girl who lived on a 160-acre homestead near the Lazy B. When Sandra's father would occasionally stop to talk cattle with the man who owned the homestead, she would try to talk to the child, who would never answer. Occasionally, Sandra would notice that the child's timid mother looked as if she had been in a bad auto accident. When she badgered her father to know what had happened, her father finally said he thought the man had been drinking and beat his wife. Horrified, twelve-year-old Sandra demanded that they tell the sheriff. Her father, who would later buy the man's land, firmly said that there was nothing they could do. She never forgot her frustration or, she would say later, her first view of what it was to fail in life.

She learned that year that her life would be happier if she had new challenges. Taking a horrendously long and excruciatingly boring bus ride to and from school, she had only one real friend to talk to, a girl named Helen who lived miles away. Sandra was even bored at school; the little school at Lordsburg could not provide what her active mind craved: a rich educational environment with stimulating classmates and teachers. Even today she says that academically, it was a wasted year because she learned basically nothing.

When Sandra was ready for high school, she went back to El Paso, taking the long train ride from home to attend Austin High School. She had grown up enough to know she would always miss the ranch, but that it had left its mark on her.

Reviewing O'Connor's book *Lazy B*, historian Doris Kearns Goodwin said the book was "an endearing memoir about a vanishing era, a place and a family that nurtured the feisty young girl who became an extraordinary woman." Every reviewer was struck by how the West and O'Connor's relationship to the arid, beautiful expanse of land along the Gila River shaped not only her personality but also her no-nonsense, energetic, hard-working approach to the law and the business of getting on with life. O'Connor and her brother, Alan, who managed the ranch for much of his life before subdividing and selling it in 1993, wrote that the stark and isolated desert of the American Southwest "was no country for sissies, then or now." She grew up determined to gain the respect of her taciturn father and her best friends, the "cowhands."

In booming El Paso, Sandra Day went to high school, where she set her own study habits, developed her own sense of where she was going in life, and heard constantly from her adoring grandmother that there was nothing she could not do, nothing she could not accomplish. While the teenaged, slightly self-conscious Sandra didn't really believe that, the message was subconsciously and irrevocably imprinted in her mind.

Childhood photos of her almost never show her laughing. Her lips were always pressed together, lifted at the corners in a faint smile, but her dark, expressive eyes seemed far more serious and mature than those of most children her age. Her formal portraits as a justice of the Supreme Court show almost exactly the same expression—serious, firm mouth, a steady, pleasant gaze straight into the camera. This was not a little girl given to uncontrolled mirth. This is not a woman who treats life lightly although she has a fine sense of humor and irony. Pictures of Sandra as a teenager show the trademark wide forehead, dark curly hair, keen eyes, and a shy yet serious smile. Her friends at the time, who are still her friends, say she was not a risk-taker but was fiercely loyal to them, a natural leader in planning events and having fun despite her shyness, and always, always, studying.

She was known even then as an independent, responsible young woman. She was impatient with girls who acted helpless or who complained. The memory of a woman beaten black and blue and her sad little daughter standing mutely by her side continued to haunt her. She resolved she would always be in control of her life. She hated it when she heard whining or heard classmates insist they couldn't do something. That wasn't how she had been reared. She had become a strong believer in being strong—physically, mentally, morally. She believed in teamwork, telling her friends that if she hadn't done her part during cattle roundups, the whole roundup could have failed. She learned early in life there were no excuses, only results. She never forgot being called away from reading a Nancy Drew mystery one day by her father, who wanted her to see how to shoot a wounded animal—a calf that had been half-eaten by a coyote.

She learned on the ranch that what made a man—or woman—successful was how well he or she did the job. She writes fondly of Rastus, born Rafael Estrada, a Mexican-American ranch hand who could not read but who could identify every one of about one thousand head of cattle. "He knew he was very good at what he did, and he demanded a high standard from those around him," she wrote. Rastus was "dealt what many would say was a poor hand in life—he was small, crippled, fatherless, a minority race in his birth land [but] he played the hand he was dealt like a master." From Rastus, she said, "we learned the contentment of doing the best you can with what you have."

After her unhappy year in eighth grade in Lordsburg, eager to learn, she was shocked at public Austin High School to find out that getting good grades marked you as a "nerd," she recalls sheepishly. Trying to hide her intellect and fit in, she did what other teens were doing. Going to the movies—Mickey Rooney and Shirley Temple were hot teen stars of the era—was a favorite pastime. She belonged to a few clubs but not in a leadership way. Oddly, perhaps, Sandra does not talk much about World War II as a major influence on her high school years, perhaps because Europe seemed so far away from El Paso, even in the turbulent 1940s. The world was at war and nobody escaped. Sandra and her father had even seen an explosion 180 miles from the ranch one morning that they later learned was the first test of an atomic bomb at Alamogordo, New Mexico.

The West would always be part of Sandra Day O'Connor's psyche and her life. She had seen the swift retribution when Mother Earth is offended, when sky and land combined to smite the unready, the unwise, the careless. She had seen foolishness in her father's ranch hands. She had seen wisdom. She had seen competence. She had seen laziness. Even at fourteen she yearned for order, for rules, for life to make sense. One of her most vivid memories of her high school years was, again, not in school but back at the ranch during the summer before her senior year. She rose early to help fix lunch for the cattle hands and her father and drove a truck to deliver it. She had a flat tire. Struggling to get the lug nuts off and change the tire in the blazing sun, she arrived late with the lunch. Expecting praise from her father for having changed the tire, she got none. The lesson she learned? "No excuses accepted."

Religion was not a big issue on the vast Lazy B, a surprise to some who note that religion was destined to play a dominant role in a number of key decisions O'Connor made as a Supreme Court justice. Her father told reporters that although the family was Episcopalian, the closer Methodist Church would do just fine when M.O. decided a church outing was a necessity that week. D.A. taught his children that nature was religion, that the ranch and, by extension, the universe was their church. But O'Connor says she is Episcopalian and will remain so.

She has spoken and written little of her high school days. She continued to live with Grandmother Wilkey, which undoubtedly meant there was not much rebellion or foolishness. She had a moderately wide circle of friends and she did exceedingly well in school, even though it was an era when smart girls were not particularly popular. But her high school pictures gradually show a happier girl as she grew up; sometimes she even opened her mouth in a wide smile.

As she grew into a curious, determined teenager, it was clear to everyone in the family that she was her father's daughter, possessing a special bond with him developed when she was the only child for nine years and they spent hours talking, a bond he did not have with his two younger children. "Any young girl would feel so blessed to have a relationship like that," her brother told an interviewer when their book on the Lazy B was published. As for Alan, he frequently clashed with his father, especially on how to manage the ranch.

The Days were by no means poor, although they took government subsidies when cattle prices were low, slaughtering eight hundred head of cattle for $12 a head, paid by the government in 1934. They had local positions of social and economic leadership. They took their children to Cuba on a banana boat, to visit the exotic playground of the Western Hemisphere long before the days of Fidel Castro. They even went to Alaska, where young Sandra fell in love with the mountains but not the mosquitoes.

O'Connor was proud of being the only female during the semiannual roundup—her mother refused to participate. "Changing [the roundup] to accommodate a female was probably my first initiation into joining an all-men's club, something I did more than once in my life," she wrote. "After the cowboys understood that a girl could hold up her end, it was much easier for my sister, my niece, and the other girls and young women who followed to be accepted in that rough-and-tumble world." When Fort Worth's $21 million National Cowgirl Museum opened, Susan Fine, director of development and marketing at the museum, said, "These women were doing ordinary things back then that were absolutely extraordinary." The museum was dedicated to the power and passion of pioneering women and to dispelling the image of women inside their dark prairie houses while the men rode the range. When O'Connor was inducted as the 159th member into the hall of fame on June 7, 2002, receiving a medal and a pair of custom-made cowgirl boots, she recalled, somewhat wistfully, that she had yearned for much of her early life to grow up to be a cattle rancher herself, riding the range, mending fences, putting her feet up on the front porch after a long day, sunburned, tired, and satisfied. "It is such an honor to be made a member of this honored group of cowgirls," she said. "These women sitting here today are so special, and I am so thrilled that they will have me as one of them." Inducted with her were four other women—a quarter-horse breeder, two riding champions, and a stuntwoman, sporting ten-gallon hats and shiny belt buckles. A year earlier O'Connor had been inducted into the Hall of Great Westerners for her "significant contribution to the nation's Western heritage." Honored posthumously with her was Spencer Penrose, who founded the Broadmoor Hotel and much of Colorado Springs, Colorado, and York, the manservant who accompanied Lewis and Clark on the 1803–6 expedition to the Pacific Ocean, saving their lives and becoming the first black man to cross the American West.

When Sandra was ready for college, the idea of going to Stanford came from her father, who had grown up in Pasadena, California, and always regretted that he had not gone to college. She had seen some of the country—she had driven with her family the entire length of the Mississippi River, stopping at every state capital along the way—and had visited relatives in California. So the idea of school in California—not too far away and still in the West—appealed to her.

At seventeen, Sandra was ready to get to the next chapter of her life. In the autumn of 1946, her parents drove her to Palo Alto to Stanford University, where she would forget that study was for "nerds" and would work hard to cram an undergraduate degree into three years. But growing up on the ranch had marked her forever, giving her a skepticism about the federal government and a deep belief in states' rights. She has written that what she learned most from the ranch was that the "personal qualities of honesty, dependability, competence and good humor were valued most" on the farm and, she would decide, in life.

But the character trait she most cherished from her ranch life as she left for college was a zest for freedom that she feared was disappearing in American life. Years later, in a speech in October 2001, about six weeks after the terrorist attacks of September 11, 2001, which killed more than three thousand people in New York, at the Pentagon in Virginia, and over southwestern Pennsylvania, O'Connor said with great sadness that Americans should be prepared for a long period during which "we are likely to experience more restrictions on our freedom" because of the attacks. The woman who used to ride horses freely through the West and gloried in the rain and the freedom of the boundless skies warned a new generation of Americans at Principia College in Elsah, Illinois, that every one of the rights in the

Declaration of Independence is "under attack by the terrorists." She had seen the swift retribution of justice when cowboys failed to do their job properly, permitting livestock or their comrades to come into jeopardy, and she had no doubts but that the legal system would have to change. "Our legal system abhors punishment without due process, but no single approach is appropriate to all situations," she said. Acts of war are sometimes required, she said. Increased surveillance and wiretapping are a price of being at war, she said sadly.

Her personal world changed forever, she would say often, when her brother split her beloved ranch up into five parcels and sold them, the last going when their mother died in 1989. "I feel like part of my heart and soul is gone," she said, saying it was hard to believe the ranch would no longer be part of her life. "No matter where I was in my life, whether it was at Stanford or in Germany or wherever it was, I knew the ranch was there. I knew my parents were there. I knew we were welcome there as often as we could go and for as long as we could stay. I knew our children and our children's children would be welcome there, always." She often recalls that her brother, the rancher, routinely tells her, "Sandra, you have the glamour job, and I have the good job."

But once the ranch was sold, she never went back. Once, in an interview on National Public Radio, she said, "If I loved something very much and if it has been extremely important to me, I prefer to keep it in my memory as I remember than risk seeing it again" and being disappointed.

CHAPTER THREE

No Women Need Apply

> The more education a woman has, the wider the gap between men's and women's earnings for the same work.
>
> —Sandra Day O'Connor

Life at Stanford University at age seventeen for Sandra Day O'Connor was heady. Always hungry for knowledge and new experiences and challenges, she was thrilled at the intellectual life, the social life, the professors, the freedom. Unlike some eastern colleges, which specialized in turning out young women for marriage, Stanford was a co-ed that treated women as equals. And by succeeding in the difficult subject of economics, then mostly male terrain, chosen because she had seen the importance of economics to make a ranch run well, Sandra had proven that she had a good mind. Physically imposing at five feet eight inches, she had long shed her early high school wallflower image. The often maligned late 1940s and early 1950s were the years when America was still recuperating from World War II but not yet ready for the rebellion of the rock-and-roll era or the social upheaval of the 1960s. World War II veterans were flocking to college campuses, courtesy of the GI bill. And women, too, were discovering the joys of college life. Of the 826 freshmen in O'Connor's class at Stanford, an impressive one-third were women. Before the war, female enrollment had never reached that high.

Sandra, fresh from El Paso, was somewhat taken aback by Stanford. While she was ready to work hard—really hard—she felt like a fish out of water when it came to socializing with many of the far more sophisticated female students. She was a year younger than most of the freshmen women she met, and, to her, it felt like five years. She does not dwell on this period except to say she felt "poorly prepared compared to other freshmen I met." It was in college that she developed her penchant for long, frequently tedious hours of bookwork. With Sandra, "there ain't no Miller Time," she said a friend had once told her in mock exasperation.

Yet there was no thought by anyone who knew Sandra that she wouldn't succeed at Stanford, and certainly her father conveyed to her that he expected great things. Her brother Alan once said, "From head to toe, [their father] was filled with the spirit of the people who carved their place in the West. Sandra was the apple of his eye, and the great lesson he taught us was you didn't make excuses, you didn't ask for someone to bail you out, you simply did the job yourself."

At Stanford, as she had before in El Paso, O'Connor came under the spell of an influential teacher, one of those who "makes all the difference." Nearly all great men and women have said that they had one teacher at each stage of their scholarly life who influenced them to do their best. For O'Connor, as an undergraduate, the teacher was Harry Rathburn. His specialty was business law, and his avocation was his "soirees" on Sunday night, evenings of quick, easy food and long, difficult conversations about personal ethics, psychology, and religion. One of O'Connor's classmates, Mary Beth Growden, has told interviewers that such metaphysical discussions of life's meanings were a dramatic, intellectual awakening for O'Connor. She has often expressed her gratitude to his Sunday evenings of study and scholarly questioning for propelling her into law school, calling him "terrific" for pointing out to her that one person has the power to make an immense difference in the lives of others and for teaching her that women, just as much as men, are empowered to make that difference. One of Rathburn's most famous exercises was his lecture at the end of each course, when he would discuss not just the lessons of the past semester but the meaning of life and the role each person plays in making society either better or worse. As Sandra listened to him week after week, she began to think of giving up her dream of becoming a rancher. "I wanted to be a cattle rancher when I was young, because it was what I knew and I loved it," she said in 2003, reflecting on her life. But listening to Rathburn, she began wondering if she would be a good lawyer. Rathburn told her she would, based on her penchant for hard work, for doing things the right way, and for thinking things through logically.

Finishing her university work in just three years and graduating magna cum laude, Sandra had decided from her dealings with Rathburn that she wanted to go to law school. "He spent a lot of time convincing students that they could make a difference, that a single individual could make a difference. Really, because of him, I decided to go to law school." She had no trouble being admitted to Stanford Law School, which turned out to be a "great experience," she said. Although one law professor would one day say in disgust her class was the "dumbest" he had ever encountered, it would eventually produce two Supreme Court justices—Chief Justice William Rehnquist, first in their class, and Sandra Day O'Connor, who was third.

Rehnquist and O'Connor briefly dated but it never was serious. "We went to a few movies and one thing and another," she recalls. "He was a star [on campus], a total star." They would remain lifelong friends, with Rehnquist and his wife, Nan, and John and Sandra often socializing. And it would be Rehnquist, along with Barry Goldwater, who urged Ronald Reagan to consider his tall, athletic, conservative friend from college to be the first woman on the Supreme Court.

O'Connor excelled in law school, finally coming into her own intellectually. She thrived on the give-and-take of law school classes, the competition, and the connection with professors. She would later be considered for the Supreme Court because she had gone to Stanford, one of the nation's top law schools. But she would be considered seriously also because she was on the Board of Editors of the *Stanford Law Review*, a plum in anyone's law school career, and she was inducted into the Order of the Coif, a legal honorary society. Most impressive of all, she completed law school in only two years, instead of the customary three. When she finished law school, she was only twenty-two years old.

But she already had found the love of her life: John Jay O'Connor III, her age but one year behind her in law school. They began as law review buddies, but it rapidly blossomed into romance. When they began dating, he asked her out forty nights in a row. "And then John decided he needed to get some rest," she says, laughing. When she finally took him to the ranch, she says, "We arrived one afternoon, and my father and the cowboys were down in the corral. They were branding calves and castrating the bull calves and tossing the testicles in the bucket on the side. And my father went over and got some baling wire off the fence, made kind of a long skewer out of it, took a couple of these things out of the bucket, trimmed them a little with his pocket knife, stuck them on this baling wire skewer and put them in a branding fire where they sizzled away and eventually he held them out, 'Here, John, try these.' Poor John. He had to take one, gulp, 'very good, Mr. Day.' It must have been a miserable moment." The Days were used to eating the so-called delicacy. "My mother knew how to fix them pretty well. We used to have them for the cocktail hour." Clearly, the event didn't traumatize John O'Connor or dim his ardor. The two were married about six months after her graduation, on December 20, 1952, in a ceremony at her beloved Lazy B.

Often when someone becomes famous, unflattering reminiscences spring forth from those who knew them along the way. That has rarely happened to O'Connor, although a former friend at Stanford did turn on her. In 1985, Mary C. Scarlott, who had once been a dorm mate of O'Connor's at Stanford, became an outspoken critic. She wrote a letter to Connecticut's *Stamford Advocate* newspaper claiming that O'Connor once neglected to pay the bill for a long-distance phone call. "You called long distance from a pay telephone in Kansas," Scarlott wrote in an open letter to O'Connor, "and declined payment." When the phone company called Scarlott to ask her to identify the caller, she says she refused. "Did I do the right thing? Given the value you have come to place on worldly goods, I assume you would now lament such reticence," she wrote. Scarlott accused O'Connor of hypocrisy in recent high court decisions on crime. In *Tennessee v. Garner*, she wrote, "an unarmed fleeing child is shot dead by a policeman who suspects him of stealing. The Court held it improper for the police to execute a person in such circumstances . . . But it was not tough enough for the Court's first woman." (O'Connor had dissented from the majority.) "Odd that I should have so wildly misjudged you," Scarlott wrote, "or that your values have changed so greatly. Could this be the dorm mate with whom I had enjoyed reading aloud from *Winnie the Pooh*?"

After all her academic successes in college, it had not occurred to Sandra Day that when she graduated from law school in 1952, the only job she would be offered was a secretarial job with a Los Angeles law firm even though she had been third in her class of 102 and had completed law school in just two years. One of the ironies of Sandra's lucky life was that a person who would be most helpful to her thirty years later when she was nominated for the Supreme Court was William French Smith, then the U.S. attorney general. He had been a former senior partner of the California law firm that once told her she could work as a secretary but not as a lawyer.

She still recalls that moment vividly. "I was shocked. I think I was naïve. I had never stopped to think that it might be hard to get a job. The partner who interviewed me said, 'Miss Day, how do you type?' And I said 'Well, fair, not great, I can get by.' He said, 'Well if you type well enough, I might be able to get you a job as a legal secretary. But we have never hired a woman as a lawyer here. And we don't anticipate doing it.'"

O'Connor, by then married, grew frantic. Her husband was still finishing up law school, and one of them needed to work. She finally heard that the district attorney of San Mateo County had once hired a woman lawyer. She made an appointment with him and ended up pleading with him for a job, even if he didn't pay her. And, for a short period, he didn't, saying he didn't have the money to hire another lawyer and didn't even have room for her in his office. She said she would sit with his secretary and, briefly, she did. In a way, her determination may have sprung not just from her desperation for a job, but a hidden desire to follow her father's dream of striking out on his own in California, a state he thought offered young people a great future. And, in truth, in California she found her future. From her first day as an unpaid intern, she loved being a lawyer and, even more, loved the joy she found in public service. The cattle ranching business had lost her.

A year later, after she began working, her husband became a lawyer with the army's Judge Advocate General Corps and was stationed in Frankfurt, Germany. Without a question about leaving her own job, his wife went with him, eventually getting a job as a civilian lawyer with the Quartermaster Corps. She doesn't talk much about those years, perhaps because the work was often routine and didn't interest her as much as her first and later jobs in public service. After Germany, her husband, who had not had the grades his wife did at Stanford, had no trouble getting a good job with a law firm in Phoenix. Sandra was offered nothing. Once again she improvised and hung out a shingle in her own two-person office with a partner, Tom Tobin.

Speaking to graduates at George Mason University in May 2000, she said that the two shared a small office in a shopping center in a small community in Arizona. "Other people who had offices in the same shopping mall repaired TVs, cleaned clothes, or loaned money. It was not a high-rent district. I got walk-in business. People came in to see me about grocery bills they couldn't collect, landlord-tenant problems, family members and other everyday things not usually considered by the United States Supreme Court. But I always did the best I could with what I had. I learned how the law affects the average citizen and how a lawyer can help solve day-to-day problems."

O'Connor also settled into the routine of being a mother. After the O'Connors moved back to the United States from Germany in 1957, choosing to live in Phoenix, her three sons, Scott, Brian, and Jay, were all born within the next six years. Even though she loved to work outside the home, she gave up her law firm in 1962 when her second son, Brian, was born. For five years, her primary goal was to rear her sons. But, in addition to her family, she found a new passion—volunteer work. The Supreme Court Historical Society notes that she wrote questions for the Arizona Bar exam, was on the Maricopa County Board of Adjustments and Appeals, served on the Governor's Committee on Marriage and the Family, worked as an administrative assistant of the Arizona State Hospital, was an adviser to the Salvation Army, and volunteered in a school for blacks and Hispanics.

Her official biography lists an amazing number of extracurricular activities. She was on the National Board of the Smithsonian, the Board of Trustees of the Heard Museum, the Advisory Board of the Salvation Army, vice president of the Soroptimist Club of Phoenix, the Board of Visitors of Arizona State University Law School, vice president of the National Conference of Christians and Jews of Maricopa County, the Board of Trustees of Stanford, secretary of the Arizona Academy, the board of Junior Achievement, the Board of Directors of the Phoenix Historical Society.

And that was not all. She was on the Anglo-American Exchange, the Maricopa County Bar Association Lawyer Referral Service, various committees of the state bar, chairman of the Maricopa County Juvenile Detention Home Visiting Board, the National Defense Advisory Committee on Women in the Services, vice chairman of the Arizona Select Law Enforcement Review Committee, a member of the county board of adjustments and appeals, the Arizona Criminal Code Commission. And she was a member of just about every bar group and judges group and women lawyers' group.

In 1965, she was ready to go back to work full time. She recalls that she decided to return to government, still having been unsuccessful at getting a law firm to hire her, and applied to the Arizona attorney general's office for a job. "They didn't have a place for me. I persisted, however, and got a temporary job and quickly rose all the way to the bottom of the totem pole in that office. As was normal for a beginner, I got the least desirable assignments. But that was all right because I managed to take away from those rather humble professional beginnings some valuable lessons. I learned, for example, the habit of always doing the best I could with every task no matter how unimportant it might seem at the time. Such habits can breed future success."

She often quoted Abraham Lincoln's observation that he always prepared himself for the opportunity he knew would come his way. "As his career attests, devotion to excellence in all things even when it seems, as he put it, the world will little note nor long remember the same tasks in which you find yourself engaged it can have its rewards."

She has often said that starting at the bottom and working hard pays off because "you will quickly learn as I did that the person at the bottom, despite the low rank on the totem pole can develop skills and earn respect." When her audience invariably looked quizzical at that point, she would explain, "The person at the bottom gets the first opportunity to propose a solution to whatever the problem is. That first proposed solution—if supported by the right facts and logic—often will be the one that is adopted. Although it may be years before you have the authority to decide which solutions will be adopted, you can start right away to generate the ideas that make those solutions feasible. So for those of you who are disappointed not to be moving from your graduation directly into a partnership in a 200-person firm or a Cabinet-level position in government, this ought to give you some solace."

With three active young boys at home, as an assistant state attorney general, she decided her best approach to get back into the workforce was to carve out a specialty and began learning all she could about mental health regulations. But soon she was the go-to person for just about every kind of case. She amazed her friends and colleagues with her stellar energy and her ability to organize her children's busy, active lives with their extracurricular sports activities, and her work life and the O'Connors' busy social life.

In 1969, after gaining a solid reputation as a hard-working lawyer, she was appointed to a vacancy in the Arizona state senate. She campaigned for reelection twice and won both times, and became the first woman in the nation to hold the post of majority leader in a state legislature, to which she was elected twice. Reporters poring over her record when she was nominated to the Supreme Court found her to be a conservative with a mixed record—she was a strong supporter of Richard Nixon—but she also favored the Equal Rights Amendment, which narrowly failed to be ratified by the states. She is still famous for once having forced a vote over an amendment to a long-forgotten bill to insert a comma she alone felt changed the meaning of the new statute. But now she had a solid reputation not just as a hard worker but as a tough, no-nonsense legislator. A fellow state senator, Alfredo Gutierrez, told interviewers much later, "It was impossible to win a debate with her. We'd go on the floor with a few facts and let rhetoric do the rest. Not Sandy. She would overwhelm you with her knowledge." William Jacquin, a former state senator who went on to head the Arizona Chamber of Commerce, told the *New York Times* that O'Connor was "a super floor leader. She was devoted to the law by the nature of her own professionalism and was extraordinarily thorough in drafting legislation."

And she quickly gained a reputation for being open-minded. A Democrat in the senate said, "She's not your far-out Republican." During that period, she did, for example, support the Equal Rights Amendment for women, although it failed, and she helped repeal a state law that limited women to working no more than eight hours a day, which had been used to keep them out of certain well-paid jobs. She worked to provide regular reviews for those committed to mental institutions. She pushed probate code reform. She helped establish no-fault divorces in Arizona. And she made certain that judges for Superior Court were selected on merit. She pushed for a sunshine law, making it mandatory for public meetings to be held in the open. She pushed for reining in spending so that it matched revenues. She tried but failed to get a state Medicaid program to help the poor afford medical care.

Her first taste of judicial work came in 1974 when she decided to run for Maricopa County Superior Court. She narrowly won and served for five years. She loved the bench from the first. It gave her control. It was a life of organization and discipline. And it also gave her weekends and time with her family.

In 1979, a Democratic governor, Bruce Babbitt, appointed her to the Arizona Court of Appeals. Speculation was rampant that Babbitt made the bold bipartisan move at least in part to remove O'Connor as a potential rival in the next gubernatorial race, a motive that he denied. In 1978 Republicans had pressed O'Connor to challenge Babbitt but she declined, thinking the timing was not right and not at all convinced that she wanted to be governor. One of those who pushed her hard was the formidable Barry Goldwater, who, more than a decade after his death, was still lionized by Arizonians in a state poll as one of Arizona's most influential politicians ever.

In O'Connor's eighteen months on the Arizona appeals court, she displayed invariably careful reasoning, with a large reliance on precedent. Her legal writings were considered not brilliant, but workmanlike and thoughtful. She almost never revealed her attitude on the controversial constitutional issues she would encounter on the Supreme Court. Of her twenty-nine opinions while serving on the Arizona Court of Appeals, none indicated her opinions on abortion, busing as a way to desegregate schools, school prayer, the death penalty, affirmative action, or the rights of criminals. She wrote one article in the *William and Mary Law Review* that applauded Supreme Court decisions that required federal judges to defer to determinations by state courts, an early indication of her views on federalism.

Alan Freeman and Elizabeth Mensch, analyzing her court decisions on the appeals court, said they spotted the "basic methodological blueprint" she would take with her to the nation's highest court. "She always sought to identify the extreme positions on each side and then sought to find the precise fault line between them. Facts were carefully described and compared to those of other decided cases." On the other hand, they said, she was not a mechanical formalist but paid "a legal realist's attention to underlying purposes of both statutes and common law doctrines."

They argued that one case typified her style. It was *Food Products Corp. v. Industrial Commission of Arizona*, in which the question was whether an injury had arisen because of the job. A deliveryman had stopped to help the driver of a stalled car push it to the curb. A child was in the car, and the woman driver was trying without success to push the car out of the fast lane of a six-lane highway. As the deliveryman was pushing her car, he was struck by another car. At issue was whether the deliveryman's stopping to help a stranded motorist arose out of his duties on the job although he was forbidden to conduct any personal business while working. O'Connor's ruling held that the deliveryman had acted reasonably and thus, even though he had not been given express or specific authorization by his employer to go to the aid of the stranded driver, his act of kindness was one that arose from his employment. Thus he was entitled to compensation for his injuries. But, she stressed, if he had gone to the rescue of a stranded motorist while on vacation, that would not be covered under his employer's insurance.

Sandra Day O'Connor was traveling a path that few women had trodden before. Until Esther Morris was named justice of the peace at South Pass Mining Camp in Wyoming Territory in 1870, women were unknown in law enforcement in the West. Indeed, the first woman licensed to practice law, Arabelle A. Mansfield of Iowa, did not get that license until 1869. And a hundred years later, women were still not readily accepted in law. As O'Connor had learned in her futile hunt for a job as lawyer in the private sector right after law school, the attitudes of many men hindered women from a career in law. In 1875 Chief Judge C. J. Ryan of the Wisconsin Supreme Court sealed his reputation for all time when he said, "Our profession has essentially and habitually to do with all that is selfish and extortionate, knavish and criminal, coarse and brutal, repulsive and obscene. Nature has tempered woman as little for the judicial conflicts of the courtroom as for the physical conflicts of the battlefield."

Before O'Connor became the first woman on the Supreme Court, the laurels for the woman to rise highest in the judicial system went to Florence Ellinwood Allen, born in 1884, who was the first woman in Ohio to be a public prosecutor, the first woman in Ohio to sit on a common pleas court, the first woman on the Ohio Supreme Court, the first woman on the U.S. Court of Appeals, and the first woman to serve as chief judge of a federal court of appeals. Perhaps not surprisingly, like O'Connor, she also was born in the West, in Salt Lake City, Utah. Daughter of the first congressman from Utah, she, like O'Connor, had a strong mother. Florence Allen's mother was the first woman to enroll in Smith College. According to one of her biographers, writer Kristie Miller, Florence Allen became the first woman in America to preside over a first-degree murder trial and the first woman to pronounce the death sentence. Eleanor Roosevelt once wrote that if a president of the United States "should decide to nominate a woman for the Supreme Court, it should be Judge Allen."

But Allen herself knew that would not happen in her lifetime, and, by the time she died in 1966, no woman had been appointed to the Supreme Court. She had fought too many battles with men such as Ryan, the biased Wisconsin justice.

With the struggles of her forebears such as Allen in mind, in 1979 O'Connor helped found the National Association of Women Judges, with the hope that the organization would someday—soon, she hoped—be obsolete. Just two years later, the fledgling organization represented half of the nation's eight hundred female jurists, 5 percent of the nation's judges, and she was named the group's first "Judge of the Year."

With Sandra on the prestigious appeals court and John making serious money with a private law firm, the O'Connors were part of the intense Phoenix social life that revolved around polo, golf, country club dinners, and benefits. Their good friends and frequent companions were the Rehnquists and the Goldwaters, who loved evenings talking about politics and the law. Both Barry Goldwater and William Rehnquist openly speculated about a possible future for O'Connor as the first woman on the Supreme Court if they couldn't convince her to run for higher office in Arizona, which the three couples mulled over on occasion. But much as she had loved the intrigue and power of the Arizona senate, O'Connor never told any of them she would consider running for governor. But she did want to make contributions to society, especially for women.

The issue of O'Connor's higher political ambitions, if any, soon became moot when Reagan tapped her to become the first woman to sit on the Supreme Court in 1981, only eighteen months after she had joined the state court of appeals. Impressed with her background and loving the fact that she was from a real ranch, Reagan called her a "person for all seasons." He quite pointedly did not say "woman" for all seasons.

But it was because she was a woman that she had a chance to help other women. Thirty years after she was offered a job as a legal secretary and was told she'd never work as a lawyer, she would sit on a case on the Supreme Court in which major law firms would still be arguing that they did not have to offer women partnerships under the same conditions as they were offered to male attorneys. After lawyers for an influential law firm argued that the Civil Rights Act's Title VII did not apply to women seeking equal opportunity from their employers and that as enforcers of the Constitution, lawyers deserve, O'Connor replied in what was described as a "tone of strained patience." She said, "Congress well knew how to write exemptions into the law when it wanted to. You are asking us to create one ourselves."

She recalled her own struggles that day, starting with begging the district attorney of San Mateo County for a job, even if he didn't pay her, terms he found too enticing to pass up. From that first, less than auspicious start, she thrived, partly out of determination, she once said, to show that she could do the job as well as if not better than any man. She had impressed the San Mateo's district attorney with her hard work and soon got not only a salary but an office and the title of deputy district attorney, a job that started her on her career and convinced her forever that hard work would win over prejudice any day.

But she also decided that even though the experience would stay with her forever, she would fight the system from within and win, not making waves. Just as she does not look back over her shoulder when she has made a judicial or personal decision but gets on with the next task, she does not dwell on social inequality. She decided that everyone in life has challenges and obstacles and that hers was being a woman in a man's world and she was not going to let it defeat her. She has little sympathy for women who don't struggle to overcome their problems, but all the respect in the world for those who fight hard and beat the odds.

In her book *The Majesty of the Law: Reflections of a Supreme Court Justice*, published in 2003, she reflected on the women's rights movement in America. It is "by no means a coherent or uniform endeavor," she wrote. "Perhaps because women have advanced so dramatically in the working world in recent decades, the sense of urgency that prevailed in the 1960s and 1970s has given way to fragmentation along traditional lines."

American women, unlike American men, must still "juggle" their work lives and their family lives, she said. For some women, it is just easier to forego a family life, she mused. "Personally, I chose to have and enjoy my family early on and to resume my career path somewhat later. But the ideal choice, to the extent that it exists, is certainly not self-evident, and American women are forced to make substantial trade-offs that American men largely bypass."

Yet with all the pain of her first rejections still with her, the experience simply did not generate an empathy in her that discrimination did on her colleague, Justice Ruth Bader Ginsburg. Confirmed in 1993 after being nominated by President Bill Clinton, Ginsburg had become emotionally and immediately identified with women's liberation in a way that Sandra Day O'Connor never was, although O'Connor rejoiced at having a "sister" on the bench. She once told an audience at William and Mary College in Virginia that before Justice Ginsburg arrived, "People would say, 'You've seen one female Supreme Court justice, you've seen them all.' They can't say that anymore." Yet Ginsburg's first words on the national scene would never have been uttered by O'Connor. Ginsburg paid tribute to her own mother and said, "I pray that I may be all that she would have been had she lived in an age when women could aspire and achieve, and daughters are cherished as much as sons." O'Connor repeated regularly that having another woman on the Court was a blessing because it relieved her of the public pressure of being the only woman. But the two women had completely different styles. A University of Minnesota law professor, Suzanna Sherry, told the *Washington Post*, "I can't think of any justice who is like Ginsburg in using the Court as a bully pulpit." Ginsburg once said, according to the Court's in-house newsletter *Oyez, Oyez* (an English expression that dates back to the fifteenth century and means "hear, hear"), that "No one here has risen as far as I. I started out as a GS-2 [one of the lowest clerk levels in government]!" Some, such as veteran Supreme Court analyst Joan Biskupic, think O'Connor learned from her western roots to fight sexism from the inside, while Ginsburg, who is three years younger and grew up in a working-class family in Brooklyn, learned to fight sexism from the outside.

O'Connor once told the American Bar Association's *ABA Journal* that intrinsically she thinks many women are better than men at handling the demands of their lives and that they have to work harder to succeed. "I think that many women have a great amount of energy, which I have been blessed with, and sturdy constitutions. I think many women are happier juggling various roles than not having the opportunity. I'm like that." But, she also added, "It is true that women have to perform better than their male counterparts to succeed in competition."

Her rulings have sometimes shocked feminists who think she should always side with them. In her first year on the high bench, O'Connor wrote the majority opinion that said, 5 to 4, that the nursing school at the Mississippi University for Women could not refuse to admit a male student. O'Connor said that Joe Hogan, a licensed practical nurse who had been twice denied admission to the university's nursing program because he was male, had to be admitted because Mississippi had "fallen short of establishing the exceedingly persuasive justification needed to sustain the gender-based classification." She said, furthermore, in an interesting argument that had rarely been made in the Supreme Court that the university was actually perpetuating a stereotype hurtful to women that nursing was an "exclusively women's job."

In 2002, the Supreme Court, with O'Connor writing the opinion, made it more difficult for employees to demand special treatment when they suffer partial physical disabilities. She ruled that Ella Williams, a five-foot-tall Kentucky mother who spent her working life on the Toyota assembly until she developed acute pain and spasm in her hands and arms from working with pneumatic tools, later diagnosed as carpal tunnel syndrome, was not entitled to a less physically demanding job with Toyota. O'Connor—her western heritage showing, perhaps—wrote that Williams was still able to brush her teeth, wash her face, bathe, tend her flower garden, fix breakfast, and do light housework. National Public Radio's Supreme Court reporter Nina Totenberg noted, somewhat wryly, "True, Justice O'Connor said, she stopped sweeping and dancing. She occasionally needed help in dressing and had to reduce how often she could play with her children, garden or drive long distances. But, said the justice, these changes in her life did not amount to such severe restrictions in activities that are of central importance in most people's daily lives that they establish your status as disabled under the [Americans With

Disabilities Act] law." Thus, O'Connor said, Williams had not met what should be a consistently high standard for qualifying as "disabled" under the law. She said that the disabilities act requires a case-by-case analysis of who is disabled and who is not. Thus, employers are not required to make accommodations for workers unless their symptoms are severe enough to limit a major life activity outside of work.

Representative Steny Hoyer, a Maryland Democrat and one of the authors of the Americans With Disabilities Act of 1990, said that O'Connor was clearly not dealing with what the intent of Congress was when she wrote her decision. He noted that the impetus of the law came from Tony Coelho, then a California Democrat and majority whip in the House, who had epilepsy after a childhood head injury. Under O'Connor's definition of a disability as excluding someone from major life activities, Coelho was not disabled. Yet, said Hoyer, "he had been expelled from a seminary, had his driver's license revoked, been discriminated against by health insurers and rejected by the armed services." Hoyer asked, with some aggravation, "Is this what we had in mind when we passed the ADA—that lawyers for businesses and individuals should spend time and money arguing about whether people can brush their teeth and take out the garbage? Not at all."

O'Connor is decidedly uncomfortable with the idea that male judges and female judges might rule differently. So, too, is Ginsburg, whose husband, Martin, a tax attorney and Georgetown University law professor, once wrote the *Washington Post* a letter to say that his wife does not think women speak in a different "voice" on the bench. In fact, he said, "I am sure she believes quite the opposite."

In a talk to the American Jewish Committee, Ginsburg said that after she was appointed in 1993, she was often asked whether the Court would be different with two women as members. The following year, after Stephen Breyer was appointed, she was asked if having two Jews on the Court would make a difference. She said that when asked the question about two women, "Justice O'Connor has several times quoted, as have I, the reply of Minnesota Supreme Court Justice Jeanne Coyne. In her experience, Justice Coyne said, 'A wise old man and a wise old woman reach the same conclusion.'" But, Ginsburg went on, "It is also true, I am convinced, that women, like persons of different racial groups and ethnic origins, contribute to the United States judiciary what a brilliant jurist, the late U.S. Court of Appeals Judge Alvin Rubin, described as 'a distinctive medley of views influenced by differences in biology, cultural impact, and life experience.' In this sense, Jewish judges, too, have indeed enriched the U.S. system of justice."

And then, Ginsburg, always the proselytizer, put in a plug for then President Bill Clinton's judicial appointments. Nearly one-third of his 162 judicial nominees are women, Ginsburg said, and women and minorities together constitute 54 percent of the nominees. Even though O'Connor regularly quotes Coyne's observation that wise men and wise women will rule the same way, she also once said, "This so-called new feminism is interesting but troubling," adding that she never wants to return to the days when some thought female judges were better able to rule on child custody cases than on tough criminal cases.

And there, despite their many differences, she and Ginsburg are in total agreement. "Theoretical discussions are ongoing today—particularly in academic circles—about differences in the voices women and men hear, or in their moral perceptions," O'Connor once said. "When asked about such things, I usually abstain. Generalizations about the way women or men are—my life's experience bears out—cannot guide me reliably in making decisions about particular individuals."

Yet the person in the Reagan administration charged with finding federal court nominees, Jonathan Rose, who as head of the Justice Department's Office of Legal Policy had a leading role in the screening of candidates, told the *National Law Journal* in 1983 that Sandra Day O'Connor was partially an anomaly because she wasn't interested in being a judicial activist, which, he said, too many blacks and women strive to be. "We appointed Sandra Day O'Connor to the Supreme Court, but we won't appoint anyone who wants to be a substitute legislator on the bench," Rose told the law journal. While he got hundreds of names of potential judicial nominees from a variety of sources—Republican senators and representatives in the circuit area, judges, academics, and interested groups, he said,

"It's futile to propose a candidate who doesn't share the president's philosophy." Asked if female and minority lawyers tend to be judicial activists, Rose answered, "The net result of the people Carter appointed, the composite, tended to be more in the direction" of judicial activism.

His boss, President Reagan, put a nicer spin on it when he told the American Bar Association that year in Atlanta, "We aim for a cross-section of appointments that fully reflects the rich diversity and talent of our people. But we do not, and we never will, select individuals just because they are men or women, whites or blacks, Jews, Catholics or whatever . . . I believe you rob people of their dignity and confidence when you impose quotas."

O'Connor felt that she was a result of Reagan's campaign promise to appoint a woman to the Supreme Court, but it never crossed her mind that she was any part of a quota, even though she would often say she was "lucky" to have been appointed. Of her own career in Arizona's politics and courts and then moving onto the Supreme Court and having a family, O'Connor repeatedly said that her main gifts in life were her energy and stamina. But she would then invariably add that women still have to perform better than their male counterparts to succeed.

In 1992, when her family and her brother's family and her sister, Ann Day, who had become a successful politician in Arizona, gathered for a Thanksgiving reunion at the Lazy B ranch, O'Connor realized she had many, many reasons to be thankful. She and John had been married for forty years. Her three sons, Scott, Brian, and Jay, were all launched and doing well in their own professional careers, living in Arizona. And while she might not have said this aloud, she was by many arguments the most powerful woman in the nation, with many of the most controversial issues of the day decided by her "swing" vote.

There should be no doubt: O'Connor loves to be first. On April 3, 1995, she became the first woman in U.S. history not just to be on the nation's highest court but to preside over it, when in a routine swearing-in of 131 lawyers to practice before the Court, she sat in Rehnquist's seat of honor when he and the second in seniority, John Paul Stevens, were out of town. It was a small moment, but also, for O'Connor, yet another first. The public spokesman for the Court, Toni House, a former reporter and a feminist who herself loved "firsts," told reporters, "I think she had a lot of fun."

O'Connor may often have deferred to Ginsburg on overt feminism, but she clearly had her views. In 1994, in a commencement address to 2,428 Brigham Young University summer-session graduates, in remarks aimed at the 1,137 women in the class, she said, "As students today, your challenges will come not so much in breaking new paths as your mothers, grandmothers and I have done, but in deciding which of the many paths now open to you to choose and in knowing how you should travel along them."

O'Connor has tried to treat feminism as a cause but not a burning issue, preferably one that can elicit some lightness. Shortly after she was sworn in O'Connor received a present from the Woman's Law Caucus of Northern Kentucky University's Chase Law School. It was a T-shirt that pictured one woman justice and her eight male colleagues. The shirt read: "One down, eight to go." She wrote back, "The T-shirt is terrific. Forgive me if I don't wear it around my colleagues just yet, but it will be nice to get some female companions in the future."

She also enjoyed the story relayed in *TV Guide* magazine about a young teenage actress who kept muffing her lines while rehearsing a sitcom, which ended with a mention of Sandra Day O'Connor. Finally, she complained, "Can't we just change the name?" Her fellow actor asked in disbelief, "Don't you know who Sandra Day O'Connor is?" The actress said that, yes, she did know—Sandra Day O'Connor was the first woman astronaut.

Several years before O'Connor was sworn in as a Supreme Court justice she saw a play, *First Monday in October*, which starred Jane Alexander and Henry Fonda. After she was confirmed, she wrote the actress praising her performance and said she hoped to pattern her behavior after Alexander's self-possessed, dignified, independent manner. The two became pen pals.

For two decades, from a window at the Court, O'Connor could see a brick house that for more than sixty years has been the headquarters of the National Women's Party. She sometimes mentions this in her many speeches. It served as a daily reminder to her, she has said, that women did not have the most basic civil right, the right to vote, until just shortly before she was born.

In 1873, in a case known as *Bradwell v. Illinois*, the U.S. Supreme Court held that Illinois had not violated the Constitution when it said Myra Bradwell could not practice law because she was female. One justice, Joseph P. Bradley, felt compelled to say in his concurring opinion that the "natural and proper timidity and delicacy" of women made them unfit for many occupations. One wonders how he would have explained Sandra Day O'Connor, who would sit in the seat he once held.

Alan Freeman and Elizabeth Mensch, in their analysis of O'Connor in *The Justices of the United States Supreme Court*, noted that exactly 120 years later the *National Law Journal* named Sandra Day O'Connor the "lawyer of the year" and the occupant of the "lawyer's seat" on the Supreme Court because she was "moved by the facts of the case and existing law" instead of by ideology.

It was a proud moment for the independent woman from the West.

CHAPTER FOUR

Shall We Call You Madam Justice?

My power on the Court depends on the strength of my arguments, not on my gender.

—Sandra Day O'Connor

William Rehnquist, in his book *The Supreme Court*, noted that when the Court first began to hand down written opinions in the last decade of the eighteenth century, the author of each opinion was designated, for example, "Cushing, Justice." This form continued until the February 1820, term, when it was replaced by the form, for example, "Mr. Justice Johnson." That designation continued for more than 150 years. Then in 1980, Justice Byron White, "with great prescience, suggested to the conference that since in the very near future a woman was bound to be appointed, we ought to avoid the embarrassment of having to change the style of designating the author of an opinion at that time by making the change before the event. The conference was in entire agreement, and shortly thereafter, without any explanation, the manner of designating the author of an opinion became simply, for example, 'Justice Brennan.'"

Nonetheless, when Sandra Day O'Connor arrived in Washington, taking the oath of office on Friday, September 25, 1981, she was an instant celebrity, a curiosity and a worry to her fellow justices. They had many worries. For one thing, her fellow justices weren't exactly certain how to address her. Mrs. Justice O'Connor? Madame O'Connor? Justice O'Connor? They had discussed the matter of what to call a female justice before she had been nominated, but they weren't certain what O'Connor would think. They worried that she would disrupt their closed circle. While intellectually they were ready for a female colleague, personally, they weren't certain. Some even confessed later they were mildly terrified she would cause chaos in their silent fiefdom and "be difficult" to deal with. They were concerned that even though she had been in the same Stanford law school class as William Rehnquist, the Court's most dogged conservative, she would disrupt the careful philosophical balance on the Court. She had been a majority leader of the Arizona state senate. Did that mean she would be a more political justice than the Court was used to encountering? She had been a prosecutor in the Arizona attorney general's office. How would that affect her opinions? Would she be tough on law-and-order issues? Would she side with the government? She had been a state judge, known as the "Iron Lady." Did that mean she would be distant, changing the collegiality on the Court? Her more liberal new colleagues worried that she would be disinclined to permit any federal supervision of the states. They feared she would be a William Rehnquist clone. The conservative faction of the Court worried that she might be difficult to predict, going "off the reservation" on critical issues such as abortion and affirmative action.

In the preface to her book *The Majesty of the Law*, O'Connor said she and her husband were both excited at the prospect of "new and wonderful friends," such as meeting "presidents, vice presidents, Cabinet members, ambassadors, and other justices and judges from around the world." But she was also determined not to shrink from immediately embracing the challenge of addressing "the toughest legal issues in our nation" and "helping shape the development and explanation of the principles of federal law required to resolve these issues." She would be no clone. She would be warm but principled. She would be friendly but hold her ground. She would not, above all, she hoped, be predictable.

She noted that the nation gets a Supreme Court justice on average every two years—she was only the 102nd justice in U.S. history—but because the process involves little public participation, there is little "releasing of balloons" when a new Supreme Court justice is seated. Metaphorically, however, that was not true in her case. She was the first woman (and mother) to sit on the Court. She was the first appointee of a new and untested president—an actor and former governor of a huge western state, California. And she was certain to affect the ideological balance of the Court. At the relatively young age of fifty-one, she would conceivably be on the high bench for years to come. If the nation was surprised at her nomination and confirmation, she was even more surprised. "My former colleague, Justice Lewis Powell, once said that being appointed to the Court was a little like being struck by lightning in both the suddenness and the improbability of the event."

As she had before her confirmation, she was worried about her reception in Washington. She worried a little about how she would be treated. She worried about missing her pleasant country-club existence in Arizona. She even worried about how she would adjust to no longer seeing the sun rise at 4 A.M. and not set until 10 P.M. She worried about her husband's adjustment to a new law firm, Miller & Chevalier. She worried that she would rarely see her sons, who clearly intended to live their lives in the West. She had never even practiced before the Supreme Court. How hard would it be to figure it all out? The Court gets more than seven thousand applications for review of a case each year but accepts only one hundred cases each term that involve federal law, reversing lower court decisions in about two-thirds of them. The paperwork would be monumental! The workload would be staggering!

On the day of her swearing in, she and her husband, John, rode with President Reagan and his wife, Nancy, in their shiny black limousine in a motorcade from the White House to the Supreme Court. After taking the oath of office from Chief Justice Warren Burger on two Bibles held by her smiling husband, swearing to protect and defend the Constitution, she took her seat at the end of the bench—the farthest from the chief justice since she was the newest and thus lowliest member. She said she looked down at her parents, her husband, and her three adult children with a bursting heart. "I will never forget that moment," she said.

While she was arguably the nation's hottest celebrity, there were many who didn't want a woman on the bench. She never grew tired of quoting the senior citizen who wrote, "Back to your kitchen and home, female! This is a job for a man and only he can make the tough decisions. Take care of your grandchildren and husband." But she also relished the many men who told her, repeatedly, wherever she went, that they were delighted that President Reagan, at the behest of Justice Potter Stewart, had put a woman on the Court. She likes to recite this poem: "A toast to Potter Stewart, his chivalry can't be beat. The first Supreme Court Justice, to give a lady his seat."

Indeed, it was the civility of the Court that struck her from the very first oral argument she attended. Whenever the Court hears oral arguments, it is customary for every justice to shake the hand of every other justice—nine times nine. "To an outsider, this may seem baroque and unnecessary," she writes. "But you must realize we are a very small group. We see and interact with one another often, and we all know we will continue to do so for the rest of our professional lives. It is important that we *get* along together so we can *go* along together."

Her secret apprehensions that she might be ostracized—subtly, of course—did not materialize. Her new colleagues proved to be far more resilient and open to change than the senior citizen who wanted her banished back to the female fiefdom. And it helped that William Rehnquist, who would become the next chief justice, was her friend and mentor. He calmed their fears that she would be a "wild card" in the decision-making or possibly a disruptive force. He delighted in shepherding her around.

The courtly Powell proved to be her salvation when she first arrived at the Supreme Court. He helped Sandra and her husband find a temporary apartment in the Watergate to live in before they decided where they wanted to rent or buy a house. He loaned her his own secretary, who steered the baffled new justice along the rocky path of figuring how to deal with the voluminous avalanche of paper that descended on her from day one and counseled O'Connor on how to handle the bright but sometimes difficult young clerks under her wing. "I felt very close to him [Powell] because he called immediately and offered to help," she says affectionately. Right from the beginning, O'Connor realized that this new job was a seven-day-a-week proposition. She found herself meeting with clerks on Saturday mornings to go over cases to be argued the next week, sometimes fixing them lunch after they worked.

Powell also taught her a lesson inadvertently. When she was new on the bench, she disagreed strenuously on a Powell draft opinion. She was so opposed that she proposed holding the case over for reargument to give the other members a chance to change the draft. She later wrote that her method "upset Lewis dreadfully. It was the only time I've seen him upset." She soon learned that a dissenter who tried to hold a case over would be regarded as using a grossly unacceptable tactic. She apologized and the two resumed their friendship.

It helped that while her legal personality had been forged in the rough-and-tumble states' rights atmosphere of Arizona politics, her social personality was forged in the country-club atmosphere of wealthy Phoenix. She was a hard-working, tough judge but she also wore pearls and earrings and cooked and was a mom and knew when to listen and when to speak. She had been an army wife in Germany and knew what it was like to be "spouse of." Victoria Toensing, an outspoken Republican often on television talk shows for her strongly worded views and a well-known former federal prosecutor and legal partner of her husband, recalled how stunned she was that at a dinner party of prominent Washingtonians O'Connor said nothing when it was suggested—à la nineteenth century—that the men and women adjourn for separate after-dinner drinks. O'Connor dutifully went off with the women.

Her new colleagues were curious about her background growing up on a 250-square-mile cattle ranch, bereft of electricity and running water. When they visited her office, they couldn't help but notice her Native American baskets. She is often given gifts in her travels and loves to put them in her large office overlooking the Capitol, including a handmade quilt from a village she visited in Mongolia. She is essentially a private woman who does not disclose her deepest feelings with anyone. Yet her new colleagues saw that she would quickly become dismissive and sarcastic about sloppily worded appeals. But she was candid with her new friends about one thing: her love of the West. Wherever she went in the world, she would tell them, she always knew the Lazy B would be there. And when her mother died in 1989, she was heartbroken, because after 113 years in the Day family, the ranch had been broken up and sold. "I feel like part of my heart and soul is gone," she said after her memoir about life on the ranch was published in 2002. She told some of her new friends that she always expected to grow up to be a cattle rancher or a rancher's wife. With a slight shrug, she would say, "But it didn't work out that way."

With Ruth Bader Ginsburg and O'Connor the only non-male justices on the Rehnquist Court and Clarence Thomas the only non-white member, one wonders if in the heat of debate they ever encountered subtle discriminatory comments or behavior suggestive of less tolerant times. If so, they have been careful not to talk about it. It is interesting that Ginsburg and O'Connor are friendly but not close friends. Ginsburg was head of the Women's Rights Project of the American Civil Liberties Union and brought a number of sex discrimination cases to the Supreme Court in the 1970s. That is something that would never have occurred to O'Connor to do. Yet she often says that she is delighted to have another woman on the Court because it takes much pressure off of her.

O'Connor is often asked whether she thinks women lawyers see the law differently than their male counterparts do. In *Majesty of the Law*, she wrote that while women attorneys have been characterized as more eager to mediate than litigate, she does not find that to be true. "There is simply no empirical evidence that gender differences lead to discernible differences in rendering judgments."

Pressing further, along a line of thought that clearly interests her, she decided, "whatever our gender or background, [our aspiration should be that] we all may become wise—wise through our different struggles and different victories, wise through work and play, wise through profession and family."

She added that she works with eight strong-willed colleagues. "I don't think any of us exerts much power over the others. I certainly haven't found any justice more or less willing to be persuaded by me because I am a woman. My power on the Court depends on the strength of my arguments, not on my gender."

Yet the reason she was nominated to the Court by Reagan, who had only briefly met her and didn't remember, and although she had only six and a half years of judicial experience total, was her gender. Reagan had promised to name a woman. Chief Justice Warren Burger and Justice William Rehnquist told the president she was a team player and a conservative Republican. Although she won 99 votes in the Senate compared with John Paul Stewart's 98 votes, he got the American Bar Association's top rating while O'Connor got a more guarded rating of "highest standards of judicial temperament and integrity" and "qualified from the standpoint of professional competence for appointment to the Supreme Court."

Despite her relative inexperience as a judge, O'Connor arrived at the highest court with decided views on American jurisprudence. "Americans are the most litigious people in the world today. Our judicial system has been too successful in some ways," she said in a speech on February 8, 1999, in Pasadena, California, at the dedication of the Friends Building of the Western Justice Center Foundation. O'Connor is the Ninth Circuit Justice, which means she keeps an eye on litigation arising in the Far West, but she had special interest in the Western Justice Center because its aim is to promote peaceful resolution of disputes and innovative ways to improve the American justice system. The longer she was on the highest bench, parsing the laws with her eight colleagues, the more she worried that Americans are prone to try to solve their disputes with violence.

In that speech, she said, "Without our communities, disputes between neighbors and citizens are common. Squabbles between neighbors over yards, dogs, fences, and boundaries have always existed. But in the past few years, we have witnessed rioting in the streets of major cities, and frequent breakdowns in the relationships between employers and their employees. We have been made painfully aware of the violence within our schools by the ghastly school shootings in Oregon and Arkansas. Even within churches, disputes have arisen between ministers and congregations, retiring pastors and new pastors and members of a religious institution's hierarchy." She added,

> I have even read a report of a conflict arising from a congregation's accusation that its minister had an 'unbending' biblical interpretation. In short, conflict can be found throughout our community, including those parts of our community—families, schools, and churches—that for a long time, have functioned to resolve disputes, not initiate them. Pundits have suggested a number of theories to explain the growing number of conflicts within our community, ranging from rapid industrialization and urbanization to a general breakdown in societal mores. While it is important to identify the causes of conflict in our society, regardless of the cause, we must find ways to mend the tears in our social fabric arising from these disputes. In short, we must find ways to resolve more of the disputes that permeate our society and do so effectively and nonviolently.

Despite the civility on the Court, there is evidence of increasing resentment among some of the justices that, in the words of Jeffrey Rosen, a professor at George Washington University Law School, "we are all living now in Sandra Day O'Connor's America." In an article in 2001 in the *New York Times Magazine*, he said, "Take almost any of the most divisive questions of American life, and Justice O'Connor either has decided it or is about to decide it on our behalf." While their arguments are, of course, behind closed doors, their questions in oral arguments are public and their written opinions are now even on the Internet for all the world to read and parse. And, increasingly, the dissents contain bitter, acerbic language, probably none more so than Antonin Scalia's.

O'Connor outshone all the other justices, becoming the most powerful woman in America, not by virtue of outstanding intelligence or cleverness but because of the nature of the Rehnquist Court, which increasingly began deciding its most controversial decisions by just one vote. William

Rehnquist, Clarence Thomas, and Antonin Scalia, the Court's most conservative members both on social issues and in their antigovernment views, almost always voted the same way. John Paul Stevens, David Souter, Ruth Bader Ginsburg, and Stephen Breyer, the four most liberal members of the Court, tended to vote against the other three. That left Anthony Kennedy and O'Connor as the swing votes. O'Connor, even more than Kennedy, became the justice that lawyers before the Court tried to influence. She was unique because when she joined the majority, she wrote a concurring opinion that, as Jeffrey Rosen said, "seems designed to drain her colleagues' reasoning of its more general implications." He went on, "She has a habit of confining her vote to the case at hand. Her views are so exquisitely calibrated that once in a voting rights case she wrote a separate concurrence to her own opinion, prompting Pam Karlan, a voting rights scholar at Stanford Law School, to say, 'At last, O'Connor has found someone she can agree with: herself.'"

It is a tricky, risky, and pointless business to try to psychoanalyze the justices or to figure out why they rule the way they do. But, like us all, they are products of their environment, their childhoods, their life experiences. Even in their hallowed halls, they do not exist in a vacuum. Who were O'Connor's colleagues as the Court marched into the twenty-first century? Many of the biographical details are provided by the Supreme Court Historical Society in its excellent volume *The Supreme Court Justices*, edited by Clare Cushman.

Rehnquist was born in Milwaukee, Wisconsin, on October 1, 1924, and grew up in the pleasant, well-to-do suburb of Shorewood, the son of a paper salesman. He confirms that when he was a young boy, horrified by Franklin D. Roosevelt's big government ideology, he told an elementary school teacher that he was going to "change the government" when he grew up. An Army Air Corpsman in World War II in North Africa, he went to college at Stanford University on the GI bill, becoming a Phi Beta Kappa as he earned bachelor's and master's degrees in political science. He then went on to Harvard to get a second master's in government and to Stanford Law School, where he graduated first in his class. He was known for his strong conservative views and was clearly going to become a formidable lawyer. He became a clerk to Justice Robert Jackson, a moderate, but was much more interested in Felix Frankfurter and his "magnetic personality." He was distressed by the liberal views of the other clerks at the time and wrote an article in *U.S. News and World Report* criticizing their "extreme solicitude for the claims of Communists and other criminal defendants, expansion of federal power at the expense of [the power of the states], great sympathy toward any government regulation of business—in short, the political philosophy now espoused by the Court under Chief Justice [Earl] Warren." One of Rehnquist's passions in life would be to undo as much as he could of the Warren Court's "excesses."

Rehnquist then met and married the love of his life, Natalie Cornell, known as "Nan," and they had a son and two daughters and, he says, an idyllic family life until she died in October 1991. He started his law career in Phoenix, partly because of O'Connor's glowing accounts of her state, and became a Republican Party official. Rehnquist became a friend of Richard Kleindienst, who was appointed deputy attorney general in Richard Nixon's administration and brought Rehnquist to the Justice Department to run the Office of Legal Counsel. Shortly after that, when he was forty-seven, Rehnquist was told by Kleindienst the administration had decided to put him on the Supreme Court. He was confirmed by a vote of 68 to 26 on December 10, 1971. He joined the Court on January 7, 1972, ironically, the same day as Lewis F. Powell Jr., who was considered a conservative but who often voted with the Court's liberals on such issues as the separation of church and state and affirmative action.

Rehnquist quickly became known as one of the Court's most conservative justices, constantly battling William O. Douglas, William J. Brennan Jr., and Thurgood Marshall, the Court's liberals. Rehnquist argued again and again that achieving desirable social goals was not permissible if the Constitution and statutory laws did not permit it. He argued that affirmative action was wrong. He argued that abortion was wrong. He did not think that police officers should have to tell suspects their legal rights upon arrest. When Ronald Reagan nominated him to be the nation's sixteenth chief justice upon Warren Burger's retirement, in 1986, Rehnquist was branded a "right-wing extremist" by liberals across the country. His confirmation hearings were bitter and divisive, but he was confirmed by a 65 to 33 vote.

In John W. Dean's book *The Rehnquist Choice: The Untold Story of the Nixon Appointment That Redefined the Supreme Court*, Dean quotes Joseph Rauh, a liberal lawyer who represented civil rights groups before the Court, as saying that it was not Rehnquist's conservatism that angered so many but the "incontestable" evidence that Rehnquist did not tell the truth in his confirmation hearings about a 1952 memo he had written as a law clerk to Justice Jackson in which he urged Jackson to vote against *Brown v. Board of Education*, the landmark school desegregation case, and to reaffirm the notorious *Plessy v. Ferguson* case that decreed the separate-but-equal doctrine toward race in America. Dean, who was Nixon's general counsel, who was heavily involved in Rehnquist's nomination, and who revealed the existence of the Watergate tapes in the Oval Office, agreed that Rehnquist lied when he insisted that he wrote the memo as an expression of Jackson's views, not his own. Dean concluded, "It did not pass the smell test." For one thing, Jackson did not approve of *Plessy v. Ferguson*.

On December 10, 1971, Nixon told Rehnquist in what Dean describes as their only private conversation, "I will give you one last bit of advice, because you're going to be independent, naturally. And that is don't let the fact that you're under heat change any of your views.... So just be as mean and rough as they said you were."

Liberals continued to denounce Rehnquist. In a collection of essays by liberals called *The Rehnquist Court: Judicial Activism on the Right*, the editor, Herman Schwartz, wrote, "The Rehnquist Court is the most conservative Supreme Court since before the New Deal. Ronald Reagan's efforts to reshape the American judiciary have succeeded." He added that the Court persistently used its one-vote margin to move the "constitutional and legal clock back toward the 1920s and 1930s."

Despite all the contentiousness surrounding him, Rehnquist became known as an effective and collegial manager, well liked by his colleagues, even the most liberal ones who disdained his legal opinions. He wrote two books about the Supreme Court aimed at the general public and pursues oil painting, poker, and stamp collecting.

Rehnquist and O'Connor became fast friends in Arizona, but just as they had wonderful debates while dating and as couples when they married other people, they did not always agree on the bench. In fact, they often did not, because O'Connor, from college on, found herself more middle-of-the-road than some of her intellectual friends. The justices call each other by their first names or even nicknames (although it was always Sandra, never Sandy), and O'Connor sometimes called Rehnquist "CJ" for Chief Justice. Once Rehnquist was desperately trying to convince O'Connor in an abortion case to overturn the landmark 1973 *Roe v. Wade* case legalizing abortion, and reportedly rewrote his opinion four times, hoping to win her over. He did not. Justice Harry Blackmun, who had written the opinion in the landmark *Roe v. Wade* case and considered it one of his most important contributions to the nation, was so certain Rehnquist would convince O'Connor that he wrote in his own opinion, "I rue this day." Delighted when O'Connor broke with Rehnquist, Blackmun changed his language to "I fear for the future."

Antonin "Nino" Scalia, perhaps the most vocal conservative on the Court and possibly its most formidable intellectual, was born March 11, 1936, in Trenton, New Jersey, the son of an Italian immigrant who became a professor of languages and a schoolteacher. The family moved to Queens. Scalia was first in his class at St. Francis Xavier military prep school in Manhattan. He was graduated summa cum laude from Georgetown University in 1957 and magna cum laude from Harvard Law School, where he was editor of the *Harvard Law Review*. He married Maureen McCarthy, an English major at Radcliffe College, and the couple had nine children.

A devout Catholic, he began his law career with a prestigious firm in Cleveland, Ohio, and in 1967 left the practice of law to become a professor of law at the University of Virginia. In Nixon's administration, he became general counsel for the Office of Telecommunications Policy, helping ensure the growth of cable television. Then he was chairman of the Administrative Conference of the United States, which is an independent body promoting more effective administration. Under President Gerald Ford he was assistant attorney general for the Office of Legal Counsel in the Justice Department, Rehnquist's old post. He next taught at George Washington University Law Center, the University of Chicago, and Stanford University, and became head of the American Bar Association's section on administrative law and chairman of the Conference of Section Chairs, a high honor in the ABA.

In 1982 President Reagan appointed him to the U.S. Court of Appeals for the District of Columbia circuit. On June 17, 1986, Reagan nominated Scalia to the Supreme Court, when Rehnquist became chief justice. Scalia was confirmed by a vote of 98 to 0. It quickly became clear that he had well honed his beliefs in strict constructionism—taking the Constitution at its exact word—and that he believed judicial activism is a form of societal evil. He is arguably the most outspoken justice on the need for abiding by precedent and limiting judicial excess. He argues that judges are in place to ensure that the executive, judicial, and legislative branches of the government stay equal. He is vehemently anti-abortion and was in solid disagreement when the Supreme Court in 1990 permitted children in abuse cases to testify on closed-circuit television. He argued that the Sixth Amendment says the defendant has a right to confront his or her accuser.

Scalia and his young family were the model for a short-lived television series about the Supreme Court, *First Monday*, a reference to the Court's beginning each term on the first Monday in October. He was played by the actor Joe Mantegna, but his character on television, "Joe Novelli," emerged as far less confrontational, bombastic, and brash and more tormented about decisions than Scalia is in real life. His legendary sarcasm is one reason that many Court watchers began to think he would never be appointed chief justice. His hobbies are tennis, the piano, and opera, a love he shares with the liberal Ginsburg.

Anthony Kennedy was born July 23, 1936, in Sacramento, California, the son of a dockworker who put himself through college and law school and founded his own practice. Kennedy's mother, a Stanford University graduate in the class of 1928, worked in the California Senate and became a local civic leader. One of three children, Kennedy grew up knowing Earl Warren, who would become a chief justice of the Supreme Court. Kennedy was a Phi Beta Kappa graduate of Stanford University, went to the London School of Economics and then Harvard Law School, graduating cum laude. He practiced law with a San Francisco firm, served in the Army National Guard, and then took over his father's law practice. He married his childhood sweetheart, Mary Davis, a teacher and librarian, and the couple had three children, two boys and a girl, all of whom attended Stanford. He taught a constitutional law class at the University of the Pacific and did legal work for members of Ronald Reagan's gubernatorial staff. Reagan recommended him to President Ford for the U.S. Court of Appeals for the Ninth Circuit and the Senate confirmed him in April 1975. For his twelve-year tenure, he was known as a conservative judge but was not "confrontational," said one biographer.

When the controversial Robert Bork was rejected for the Supreme Court and Douglas Ginsburg's nomination was withdrawn after he admitted using marijuana as a young man, Reagan then turned to Kennedy to replace Justice Lewis F. Powell Jr. on November 30, 1987. The amiable Kennedy sailed through the confirmation process with a unanimous vote.

Kennedy is the Court's other "swing" voter, and, like O'Connor, does not seem to like broad interpretations of the law, preferring to go case by case. He tends to vote conservatively, particularly on criminals' rights, as did O'Connor, but he is also pragmatic and even-handed. A passionate advocate of free speech, he angered many conservatives by insisting that flag burning is symbolic speech protected by the First Amendment. He once wrote that the First Amendment freedoms are most in danger when the government seeks to control thought or to justify its laws for that impermissible end. With *Roe v. Wade* the law of the land for three decades, he has not voted to ban it, angering some conservatives. A Catholic, he shares a love of tennis with Scalia but is far less competitive on the tennis court. He also likes recreational reading, and, like O'Connor, plays golf, swims, and is into physical fitness.

John Paul Stevens was born in Chicago on April 20, 1920. His father was a lawyer, wealthy hotelier, and insurance magnate who owned an estate next to the University of Chicago, where Stevens went to college and became a

Phi Beta Kappa graduate in 1941. Stevens married Elizabeth Jane Sheeren, and the couple had four children, but divorced in 1979, four years after Stevens went to the Supreme Court. In 1980 he married Maryan Mulholland Simon. He served in the navy in World War II and was awarded the Bronze Star. He went to Northwestern University School of Law and was editor in chief of the law review and first in his class. He clerked for Supreme Court Justice Wiley Rutledge, a liberal vote on the Court. He became a well-known antitrust lawyer in Chicago, taught antitrust law, and became a sought-after expert in Washington. In 1970 Nixon appointed him to the Seventh Circuit Court of Appeals, and he became known as a serious, dependable moderate. He was a Republican but not an active one. In 1975 President Ford nominated him to replace the liberal William O. Douglas, and he was confirmed 98 to 0.

Like Kennedy, Stevens tends to go for the pragmatic angle, but he is less conservative. He does not appear to have his own agenda. One of his most famous opinions came in 1978 when he said that because of an afternoon radio broadcast of comedian George Carlin's seven dirty words you can't say on TV, when children were listening, the government could regulate the repetitious use of indecent language on the air. However because of the invasion of privacy the government may not ban such language. Like O'Connor, he has a zealous regard for getting the facts of each case straight and trying to divine congressional intent before deciding what to do. He is known for writing more concurring and dissenting opinions than his fellow justices. He wears bow ties and is the only justice who owned and flew his own airplane.

David Souter was born in Melrose, Massachusetts, on September 17, 1939, but considers his home Weare, New Hampshire, where he spent his summers with his maternal grandparents on a farm half an hour from Concord. He is the son of a banker and loved being at town meetings where the citizens of Weare engaged in New England–style self-rule. He majored in philosophy at Harvard University, graduating in 1961 magna cum laude and Phi Beta Kappa. He once wrote a thesis on Supreme Court Justice Oliver Wendell Holmes. A Rhodes scholar, he studied law at Oxford University and then went to Harvard Law School, returning to New Hampshire to practice the kind of law that tried to benefit the poor before moving to the state attorney general's office and becoming good friends with the attorney general, Warren Rudman, who would go on to become a senator. When Rudman went to Washington, Souter was appointed attorney general of New Hampshire. One of his major campaigns was to keep casino gambling out of the state.

Like the majority of Supreme Court justices on the Rehnquist Court, Souter was a Republican. But, like Kennedy, he was not particularly active in the party. In 1978 he was appointed associate justice of the New Hampshire Superior Court, traveling from county to county to hear cases, and then was named to the state supreme court. He was judged tough but fair. He was nominated to the U.S. Court of Appeals for the First Circuit by President George H. W. Bush, who just three months later was urged by Rudman to put Souter on the U.S. Supreme Court to fill the vacancy created by William Brennan's retirement. Souter was confirmed in 1990 by a 90 to 9 vote, with a number of senators concerned that he was too little known, which meant they weren't certain how he would vote on the highest Court.

Although by most standards he is a philosophical moderate, he is considered a liberal on the Rehnquist Court. He leads a spartan, lifelong bachelor's life and says he is happiest in Weare, where he can often be found in summer climbing the White Mountains.

Clarence Thomas was born June 23, 1948, in Pin Point, Georgia, a tiny town now famous only because it is his birthplace. His father left the family when he was two years old. His mother went to work as a maid. When she remarried, Clarence went to live in Savannah with his grandfather, Myers Anderson, a Catholic, a Democrat, and a strong-minded civil rights advocate. He delivered fuel and made enough money to send Clarence and his brother to St. Benedict the Moor, an elementary school for black children. In high school Thomas was the only black student at a Catholic boarding school outside of Savannah. Thomas said his grandparents taught them that discipline, a strict adherence to morality, and hard work were the paramount virtues of a good life. He at one time intended to become a Catholic priest and enrolled in Immaculate Conception Seminary in Missouri but was discouraged when he encountered racism among his fellow seminarians. In 1968 he wound up at Holy Cross in Worcester, Massachusetts, where he became a founder of the Black Student Union but insisted upon having a white roommate. He was ninth in the class of 1971.

He married Kathy Grace Ambush, and the couple had a son, Jamal. The couple was divorced in 1984. Two years later he married Virginia Lamp, who is white and who then worked for the U.S. Chamber of Commerce.

Thomas went to Yale University on an affirmative action plan, which angered him because, he said, the general assumption was that "you were dumb" and couldn't have gotten in without affirmative action. He took pains to become invisible, afraid of being singled out because of his race. His experience undoubtedly would later explain his decisive votes against affirmative action. It might also explain why he almost never asks questions during oral arguments.

After Yale, Thomas went to work for Missouri's young attorney general, John Danforth, an Episcopal priest and staunch Republican who would become a U.S. senator, where Thomas would again work for him. During this time Thomas began forging his own brand of political conservatism, believing that it was wrong to hand anyone special privileges but that everyone should improve his or her lot in life through self-reliance. Eventually Ronald Reagan heard about the rising young black conservative and named him assistant secretary for civil rights at the new Department of Education. Thomas was at first reluctant, because he did not want to become identified with the civil rights movement. After eight months, Thomas was made director of the Equal Employment Opportunity Commission, where he was reluctantly in charge of enforcing federal laws against discrimination in the workplace. He earned the ire of liberals by his opposition to quotas and timetables for racial equality and for openly declaring that racial preference programs did not help the majority of African Americans. He stopped the practice of using class-action suits at the EEOC. And nine thousand Americans who filed age discrimination suits with the EEOC found the time had elapsed without a decision, leaving them with no legal recourse.

In 1990 Thomas was appointed to the U.S. Court of Appeals for the District of Columbia, where his most notable decision was that the federal government may not give preferential treatment to women in broadcast licenses because there was no evidence this would promote greater diversity on the nation's airwaves.

In 1991 President George H. W. Bush nominated Thomas to replace the beloved liberal icon Thurgood Marshall. At a famous press conference at Bush's summer home in Kennebunkport, Maine, Bush declared that Thomas was "the best person at the right time."

His confirmation hearings were among the most circus-like and yet compelling ever held and were televised to the nation. Thomas refused to disclose any views on controversial issues such as abortion. Anita Hill, a lawyer who had worked for Thomas at the EEOC, was brought to the Judiciary Committee to testify under oath that Thomas had sexually harassed her. Nearly everyone in America had an opinion, and books have been written on both sides—against Hill and against Thomas. Thomas's longtime mentor, Danforth, also wrote a book, insisting Thomas was unfairly maligned. When President George W. Bush named Danforth to be ambassador to the United Nations, Thomas swore him in and whispered how honored he was to be doing it. Eventually, the Senate voted to confirm Thomas by the incredibly close vote of 52 to 48.

On the Court, Thomas quickly became known as a second Scalia vote, siding with Scalia repeatedly. He remained bitter and reclusive because of the contentious confirmation ordeal, declaring that he had nearly been ruined by an unfair process. A cigar-smoking fan of NASCAR races, Thomas, like the other justices, is into physical fitness. He is an avid weight lifter.

Ruth Bader Ginsburg was born Joan Ruth Bader on March 15, 1933, daughter of Jewish Americans whose families came from Central Europe and Russia and moved to Brooklyn. Her older sister died at the age of eight, so young Ruth was, in effect, an only child. Her mother, Celia, was the defining presence in the young girl's life, constantly surrounding her with books and making sure she scrimped and saved to get the money to send her smart daughter to college. Ruth did so well in high school that she won numerous scholarships, but her mother died the day before her high school graduation, and never saw her daughter graduate from Cornell University, where she was elected to Phi Beta Kappa and ranked first in the class among women. There she met Martin Ginsburg and they married in 1954, a year after graduation.

They both went to Harvard Law School—she being one of only nine women in the class of 1959. Tragedy struck the young wife and mother when her husband was diagnosed with cancer. During his rigorous treatment, she took notes in his classes and typed his papers, so that he was able to graduate with his class. She was a year behind him but still managed to make law review. When he took a job with a New York law firm, she transferred to Columbia University, where she again made law review and was tied for first place in her class. Just as O'Connor had received no job offers despite her excellent academic record at law school, neither did Ginsburg. She was also declined for a clerkship with the Supreme Court. She has said that being "a woman, a Jew and a mother to boot" was too much for many law partners. Finally, Edmund Palmieri, a district court judge in New York, gave her a clerkship and said she was among the best clerks he had ever hired.

Next she worked on a Columbia Law School project, cowriting a book on Swedish judicial procedure. She learned Swedish and went to Sweden to see its courts firsthand. She even translated the *Swedish Code of Judicial Procedure* into English.

In 1961 she joined the law faculty at Rutgers University and had a second child, disguising her pregnancy for months by wearing large-size clothes, worried she would be fired. Now she had a girl and a boy—and a passion, righting the wrongs of discrimination against women. Her next career move was to work with the American Civil Liberties Union, helping write a brief in *Reed v. Reed* of 1971, in which the Supreme Court nullified a state law that gave men preference over women as administrators of estates in death cases. In 1972 Ginsburg took over the ACLU's Women's Rights Project and for eight years argued cases before the Supreme Court, urging the justices to take a new look at sex-based legal distinctions, trying to push the Court into deciding that gender-based stereotyping hurt all of society, not just women. One of her cases was pushing the Court, successfully, into ruling that a widower was entitled to Social Security benefits based on the earnings of his diseased wife. Until then only widows had been eligible. Even as she was arguing cases for the ACLU, she was also teaching at Columbia Law School, where she became the first woman law professor to get tenure.

In 1980 President Jimmy Carter appointed her to a high-profile job as judge on the U.S. Court of Appeals for the District of Columbia. Her husband left his lucrative practice in New York to move to Washington, D.C., to teach at Georgetown University Law Center.

As a judge, Ginsburg was efficient, prompt, ordered, clear, and concise. She also became a role model for young liberal women lawyers. In 1991, when Justice Byron White resigned, she was nominated to the Supreme Court by President Bill Clinton. Introducing her in the Rose Garden to the press, Clinton extolled her for having "a fine mind, good judgment, wide experience in the law and in the problems of real people" and also being "somebody with a big heart." He called her the "Thurgood Marshall of gender equality law."

Yet some feminists were wary of her because she had expressed concerns about the Supreme Court's reasoning in *Roe v. Wade*, which legalized abortion in 1973. Ginsburg made clear that she believed "a woman's right to choose" to have an abortion was central to a woman's life and dignity. She was confirmed by a vote of 97 to 3.

On the Court she has become known for impeccable grammar and well-written, commonsense opinions. She loves opera.

Stephen Gerald Breyer was born August 15, 1938, in San Francisco, where his father was a prominent lawyer and also administrator for the city school system. His mother, the daughter of Prussian immigrants, was a civic activist, a loyal Democrat, and devoted to the League of Women Voters. She instilled in her son a passion for good government, helping others, and a life of public service. She made certain he joined the Boy Scouts.

He was a good student at the city's flagship Lowell School, a polished debater, and voted most likely to succeed. He actively practiced his Jewish faith and followed his parents' advice by going to Stanford University instead of Harvard, where he graduated with the highest honors in 1959.

After a stint at Oxford University on a Marshall Scholarship, he went to Harvard Law School, worked on the law review, and got his law degree magna cum laude. He became a clerk to Justice Arthur J. Goldberg, one of the Court's best-known liberals. In the mid 1960s, he worked in the U.S. Department of Justice on antitrust regulation. He also met and in 1967 married Joanna Freda Hare, a graduate of Oxford and daughter of a British lord who headed Britain's Conservative Party. He then went to teach at Harvard Law School.

In 1973 Breyer became assistant special prosecutor in the Watergate investigation. He went on to work for the Senate Judiciary Committee, where he took a special interest in the airline industry, becoming a strong advocate of deregulation. In 1980 President Jimmy Carter nominated Breyer for a seat on the U.S. Court of Appeals for the First Circuit, and even though many Carter nominees were stalled by Republicans in Congress, Breyer was confirmed. Five years later he was appointed to the U.S. Sentencing Commission, an independent body with the duty of making federal criminal sentencing procedures more uniform and fair.

In 1993 Clinton almost nominated Breyer instead of Ginsburg to the high court. In May 1994, when Justice Harry A. Blackmun resigned, Clinton nominated Breyer. He won confirmation on an 87 to 9 vote.

On the Court Breyer is known for his dry wit, his boundless energy, and his knowledge of regulatory and economic law. Breyer quickly became part of the liberal branch of the Court, often joining with Stevens, Souter, and Ginsburg. Like the other eight justices, who spend so much time indoors that they relish the outdoors, Breyer likes physical activity, and he and his wife and three children spend many weekends camping and going on bicycle trips.

These were the colleagues O'Connor spent most of her working years on the high court associating with, genteelly disagreeing with, sometimes socializing with, and, ultimately, coming to respect and admire. They shaped her life and thoughts; she shaped theirs.

CHAPTER FIVE

Behind Closed Doors

> Slaying the dragon of delay is no sport for the short-winded.
>
> —Sandra Day O'Connor

The nine justices may look remote and untouchable in their black robes and carefully phrased, nuanced, and sometimes robust questioning of lawyers during oral arguments. But the Rehnquist/O'Connor Court was what lawyers like to refer to as a "hot bench"—the justices like the jousting. During oral arguments, they were invariably predictable. Chief Justice William Rehnquist, who tolerated no aberrant behavior in his court, frequently got up and disappeared behind the velvet curtains to stretch his back; twenty-four seconds later he returned. Antonin Scalia loves sharp, sarcastic questioning; if the lawyers before him squirm or perceptibly pale, so much the better. Clarence Thomas says nothing. Stephen Breyer likes to be multifaceted, with hypotheticals thrown in. Ruth Bader Ginsburg usually asks a barrage of "liberal" questions, but they are carefully posed and often elicit a new understanding even for her conservative colleagues. David Souter seems uncomfortable and sometimes out of place but then will focus on the most critical issue. John Paul Stevens seems to hover over the proceedings like a benevolent but sometimes disapproving father. Anthony Kennedy ponders one side and then the other, seemingly torn by the great dilemmas of the day. Sandra Day O'Connor often looked as though she would rather be somewhere else but then suddenly leaned forward with a question that got right to the point and seemed to indicate that yes, she now understands the point of it all, even if she is playing devil's advocate. Court watchers say her questions tended to be among the most balanced. Some think that the justices generally ask more questions, and in a more confrontational manner, of the side that he or she ultimately votes against. And behind the closed doors, the chambers ooze with politics, sometimes in its rawest form. The justices strive for cool objectivity and thoughtfulness, but they are just as subject to the vagaries of human nature, conflict, and jealousy as anyone else.

Far more than most institutions in the sometimes arcane world of Washington, D.C., the Supreme Court—which looks like a Greek temple on the crest of Capitol Hill and is sometimes called "the marble palace"—has remained mysterious and confusing. Under the forty-four-foot-high ceiling of the Supreme Court hearing room, flanked by two dozen columns of Italian marble, tourists may watch the justices, who enter like magicians through a red velvet curtain and pelt questions at nervous lawyers desperate to make their points. But the tourists, while often thrilled with the spectacle, walk out unsatisfied and confused. How do the nine justices reach their decisions? Because of the current spate of kiss-and-tell books, we may know the most important secrets of what happens inside the White House within a matter of hours, weeks, or months. For Congress, it is often a matter of minutes. But in the sacrosanct world of the nine men and women who make up the Supreme Court, we may never learn how decisions are reached or at least not until decades have passed or memoirs are published or, occasionally, if someone, such as a clerk, talks. But that is rare. For one thing, those who work at the Court and know its secrets often spend as much as ninety hours a week inside its walls—giving them hardly any time to spill the beans of what they see and hear. What isn't generally known is that the justices sometimes take many votes and that they pressure each other—

subtly—to change a vote. This is the all-too-human practical politics rule of shifting alliances. Thus, on a hot case, word may leak out that the justices will rule one way but when the final vote is taken, the decision may go in exactly the opposite direction.

On September 25, 1981, the day Sandra Day O'Connor was sworn into office, the clue to 21-across, "Characterization of Supreme Court," on the *Washington Post*'s crossword puzzle was "nine old men."

When O'Connor walked into work on her first workday as a justice, September 28, 1981, arriving in a compact car shortly before 8 A.M., she was the only woman in 191 years who ever attended one of the justices' most secret conferences. They handed her a list of one thousand petitions for Court review and suggested, politely, she get to work. And if they thought she would sit back quietly until she got the lay of the land, she did not. In her first oral argument some days later, she asked her first question from the bench, a question about California's bid to obtain an offshore oil and natural gas leasing system that would bring more income into state coffers. In the front of the courtroom was her husband, John, who would soon go to work for a prestigious Washington, D.C., law firm. Nearby was Potter Stewart, whose retirement as a justice on July 3, 1981, had opened the way for Reagan to nominate her.

When network TV tried to decipher the Court for viewers, much as producer Aaron Sorkin did in *The West Wing* for the White House intrigues, the results were not impressive. The show, *First Monday*, debuting in January 2002, didn't make it. Two well-connected Washington lawyers told Tony Mauro, the veteran Supreme Court watcher for American Lawyer Media, that the show was "unbelievably smarmy" and "vomitous."

In a panel discussion in 1993, O'Connor said she remembered with "complete clarity" that what she called the most exciting moment of her nomination and first days on the Court was going to the conference table and being one of nine people to decide some very important issues of federal law.

> That feeling of awe in attending the conference stays with me today. It is by far for me the most interesting time that I spend at the Court,

it's going to those conference discussions. And even though we get to know our colleagues pretty well and, as you prepare and I think we all do prepare, it's a little like going in my view to an oral final examination. You have to prepare with some care before going in there because your expression of views has pretty serious consequences for you inasmuch as you might be asked to write an opinion either for the Court or for the dissenting justices based on what you said at the conference discussion. So this is not an idle discussion. Even today I can't go in there and predict with any great degree of accuracy how my colleagues are going to vote on a given case. There are lots of surprises, and they will surprise you in conference. And it's so interesting to see how the justices come out on it.

Generally speaking, the nine justices who make up the Supreme Court are independent, nonpartisan jurists, the best and the brightest, and make up their minds on each case based on the merits of the arguments before them. But seven of the justices on the O'Connor Court were appointed by Republican presidents. And there is often a clear cast to the ideological persuasions of the justices. The liberals, at the dawn of the twenty-first century, were Ruth Bader Ginsburg, David Souter, John Paul Stevens, and Stephen Breyer. The conservatives were Chief Justice William Rehnquist, Antonin Scalia, and Clarence Thomas. Anthony Kennedy and O'Connor, appointed by Reagan, were the "swing" voters. They think like conservatives, and they talk like conservatives. But conservatives cannot always count on them, especially in cases of social behavior. To watch a Supreme Court argument is to watch lawyers on both sides of an argument nervously watch O'Connor, eager to please her, eager to answer her questions, eager, oh very eager, to get her vote.

One Georgetown University law professor told *Washington Post* Supreme Court reporter Charles Lane that he advises lawyers arguing cases before the Court to treat every justice with the utmost respect but when O'Connor asks a question they would be "well advised to answer in full, and pause and look at her, because nothing is more important to you than making sure you've addressed her concern. With the others, it may not make a difference."

While clerks to the justices know much, see much, and hear much, few talk. Edward Lazarus, a law clerk to Justice Harry A. Blackmun from 1988 to 1989, subsequently wrote a book, *Closed Chambers: The First Eyewitness Account of the Epic Struggles Inside the Supreme Court.* Lazarus said he approached his examination of the Court with the skills of a reporter and was careful to avoid disclosing information he was privy to solely because he worked for Blackmun. He also relied on people he had come to know telling him information without attribution.

Not surprisingly, by portraying the Court as manipulated by politicians and the machinations of ideologically conservative law clerks who sometimes sway the justices, he was highly critical. The justices were not pleased by the book, even though Rehnquist, a former law clerk, had once written an article for *U.S. News & World Report* that said liberal law clerks were exercising too much power over the justices.

Lazarus wrote that it was "received wisdom among the clerks" that O'Connor distrusted the persuasive but liberal Justice William Brennan, who died in 1997, "for having hoodwinked her in some unnamed past case." Thus, Lazarus insisted, O'Connor refused to sign on to Brennan's major opinions while they were both on the Court.

The justices did not comment on the book, but the underground judgment was that Lazarus overstated the power of the clerks and that his explanation does not fit, considering that the justices rule about the same way over years while clerks stay for one year and then depart. Gerard Lynch, a Columbia University law professor and former clerk to Brennan, told *Time* magazine that a former clerk selling a book abut what he saw at the Court is a violation of "personal loyalty." The official *Supreme Court Code of Conduct* requires each law clerk to hold to "complete confidentiality" on behalf of the Court and the justice. No clerk who ever worked for O'Connor betrayed her confidence.

Nonetheless, Lazarus and others who have probed the inner sanctum of what happens when the nine men and women flay the most controversial issues of their day behind closed doors show that raw politics is never too far from the negotiations but that those who think they know what the

Court will decide are often doomed to be wrong. Nobody, however, disputes that the Court's rulings affect the lives of millions of Americans every day.

In recalling the case of *Planned Parenthood of Southeastern Pennsylvania v. Casey*, the abortion test case of 1992 that in many ways was pivotal, Lazarus noted that dozens of people lined up outside the Court for much of the rainy night before the decision was handed down, looking "like rock 'n' roll fans camped out for the night in front of a box office."

Much was at stake. The Third Circuit Court of Appeals, which covers Pennsylvania, New Jersey, and Delaware, had ruled that *Roe v. Wade* was no longer the law of the land. Opponents of abortion were jubilant, seeing at last an opportunity for them to take a major case to the Court and win; supporters of abortion rights were frantic. Whatever happened on appeal, the decision was certain to be 5 to 4, and nobody was quite certain how it would go. In April 1992, before the case was orally argued, abortion rights advocates had staged a march on Washington with 500,000 supporters to try to put as much political persuasion as possible to bear on the Court.

When the day came in July 1992 to announce its decision, the Court was as divided as it had ever been on any issue in any decade. O'Connor, who hated the whole issue of abortion and the need to rule on it in various ways and always at inopportune moments in the nation's history, had to once again become identified with the issue. Justice Anthony Kennedy felt the same way. A devout Catholic, he hated abortion and for years had mustered up compelling legal arguments against *Roe v. Wade*. But he had misgivings about the Pennsylvania law and given such a fractious issue as abortion yearned, as did O'Connor, for some way to strike a middle ground, a balance, even though in hindsight it was clear a compromise would please nobody. Justice David Souter, the mild-mannered, reclusive New Hampshire bachelor, was part of the cabal to achieve some sort of middle ground that would not rent the nation into two warring camps and stir up passions that could last for generations. Central to their argument was the belief that the Court's authority stemmed from the belief its rulings were grounded in law, not formed by social and political pressures, and that grounds for overturning *Roe v. Wade* in the case before them had not been firmly established.

O'Connor, Kennedy, and Souter had to plot and scheme behind the scenes to achieve a centrist, moderate position, agreeing it was not the best solution in an ideal world but was the best they could contrive given the passions in an election year.

As the decision was announced, O'Connor was the first of the nine justices to speak. Lazarus wrote, "Then O'Connor began, her face pressed into one hand, a small tremor in her voice. 'We conclude the central holding of Roe should be affirmed.'" In other words, women have a constitutional right to have an abortion if they choose to exercise that right. The trio also succeeded, over Chief Justice William Rehnquist's vehement objections, in opposing Pennsylvania's demand that any woman getting an abortion have the approval of her spouse. But the Pennsylvania requirement that parents of minors approve an abortion was upheld, as was the proviso that a twenty-four-hour wait was required, giving time for a woman to change her mind. Abortion rights advocates were dismayed to realize that the Court had shifted to say that a state now could legally regulate abortion, possibly even ban it in certain circumstances, if abortion was preserved as a legal remedy in the case of a woman whose life or health was at risk.

O'Connor, Kennedy, and Souter had essentially formed what Lazarus called "a troika" to defeat Rehnquist, O'Connor's good friend and mentor. Rehnquist, knowing he had the full support of the flamboyant opera buff Justice Antonin Scalia, had tried in vain for weeks to derail the case from being decided by the Court. He ridiculed the opinion as a "judicial Potemkin Village," a meaningless façade. His opinion was that the harshest aspects for women seeking abortions under the Pennsylvania law should be upheld, that *Roe v. Wade* had been wrongly decided, "and that it can and should be overruled." Abortion opponents considered the case a major defeat and were furious that three "Reagan-Bush appointees" had betrayed them and that they had lost by just one vote. They reviled O'Connor's continuing insistence that restrictions on abortion must not place an "undue burden" on the right to have an abortion. But abortion rights advocates did not claim victory, considering the decision a travesty, the first major success in the ongoing crusade to gut *Roe v. Wade* and ban legal abortions.

The decision pleased nobody and certainly did not end the divisive, passionate debate over abortion. It opened the Court to criticism from both sides that its rulings on abortion were illegitimate. And it ensured that abortion would be a central issue in forthcoming presidential campaigns. In other words, would a candidate name someone to the Supreme Court who would support the right of a woman to abortion or would deny it?

O'Connor, pondering the workings of the Court, wrote in her book *The Majesty of the Law* that she was certain "we do not always succeed in striking precisely the right balance among the competing ideals of law, freedom and justice. But we never stop trying. It is safe to say that at least one lawyer disagrees with almost every opinion we hand down; we don't take a case without two sides to it, and one side always must lose. Indeed, I have known judges whose natural temperament led them to endeavor to decide a case against the lawyers on *both* sides, but generally speaking, such efforts have not been crowned with success."

Another contentious case, *Bush v. Gore*, in which the justices, in a divisive 5 to 4 decision that has become a trademark of the Rehnquist-O'Connor Court, decided the 2000 election was a true test of the civility on which the Court prides itself. There were reports after that decision that some justices were not even speaking to each other. If true, the justices quickly got over such childish behavior—nothing interferes with the daily tradition of shaking hands, begun in the late 1800s by Chief Justice Melville Fuller. It's difficult to shake hands without speaking.

According to Rehnquist's book, *The Supreme Court*, after the justices shake hands in the conference room next to the chambers of the chief justice, they sit down at a long rectangular conference table, Rehnquist as chief justice presides and sits at one end. Everyone sits according to seniority. At the opposite end is the second most senior justice, John Paul Stevens. Next in line was Sandra Day O'Connor. She sat with the next two most senior justices. The three "junior" justices sit facing them on the opposite side of the table. Not one of the Court's four hundred staff members has ever been in the room for deliberations. If there is a knock on the door, the junior justice (Stephen Breyer during much of O'Connor's tenure) opens the door.

Rehnquist always leads the discussion. He reviews the facts of the case at hand and sets out the decisions of the lower courts. He is the first to state whether he will vote to affirm the lower court's decision or reverse it. Then Stevens gives his thoughts, followed by O'Connor, and so on down the line.

Rehnquist wrote that he was surprised and disappointed when he first went to the Supreme Court at how little interplay there was among justices during the conference. "Probably most junior justices before me must have felt as I did that they had some very significant contributions to make and were disappointed that they hardly ever seemed to influence anyone." As a result, Rehnquist lets anyone speak—in turn, of course. After discussion, Rehnquist announces what he perceives to be the final vote. Often he will say that there are some issues that need to be worked out "in the writing." That gives the justice to whom he assigns the task of writing the Court's opinion enormous latitude and enormous responsibility. A justice who disagrees with the opinion may write a dissenting opinion that is also published. The dissents are often the major key to how the justices have debated and what points they have made behind closed doors.

Math has played another important role in the Court. Statistically, with nine justices, there are 512 coalitions justices could form, with 256 of them winning coalitions, according to Paul H. Edelman and Jim Chen in "The Most Dangerous Justice: The Supreme Court and the Bar of Mathematics," in the 1996 *Southern California Law Review*. Generally, according to mathematical probability, Rehnquist wrote two-thirds of the decisions, Stevens wrote one-fourth, and O'Connor just under 10 percent.

Some of O'Connor's best arguments, according to legal scholars, have been made in her dissents. In one such case O'Connor's western heritage and passion were obvious. In 2001 the Chickasaw Nation said Indian reservations deserve the same exemption from federal wagering excise and occupation taxes that the states get from gambling revenues. The Chickasaw lawyers cited the Indian Gaming Regulatory Act of 1988 and said a parenthetical numerical cross-reference in the law gave them the exemption. The Supreme Court ruled against the Chickasaws, saying Congress didn't legislate by parenthetical references. O'Connor completely disagreed. She said,

"Exempting Nations from federal gaming taxation in the same manner as States preserves the Nations' sovereignty and avoids giving state gaming a competitive advantage that would interfere with the Nations' ability to raise revenue in this manner." She concluded that because Congress had chosen gaming as a way to enable the Indian Nations to achieve self-sufficiency, the "Indian canon rightly dictates that Congress should be presumed to have intended the Nations to receive more, rather than less, revenue from this enterprise." She lost, and Indian Nations must pay the same gambling taxes as private concerns.

In another case her dissent startled some of her most conservative admirers. In 2002 the Supreme Court ruled that high schools may require that students who want to participate in extracurricular activities submit to urinalysis testing for drugs. By 5 to 4, the Court ruled such a policy does not violate the Fourth Amendment, which says people have the right to be secure in their persons, houses, papers, and effects, against unreasonable searches and seizures. O'Connor joined the "liberal" minority of the Court to argue the Court was wrong in using a precedent that said schools may test all athletes for drugs because drug use could increase the risk of sports injuries. She wrote that requiring urinalysis of any students wanting to be in extracurricular activities was not reasonable but "capricious, even perverse." She said such a school policy was actually targeting a student population "least likely to be at risk from illicit drugs and their damaging effects."

But O'Connor's decisions were not always predictable. One might have thought that she would have taken the side of a high school student who was molested for months by a teacher she met in eighth grade when she joined his high school book discussion group, an activity subsidized in part with federal money. The girl sued, claiming her rights under Title IX of the 1972 Education Act, which forbids sex discrimination in schools. She claimed the school district was responsible since the teacher worked for the district and that it did not have an adequate sexual harassment policy for the benefit of both students and teachers. O'Connor sided with the majority of the Court in a 5 to 4 decision that the school district was not liable because it was never notified of the misconduct. She wrote that it was more important to avoid diverting education funding from beneficial uses where a recipient who is unaware of discrimination in its programs is willing to institute prompt corrective measures.

Another hot-button case in which O'Connor did not do what many expected involved guns and schools. In 1992 Alfonso Lopez took a handgun with five bullets to school in San Antonio, Texas, and was charged with violating the Gun Free School Zones Act of 1990. In another 5 to 4 decision, the Court said the Gun Free School Zones Act was unconstitutional because Congress exceeded its legislative powers under the Interstate Commerce Clause. In other words, Lopez had not been engaging in interstate commerce and that if the Court upheld his conviction, it would be saying that Congress could use the Commerce Clause of the Constitution to create "a general police power of the sort retained by the States." O'Connor agreed, infuriating those who said that education is inextricably intertwined with the nation's economy and that guns in schools significantly undermine the quality of education. Congress was so angry, it quickly passed amendments to the gun-free schools law that said the government had to prove the firearms had moved in interstate commerce or somehow that the possession of such firearms affects interstate or foreign commerce.

The Court in recent years has dealt almost regularly with the issue of gay rights. One of the most controversial involved John Geddes Lawrence and Tyron Garner, who were discovered engaging in sodomy by police responding to a fake domestic disturbance call in Texas, which had outlawed sodomy in one form or another along with twelve other states. In 1986 the Court had upheld a similar antisodomy law in Georgia. Many conservatives immediately rallied around the Texas ban on sodomy as a "pro-family" law. O'Connor joined the majority of the Court in a 6 to 3 ruling that the Texas ban on sodomy was unconstitutional because "liberty protects the person from unwarranted government intrusions into a dwelling or other private places. In our tradition the state is not omnipresent in the house." Scalia, Rehnquist, and Thomas were appalled, arguing this would end all rights of the states to enact laws based on morality. Scalia argued the Texas law rightly conveyed to its citizens that certain forms of sexual behavior are "immoral and unacceptable," akin to criminal laws barring fornication, bigamy, adultery, adult incest, bestiality, and incest.

It is both inspiring and frustrating that personalities play such a decisive role on the Court. We yearn for evidence of humanity on the part of the justices who are proscribed by ethics rules from giving their opinions on so many issues but who go to the grocery store, play tennis, and drink cocktails. Justices fear any public controversy over their lifestyle. After Justice Hugo Black of Alabama was nominated by Franklin D. Roosevelt to the Supreme Court and confirmed by the Senate, he almost had to resign when it was learned he had once belonged to the racist Ku Klux Klan. The controversy went away when World War II broke out, and Black became one of the Court's strongest civil libertarians, but it was a delicate period. Today he probably would not have survived and would have lost his tenure. Even as recently as 1986, when William Rehnquist was confirmed as chief justice, it came out that he had once tried to intimidate black voters by challenging their credentials to vote and that the deed to his summer home in Vermont, bought in 1974, had a covenant prohibiting sale or rental to "any member of the Hebrew race." Yet he was confirmed by the Senate, 65 to 33, albeit the largest "no" vote garnered thus far by any chief justice in U.S. history.

As much as anything else, personalities of Supreme Court justices frequently seem to be derived from which region of the country a justice ascends to the Court. It has often been noted that O'Connor's western roots formed the core of her distrust of the federal government, while, for example, Souter's rock-ribbed New England roots made him suspicious of the vagaries of statehouse politics, more in line with Abraham Lincoln's efforts to save the union and ban slavery and certify the rights of the downtrodden.

The Court attempts huge decisions that affect Americans in life and death, more often than not, on the basis of 5 to 4 decisions, a situation that has existed for years because of the divisions in U.S. society. It is at essence a clash of the power of the federal government vs. the authority of each state to be the "laboratory of democracy," establishing its own rules.

O'Connor, basically, agrees that the Court is giving more attention to the doctrine of separation of powers and letting states have more immunity from lawsuits brought in federal court. Tellingly, she often describes it as the "little guys" against the government. But she insists the increasing number of "federalism" cases decided by the Court is a result, not of an agenda by the justices, but of "a reflection of concerns that originate outside the Court." Others disagree.

Yet, there is little disagreement that in the decades since O'Connor ascended to the highest court in the land, it became not the Rehnquist Court, which is the usual tradition of naming the Court after the chief justice, but the O'Connor-Kennedy Court. They are the swing voters, deciding by one vote how a decision will come down. It is a tiring, exhausting, debilitating role, and it is one that neither O'Connor nor Kennedy usually enjoys. They are, at heart, two conservatives, but they are persuadable. They voted, for example, to ban Colorado from denying gays and lesbians status under civil rights laws. They agreed to vote to require Virginia Military Institute to admit women. Obviously, this position did not win them new accolades from the Court's conservatives. As Lazarus wrote, the two were increasingly at bitter odds with Rehnquist and Scalia, who bitingly accused them of not interpreting the Constitution, but creating one of their own.

Mainly because of her votes on abortion and somewhat because of her votes on gay rights, conservatives never much cared for O'Connor, said Ramesh Ponnuru, a conservative writer for the *National Review* in 2003. But, he added, "She is, in truth, both better and worse than they think she is." They like her because of her votes on racial preferences, the death penalty, criminal procedure, and, possibly most of all, her decision in *Bush v. Gore*. But they are horrified at what they perceive is her social liberalism.

But inside the Court, there is more understanding among the conservative justices of the value that O'Connor has provided. So goes O'Connor, so goes the Court. She was in the majority more often than Rehnquist, the chief justice. Ponnuru explained her value to the conservative members of the Court, saying that followers of conservative jurisprudence like her because instead of insisting the Court uphold strict secularism in government, she has helped push the Court to governmental neutrality among religions and because under her tenure the Court has moved more aggressively to limit the power of Congress and protect the prerogatives of the states. Seth Waxman, former solicitor general in the Clinton administration, noted that under Rehnquist and O'Connor, the Supreme Court struck down 28 federal laws in a six-year period compared with only 127 federal laws being struck down in the previous two hundred years.

One reason O'Connor is respected among her peers is that instead of broadly philosophical opinions, she tended to write on narrow issues of fact, which made their job of dissenting or concurring much easier. While conservatives want the Constitution "strictly constructed" instead of justices taking into consideration the practical consequences of their decisions, she has in fact been a voice for pragmatism and civility. While there are reports of increasing contempt and scorn by conservative and liberal justices for each other's opinions, particularly the didactic, iconoclastic Scalia, O'Connor is not included. Her opinions tend to be judicious, somewhat dry, and limited to the facts. She did not tend to skewer personally her colleagues' positions.

O'Connor says that little of the conflict among the justices is spoken. She calls it the "battle of the footnotes," because, said Philip J. Cooper, the Gund Professor of Liberal Arts at the University of Vermont and a specialist in the history of the Supreme Court, the confrontations took the form of "sharp exchanges in footnotes to opinions in which the justices challenge each other by name."

In an interview with Bill Moyers for public television, O'Connor was asked if the justices are deferential with each other. "Yes, very much so. Very courteous, always. I think every justice holds every other justice in very high regard and has great respect one for the other. It's a very civil group."

Moyers pressed her: "But they [her opinions] sometimes antagonize some of your colleagues, don't they?"

"That can happen too," she answered. And did she answer them back? "Oh," she said, "I think there have been occasions when I've taken a stab at responding and others when I don't."

The issue under discussion was Scalia's often sarcastic, bitter name-calling of O'Connor, in which he has not just stopped with criticizing her opinions but has made what some perceive to be stinging references about her character, saying she lacked the courage of her convictions and publicly upbraiding her. Her opinions in abortion cases, on which he is emotional, have invariably drawn his ire.

While conservatives may decry that she has not succeeded completely in overturning main tenets of the liberal Burger Court and the Warren Court, which were known for a progressive view of the Constitution and an eagerness to use the power of the Court to shake up society on issues ranging from school prayer to segregation—outlawing both—she has been in many ways an overseer of pragmatism.

Jonathan Turley, a law professor at George Washington University and a recognized constitutional law scholar and longtime watcher analyst of the Supreme Court, wrote in 2002 that because O'Connor was the perennial swing vote on the divided Court, she alone was making sweeping changes in areas ranging from drug-testing of high school students to the relationship of church and state. "We have come to accept a new reality: 'As O'Connor changes, so does the nation,'" he said. But while he is worried that the nation had become hostage to her views, he said it was a problem of what the Constitution does not say, not what it says. (Turley advocates putting nineteen justices on the Court so that there is no one swing voter. There is no law setting the number at nine—it is tradition, and the number of justices has fluctuated from five in 1801 to ten in 1863. The "court-packing" president Franklin Roosevelt once threatened to increase the Court to fifteen members but dropped that threat when a justice switched his vote and saved some of Roosevelt's New Deal programs. It was known as the "switch in time that saved nine.")

Since then no president has even contemplated changing the number of justices, and O'Connor continued to be the swing voter, with some help from Kennedy. When she first got to the bench in 1981, she found there was "not hostility" toward her, largely because, she said later, the members were tired of operating with only eight justices. "When there are only eight members, it does not function right, particularly in those days when it often divided four to four. The members of the Court were just delighted to have a ninth member, male or female. They were all kind and welcoming."

She later told David Rudenstine, professor of constitutional law at Cardozo Law School, that one thing that irritated them—and her—was what she called the "excessive amount of media attention to the appointment of the first woman and everything she did. Everywhere that Sandra went, the press was sure to go. And that got tiresome; it was stressful . . . I didn't like it. I don't think my husband liked it. It was a constant presence."

Over the years, she went on, "just because I was somehow symbolic of something different on the Court, when the Court would hand down a decision, there would be a little add-on. 'What did Justice O'Connor do in the case?' This changed dramatically with the arrival of Justice Ginsburg. All of a sudden there were two women, and we all became 'fungible' justices, and that was an enormous help. Justice Ginsburg is a very competent justice and it is a joy to have her on the Court, but particularly for me it is a pleasure to have a second woman on the Court."

One thing no new justice is quite prepared for is the huge amount of work involved in reading cases, briefs, and earlier decisions. Despite the rigor of the workload, reading thousands of cases and working through the group dynamics of the Court to reach a decision, few justices ever want to step down. Many retired justices have said that leaving the Court and the strange camaraderie it spawns was one of the most difficult decisions they ever made.

Leon Silverman, president of the Supreme Court Historical Society, wrote in 1995 that Americans should remember that the "vote of the most junior member of the nine justices, from the moment he or she takes the oath of office, counts for as much as that of the chief justice." Thus it is a rarefied atmosphere, and one that despite moments of frustration, anger, and bitterness foments strong feelings of kinship. Justice Robert Jackson once said of his brethren on the Court, "We are not final because we are infallible, but we are infallible only because we are final."

Philip J. Cooper's book *Battles on the Bench: Conflict Inside the Supreme Court* documents strong passions and burning disagreements. But ultimately, he concluded that despite the conflicts the remarkable thing is that the members of the Court "manage to avoid conflict as much as they do and find ways to work together in what could be one of the most conflict-ridden work environments imaginable." Despite all the elements that would seem to make the Court fly apart, he wrote, the Court works together reasonably well.

Rehnquist, in his book *The Supreme Court*, wrote:

> In the light of the temptations that naturally beset any human being who becomes a justice of the Supreme Court, the truly remarkable fact is not that its members may have on infrequent occasions succumbed to these temptations, but that they have by and large had the good judgment and common sense to rise above them in the overwhelming majority of the cases they have decided. The framers of our system of government may indeed have built perhaps better than they knew.
>
> They wanted a constitution that would check the excesses of majority rule, and they created an institution to enforce the commands of the Constitution. But wary of unchecked power in the judiciary, as in all other branches of government, they gave the president, with the consent of the Senate, the power to appoint members of the Court, and the people the right to amend the Constitution. They limited the Court to deciding actual cases and controversies that were brought before it, and they left it partially dependent upon the popularly elected branches of government for the enforcement of its mandates. More than two hundred years of experience now tell us that they succeeded to an extraordinary degree in accomplishing their purpose.
>
> We cannot know for certain the sort of issues with which the Court will grapple in the third century of its existence. But there is no reason to doubt that it will continue as a vital and uniquely American institutional participant in the everlasting search of civilized society for the proper balance between liberty and authority, between the state and the individual.

O'Connor as well as the other justices has given speeches saying the Court's workload is too great and that Congress must do something to help.

In 1987 she gave a speech to the Cleveland (Ohio) City Club in which she said, "The Court is operating, in my view, at maximum capacity now by taking some 150 cases a year. . . . It's a tremendous amount of work. . . . We read all the time and work very hard to keep up with that."

In her first term on the bench the Court had one thousand petitions for review; six years later it had four thousand. "With the growth in population of the United States, and with our tradition for litigation in this country, the numbers have grown very large of the cases decided in the lower courts," she said. Former chief justice Warren Burger had suggested an intercircuit panel be created as a kind of junior Supreme Court. O'Connor said she thought this was a good idea. "I trust that at some time in the future, Congress will take a serious look at such a suggestion," she said.

In the meantime, however, in 1989 she made the Hilton Hotels Corporation's first annual "Best-Stressed List," an award that recognized ten Americans for their ability to balance the pressure of daily stress with leisure and family activities. Besides O'Connor, the list included actor Michael Keaton, actress Candice Bergen, former first lady Betty Ford, hockey champion Wayne Gretzky, United Airlines captain Al Haynes, sports pro Bo Jackson, former U.S. surgeon general C. Everett Koop, *Today* show host Jane Pauley (who has since written a book about her ordeal with bipolar disorder), and opera singer Beverly Sills.

CHAPTER SIX

Party Animal

Do the best you can in every task, no matter how unimportant it may seem at the time. No one learns more about a problem than the person at the bottom.

—Sandra Day O'Connor

Sandra Day O'Connor and her husband, John, quickly made themselves at home on the social circuit when they moved to the nation's capital. Their names studded the local papers because of their frequent attendance at charity balls and cocktail parties. Those who met the new Supreme Court justice in person for the first time were invariably struck by her height (five feet eight inches), her warmth, her elegance, her remarkable cheekbones. More delicate than she seems to be when sitting on the bench next to Rehnquist, she became instantly recognizable at most of the city's major balls and dinners, her trademark blondish-gray hair serving as soft frame for her wide brow and intelligent eyes.

An early introduction to social Washington came at a Washington Press Club dinner when she was seated at a table with John Riggins, the bad boy fullback for the Washington Redskins. As the evening wore on, and adult beverages flowed, Riggins became more and more relaxed. At one point, shortly before he stretched out under the table to take a nap, he was overheard telling the nation's newest Supreme Court justice, "Loosen up, Sandy baby."

O'Connor quickly became a beacon on the social circuit, highly sought after for elite dinner parties and large black-tie events. Not only did she add class, she provided wit. While she enjoyed the acclaim to a certain extent, she still fakes a slight shudder when she recalls her first days in Washington. "Everybody wanted to see me. Everybody was thinking, 'what does she look like?'" At a white-tie Gridiron Dinner on March 9, 2002, she complained that she wasn't dressed up enough. "I was going to wear a glittery dress. But it zips up the back, and John couldn't get the zipper up." Instead, she wore a staid blue and white dress with long sleeves, a shawl, and a turquoise ring from Arizona. "I love turquoise," she said, looking at the ring fondly.

She often startled new acquaintances with her sardonic sense of humor, frequently jarring in a woman of her polite demeanor. Spying the current secretary of the army, who was having a bad spell because of connections to Enron, the failed energy company, she twitted him, "You've been in the news a lot lately." When she saw he was wearing around his neck the highest decoration the German government bestows, she was all but contemptuous. "But why did you get it? What did you do?" she kept asking him impatiently, never getting an answer she found satisfactory.

Highly solicitous of her husband, eager to make certain of his comfort, she rarely accepted invitations unless he was also invited and carefully included him in conversation in a group where he might not know anyone. Once, talking with someone who came from a family of nine children, she exclaimed, "John, she's one of nine, just like Justice Scalia." Her husband looked at the woman and said, "Oops." John O'Connor occasionally said things in public that were less than diplomatic. At a speech O'Connor was giving to the Women's Bar Association of the District of Columbia in 1983, the couple began engaging in a half-funny, half-sparring account of sustaining a two-career family. Mr. O'Connor said that his father told him to marry someone who would produce income and not be a stay-at-home wife.

He said that early in their marriage, after law school, his wife worked a newspaper delivery route. The advantages of this, John O'Connor told six hundred puzzled women, were a "steady income," "it taught her humility," and "gave her security and a sense of place." He added that she also got "regular exercise" and "it kept her close to the news."

None of the hundreds of parties O'Connor attended has been more written about because of their presence than an election-night party on November 7, 2000. While O'Connor is extremely careful to guard her views on political matters, she let her guard drop that night when she heard via television the first returns from Florida shortly before eight P.M. Seated in the den of the house where the party was being held, she was staring at a small black-and-white television set when Dan Rather, anchor for CBS, prematurely (and wrongly, as it turned out months later) called Florida for Al Gore. "This is terrible!" was her exclamation. She turned to someone next to her and said that if Gore had won Florida, the election was "over," because Gore had just carried two other battleground states, Michigan and Illinois. As she left, a look of disgust on her face, to get some food, her husband, John, told the assembled guests that she was upset because they were eager to retire to Arizona and that if Gore won, they would have to wait four more years, to make certain a Republican president would nominate her replacement. She did not want a Democrat to name her successor. This widely reported incident, which she never convincingly denied, was moot because during George W. Bush's first term, she did not retire. She waited until his second term.

But the story does encapsulate O'Connor as a consummate "party animal" not just because of the staggering number of social gatherings she attends but because of her dedication to the Republican Party, which is what vaulted her into the public eye.

In the 1970s, as her husband devoted his career to getting ahead in private practice at the law firm of Fennemore, Craig, von Ammon & Udall and her three sons began to be more independent, O'Connor became increasingly drawn to politics. Having worked her way up to a leadership post in the Arizona senate, she exulted in the life-altering experience she still calls on to craft compromises. It was in the state senate, too, that the once shy ranch girl blossomed into a "people" person as she honed her ability to read people, to figure out their motives and motivations, charming her fellow lawmakers even as she leaned in for the kill to get done what she thought necessary. Her legacy in the Arizona legislature, before she moved on to the bench, is not without critics. But hers was one of the early stories of a woman quietly and effectively amassing power before the big boys realized what was happening. When reporters and scholars examined her record as a lawmaker in Arizona, they found example after example where the paper trail on obscure pieces of legislation was scarce but suddenly her point of view prevailed. She simply possessed the knack for argument, the perseverance to continue when others gave up, and the hard work that gave her the facts to undermine unsubstantiated arguments of others. Yet much of Sandra Day O'Connor's early married life was like *Leave It to Beaver* or *Father Knows Best*, the 1950s TV sitcoms where the stay-at-home mother is always available to solve problems, contribute to the bake sale, volunteer, and be ready to party at the local country club on Saturday night.

From 1960 until 1965 O'Connor did not have a legal job or any full-time job while she took care of three sons, born between 1957 and 1963. The O'Connors are proud of their family; all three sons have been successful and all have remained in the West. Scott and Jay both went to Stanford University, following their parents. Brian, the middle child, went to Colorado College. As an adult, he became a successful Scottsdale businessman, but also fulfilled his childhood dream of being a pilot, a skydiver, and by his early forties one of only 110 people who had climbed the tallest mountain on each of the seven continents. He sounded like his mother when he said, "Perseverance is sticking with a goal and a dream no matter how long it takes." But after conquering Mount Everest on May 26, 2003, at the age of forty-three, he said he'd never again attempt such a feat, preferring to spend the time with his son Westlin, then seven years old.

By the late sixties, Sandra and John began to get more interested in Republican Party politics. There was never a question which party would get her loyalty; her self-reliant father, D.A., had instilled in her a deep distrust of too much government intrusiveness, which she associated with

Democrats. In 1964, when her friend Barry Goldwater, the "conscience-of-a-conservative," "extremism-in-the-defense-of-liberty-is-no-vice" Arizona senator, got the Republican nomination for president, the conservative wing of the Republican Party was briefly centered in Arizona. O'Connor became a precinct committee captain for Goldwater and would admire him, socializing with the Goldwaters, until he died at age eighty-nine in 1998. He would be one of her most vocal defenders when some conservatives wondered if she would be too liberal on the Supreme Court because of her apparent support for abortion rights and because Arizona governor Bruce Babbitt, a Democrat, had deemed her middle-of-the-road enough that he put her on the state appeals court. This was the period, too, when she and Rehnquist cemented their friendship, begun in law school. Charles Lane of the *Washington Post* noted in an article for his paper that Rehnquist and Goldwater worked together on developing arguments against civil rights legislation, and, wrote Lane, Rehnquist testified before the Phoenix City Council "against an ordinance that would have required hotels and restaurants to serve African Americans." But that position didn't prevent his being confirmed as chief justice.

O'Connor also became active in the Paradise Valley Country Club, to which she still belongs and where she still plays golf and has lunch with friends whenever she goes home to Arizona. She did not really learn golf until she was in her early forties. She didn't even attempt to play nine holes until she had hit buckets of balls weekend after weekend for four years, according to Howard Kohn in an article he wrote about O'Connor in the *Los Angeles Times*. But one of her former law clerks, Viet Dinh, says that when he played with her, she gave no evidence of having learned the game relatively late in life and was as formidable on the green as on the bench. On December 17, 2000, she hit her first hole-in-one at the Paradise Valley Country Club. Then seventy, with a 15 handicap, she was with her husband and two friends, Al and Ginger Moore, when she scored an ace on the 125-yard par-3. Looking into the sun, O'Connor at first didn't believe what she had done. Al Moore said, "I can't speak for what was the highlight of her week. But I'm sure the hole-in-one was more exciting and will be the most fun when she looks back on it."

O'Connor was drawn to politics as a way of solving practical problems. It was in the Arizona legislature, too, that she developed the art of charming her fellow lawmakers to support her bills. She became known as the person to go to when things had to be done. Many of the legislators considered her one of the guys, possibly because of her years on the ranch when she sometimes thought of herself as just one of the cowboys and earning their respect was her key goal. But she always attempted to "play feminine," she once said. And she herself insists about her time in the Arizona legislature, "I was never one of the boys."

Also, O'Connor was on her way to becoming a wealthy woman because of her husband's job even though her legal career was never devoted to making money. Twenty years after being nominated and confirmed as a Supreme Court justice, O'Connor was still making a salary commensurate with what many of the top law firms pay starting attorneys. She was earning $173,600 (Chief Justice Rehnquist was getting $181,400). While this salary was irritating to some justices, the majority took it in stride. Most of them have made personal fortunes and are able to exist in Washington (a very expensive city) and also have homes elsewhere. O'Connor, for example, maintained a beautiful home in Chevy Chase, Maryland, and another elegant residence in Paradise Valley, Arizona, which she always considered home. She, John Paul Stevens, David Souter, Stephen Breyer, and Ruth Bader Ginsburg are reputed to be multimillionaires, although they are not required to issue annual disclosures of their financial holdings as members of Congress and the Cabinet are. Because of her wealth and holdings in various companies, O'Connor frequently recused herself from participating in cases. In one case in which she owned stock in a company involved in a major lawsuit, and thus recused herself, the Court split 4 to 4, automatically upholding the lower court's decision. It has happened enough to infuriate some special interest groups although there is no certain way to know how she would have voted in such cases.

Much as they try to be above the fray, the justices are human beings and do not give up their extracurricular activities when they go to the Supreme Court. For example, Clarence Thomas is an enormous fan of NASCAR auto racing and once served as grand marshal of the Daytona 500. He loves Corvettes IROCs (for International Race of Champions) but drives like a turtle, a friend once told the *Washington Post.* "He obeys every speed limit." Unlike O'Connor, he doesn't read newspapers but listens to Rush Limbaugh on the radio.

O'Connor's enthusiasms are more physical, stemming from her days on the ranch. Not only did she institute fitness regimes for about twenty of the Court's female employees at eight A.M. three days a week, but her weekends, when she was not working, were devoted to being physical. She loves hiking, golf, tennis, skiing, and fishing.

When she was in her thirties, she took up serious fly-fishing, eager to try her hand in rivers and streams as far away as New Zealand. She told the *Wall Street Journal* that when she is in the mood to go after a really large fish she heads for Alaska. "It's my idea of fishing heaven. There's an abundance of fish and the place is absolutely beautiful." One of her favorite places, Unalakleet River Lodge in western Alaska, 150 miles south of the Arctic Circle, is accessible only by plane from Anchorage and then by boat. The lodge will accommodate only fourteen guests at a time. In 2004, the *Journal* reported, guests were paying $3,750 for six days. Reporter Steve Stecklow went up to see for himself and reported that the lodge has no telephones, no televisions, and no Internet access, thus no e-mail. But, he said, the water for showers was hot, the beds firm, and the food excellent—seared salmon with lime beurre blanc a specialty.

O'Connor also loved white-water rafting with her law clerks on the Youghiogheny River in Pennsylvania and backpacking with her husband in New Zealand. They once went hot-air ballooning over Kenya. Just as there is seemingly no legal problem for which she doesn't have an answer, there is no physical barrier too difficult to surmount. Her sister, Ann, once told Howard Kohn, a contributing editor for the *Los Angeles Times*, that Sandra has always been "a conciliator, a solutions person. Sandra believes there is no problem for which she can't find a solution. When you grow up in the middle of nowhere, when you don't have a phone to call for help, when the nearest town is 25 miles away, you learn to fix things by yourself."

No matter how self-reliant, no matter how important, for almost everyone the first White House State Dinner is always magical. For Sandra and John O'Connor it came November 2, 1981, a banquet in the State Dining Room in honor of the visiting King Hussein of Jordan and his Queen Noor, the former Lisa Halaby, who then was only thirty, a glamorous and sought-after celebrity. Nancy Reagan wore a slim black Galanos evening gown with rhinestones sparkling over it. O'Connor had a new dress with a polka-dotted skirt slit to above the knee. Among the guests that night, all of whom wanted to shake hands not just with the beautiful queen but with the first woman on the Supreme Court, were Frank Sinatra and Paloma Picasso, the fashion and jewelry designer. O'Connor, who loves to cook southwestern dishes and is considered a gourmet cook, found the choice of food fascinating—poached halibut in dill sauce, sliced tenderloin of beef, chestnut bombe. Circular tables were set with green moiré tablecloths with bud vases of white freesia and narcissus. The United States Army Strolling Strings played for the guests. The best part came after dinner when John and Sandra, cheek to cheek, swept dancing around the Great Hall of the White House. John O'Connor, handsome in his tux, gave a little polished kick à la Fred Astaire every few moments. Reagan, who loved dancing with Nancy, "was beaming like a movie producer who had suddenly discovered a pair of budding stars," wrote the *New York Times*. O'Connor later recalled that it was a perfect evening.

She loved parties with international guests. In 1982, she was invited to an elegant dinner with Italian Interior Minister Virginio Rognoni, honored for masterminding the rescue of an American general, James Dozier, who had been kidnapped by the Red Brigade. "We are very impressed," said O'Connor. "But you already know that, don't you." Then the guests sat down at mint-green, lace-covered tables for shrimp salad, roast veal, and a mountain of chopped chocolate candy under vanilla ice cream. No wonder the O'Connors liked going out to eat so much.

Three of the justices, including O'Connor, have written best sellers (or what passes for best sellers in the world of exploring the law). O'Connor and Rehnquist served as judges in a 1997 reenactment of Lizzie Borden's famous trial, in which she was convicted of murdering her father and stepmother. (They found her still guilty 105 years later.) Because O'Connor is the most famous member of the Court, she is often asked to give speeches and often asked to parties. Invariably, guests who have never met her before are struck by her warmth, dry sense of humor, and solicitousness of her husband. Unlike Ruth Bader Ginsburg, whose husband actively campaigned for his wife's nomination, John O'Connor was not particularly keen on moving to Washington when his wife was nominated. Neither, at first, she says, was she. "We had a wonderful life in Arizona," she said, with a slight hint of wistfulness. It is not a rare reaction. Her fellow justice, the reclusive New Englander David Souter, reportedly complained to his chief sponsor, Warren Rudman, then a Republican senator from New Hampshire, "What have you done to me now?" President George H. W. Bush nominated Souter in 1990 knowing he did not have much of a record that would make a Senate confirmation battle contentious but confident that he would be reliably conservative. Souter has, however, sided with the so-called liberal side of the Court on some issues.

If O'Connor had any serious regrets about taking the job, she never publicly expressed them. For one thing, she had instantly become a part of history, not an experience to be lightly rejected by an ambitious, intelligent woman. And everywhere she went, she was lionized, not just by her fellow Republicans, not just by fellow lawyers, but also by Democrats, and, for her more importantly, by ordinary women around the country. Since 1949 and throughout her term, no other nominated justice had gotten more votes from the Senate (99 to 0) than she did. After the contentious Thomas hearing, in which a former employee, Anita Hill, charged him with sexual harassment, his margin of victory was only four votes—52 to 48, the smallest in the entire twentieth century.

By the time O'Connor arrived in Washington, despite relatively little experience as a judge, there weren't many aspects of the law she wasn't familiar with, especially considering she was once told she would do well to aspire to being a legal secretary because she was female. She had been deputy county attorney from 1952 to 1953, a civilian attorney in the U.S. Army from

1954 to 1957, a private homemaker and volunteer and a private-practice lawyer from 1957 to 1965, an assistant state attorney general from 1965 to 1969, an Arizona legislator from 1969 to 1975, an Arizona trial judge from 1975 to 1979, and a judge on the Arizona Court of Appeals from 1979 to 1981. Most importantly, she was a female, she was Republican, and she was well liked in Arizona. Her law degree from Stanford didn't hurt either. Four of the sitting justices with her had law degrees from Harvard (Scalia, Kennedy, Souter, and Breyer), one was from Northwestern University (John Paul Stevens), one from Yale University (Thomas). Technically, the Constitution does not require a law degree, but the odds against a justice being nominated without one are considered astronomical.

All her career, however, O'Connor has found herself being criticized by some conservative Republicans that she is not truly one of them. She supported bilingual education, a non-starter with many Republicans. She favored a death penalty but "one we can live with." She opposed state financial aid to religious schools, when funding religious schools with strict values was a no-brainer for many Republicans. And worst of all, besides her ambivalence about abortion (she was said to have voted against an abortion ban while in the Arizona legislature but the vote was not recorded and she later insisted she couldn't remember how she voted), for many in her party, she was a passionate advocate of the Equal Rights Amendment.

Such positions made her acceptable to Democrats and were one reason her nomination sailed through the Senate while others, most notably the far more ideological Rehnquist, had to fight for his confirmation as chief justice.

Sandra Day O'Connor was a "party animal"—a Republican through and through as well as a social creature, always eager to go to a party to meet new people, to stretch her boundaries, to live a "real" life, straining against the limits of her incessant work load and the "apartness" that the Supreme Court demanded. Clarence Thomas reportedly needed help with his social calendar, but never O'Connor. Thomas's friend radio personality Armstrong Williams told the *Washington Post*'s Marc Fisher in 1995 that "I decided to set up meetings for him [Thomas], do whatever I could so he won't be totally isolated. He doesn't socialize. He has no chums. He has

Virginia [his wife], but she has her friends, she has her life. They may go to some events together, but that's rare. It's kind of dangerous when you insulate and isolate yourself and let the media create its own image of you. That's why I bring over young kids and stars like Charles Barkley to see him at the Court. That helps him heal" from the bruising confirmation fight he had when Anita Hill, his fellow lawyer and former employee at the Equal Employment Opportunities Commission, accused him of sexual harassment. Nobody could ever say such words about O'Connor; her social agenda was invariably too full. She decides for herself which of the thousands of invitations she receives she will accept and decline and why. And she instigates her own private social evenings, delighting in cooking for her friends, family, and law clerks.

Everyone who has gotten to know O'Connor realizes that it is the West—with its vastness decreeing isolation and needing activist intervention to defeat that—that defined her, far more than her political party. In her chambers at the Court is a Papago Indian weaving called *The Man in the Maze*. She once told an audience that it is her favorite work of art because "that's what life is after all. We're like the man walking in the maze . . . You have to go this path or that, and you don't know what it's going to lead to, but you don't worry about it. You make the best choice you can and do the best job you can." When she got to the Court in 1981, having never seen a Supreme Court oral argument and not even having anyone in her chambers who had ever been in a chambers in the Supreme Court before, she managed because she thought about how to do the job, surrounded herself with good people, worked hard, and organized her time.

Obviously, making the right choice in and of itself is not always enough. Once, asked how someone becomes a Supreme Court justice, O'Connor said simply, "You have to be lucky."

And, of course, there are always surprises along the way. The O'Connors were stunned to learn that their next-door neighbor in the adjoining apartment for at least two years when they lived in the St. Nicholas apartment building on California Street in Washington was senior diplomat Felix S. Bloch, who was under investigation by the FBI for espionage.

Describing a "typical day" in her life, O'Connor told an audience meeting at a Ninth Circuit judicial conference in 2000 that what a Supreme Court justice does most of the time is read.

> I'm a fan of reading a newspaper early in the morning. I don't know about you. I don't rely on television for news and there's something about having a big, fat, messy newspaper in your hands at the beginning of the day that has become a lifelong habit. And so, I get up very early. That must be my ranch upbringing. By five or five-thirty I'm awake and ready to get up and get going. And I'm usually outside or John is looking for the newspaper before it has even arrived. And once it does we have a little breakfast and read the paper and go down to the Court. I'm the chauffeur in the family and drive John downtown on the way to Court. I try to leave the house about 7:15 or so to beat some of the traffic. The first thing I do is half an hour of exercise, and this is really part of my life. It's been so since my days as a lawyer in Arizona many years ago. I started with early morning exercise, and I never quit. It doesn't keep the weight off any more but I feel better and it helps keep me awake the rest of the day. We lead such sedentary lives as judges and we're kind of glued to our chairs for a long period of every day. It just helps me enormously to start out with an hour of exercise, and I have persuaded a few law clerks and employees in the building and a few neighbors on Capitol Hill to join me. It's not a large group, but it's a compatible group. And that's a nice way to start the day.
>
> And when I go down to the office then I start reading again. Much of that is what has initially come into my in basket since the last time I looked at it. It has a way of growing very rapidly before my eyes. The Supreme Court, as I've often said, is the backbone of the paper industry in America. It's evidenced every day by what comes in. We receive a great deal of mail. I know I have heard from every school child in America, probably more than once. My office tries very hard to answer most of their questions and letters, but it's

hard. It's a constant effort to try to keep up with that. We receive, as most of the justices do, mail from people around the country dealing with issues before the court. I ask not to see that unless it's a letter from a personal friend and I can write the person back and explain it wouldn't be appropriate for me to consider their views on something. But I don't attempt to answer that kind of mail.

Then we have all the Court work that piles in, the petitions for certiorari and the responses, and the law clerks pool on that. There's such a lot of that to read every day. When I came to the Court in 1981, we got about 1,000 petitions asking us to take a case. This year (2000) we had well over 7,000. So that's just a daily occurrence, going through the petitions that come in. As I've often said, many are called but few are chosen. We have become increasingly selective through the years in our number of grants. Not because the standards have changed but just because all the federal judges in the country have been doing a better job so we don't have to take all of them.

And if it's a day of oral arguments, we are summoned to the Court by a big buzzer that goes off throughout all the chambers five minutes ahead. We go down and put our robes on and shake hands and go in the courtroom. The oral arguments typically in the last term or two just occur in the morning. In the early years we had arguments in the morning and then again starting at one o'clock in the afternoon. It's not often these days that we have to go back for the afternoon. So that's a lot of luxury for us. And the rest of the day is spent reading and, we hope, thinking as well and trying to work out what we think about cases that we are going to have argued or have had argued and writing of any opinions that have been assigned or anything else that comes across that desk. It helps to go home a little late so you again try to avoid the traffic. It's nice to take some of the work home and continue reading if you don't have an evening obligation. And then you get up and start the next day.

Musing once on her appointment, she told an all-girls private school in 2000 that by breaking a boundary that had held for 191 years when she became the nation's first female justice on the Supreme Court, "It opened all the doors. It had an incredible snowballing effect, not just in our country but around the world. So it made such a difference, and that makes me very proud." Then, with a twinkle in her eye, she told the students, when she first joined the Court, there were hardly any women's bathrooms, and none attached to the popular gymnasium. "There are now," she said drolly.

CHAPTER SEVEN

The "A" Word

Liberty finds no refuge in a jurisprudence of doubt. Yet, 19 years after our holding that the Constitution protects a woman's right to terminate her pregnancy in its early stages, *Roe v. Wade* (1973), that definition of liberty is still questioned.

—Sandra Day O'Connor, 1992

Shortly after Sandra Day O'Connor was confirmed in 1981, Senator Charles E. Grassley, a conservative Republican from Iowa staunchly opposed to legalized abortion, was meeting with President Reagan on the sale of fighter planes to Saudi Arabia. Grassley stunned Senate colleagues by breaching protocol to take Reagan aside and demand to know if Reagan had been satisfied with O'Connor's vague replies on abortion during her confirmation hearings. Grassley said he would feel better if Reagan telephoned O'Connor and urged her to take a stronger position against abortion once she had been sworn in.

No issue has dogged—and, many say, defined—Sandra Day O'Connor's judicial career more than the blisteringly emotional national controversy over abortion. Although she spent years in Arizona as an ardent supporter of Planned Parenthood, as a potential nominee for the Supreme Court she was determined to keep her own views private. But the moment she was appointed, anti-abortion groups feared that she would be instrumental in preserving the 1973 decision *Roe v. Wade*, which gives a woman the legal right to have an abortion through the first trimester of pregnancy.

When Reagan introduced O'Connor to the nation in the White House briefing room in July 1981 as his nominee to replace the retiring Justice Potter Stewart, he stressed that he was not nominating O'Connor just because she was a woman. Naming her just because of her gender, he said solemnly, "would not be fair to the women, nor to future generations of all Americans whose lives are so deeply affected by decisions of the Court. Rather, I pledge to appoint a woman who meets the very high standards I demand of all court appointees."

Despite what he said, Reagan was clearly pleased to be keeping his campaign pledge to nominate the first woman ever to the Supreme Court after 191 years and 101 male justices.

But White House aides at the time made crystal clear that the fifty-one-year-old Arizona jurist would not have been nominated if she could be defined as either an ardent opponent or a supporter of abortion. The issue was simply too incendiary in 1980s America. O'Connor's appeal to the Reagan White House was that she was not known as a doctrinaire conservative, although she was from the conservative wing of the Republican Party. She was known after her years on the Arizona State Court of Appeals as a scholarly, careful legal thinker—cautious but fair and a stickler for legal precedent. She also wrote relatively short opinions.

Although the instant praise that greeted Reagan's decision buoyed the president, still recovering from the assassination attempt against him just a few months earlier, he knew that her confirmation hearing in the Senate would revolve in large measure around her opinions on abortion.

Right-leaning members of his party already were annoyed with Reagan on the issue of abortion. He did not personally address their annual right-to-life rally but chose instead to speak to them by telephone. Throughout his eight-year presidency, he would stick to that precedent. Anti-abortion forces could not fault him on his rhetoric but bitterly blamed him for not doing more to further their cause. They often complained that while the former Hollywood actor gave excellent lip service to their beliefs, he was unwilling to extend himself to help them end a practice that they were adamantly convinced was murder.

When Sandra Day O'Connor was named, Reagan's conservative base was immediately suspicious, fearing that her Arizona actions indicated she was secretly in favor of abortion rights. Long before the age of e-mails, telegrams to the White House ran 10 to 1 against her. "We feel we've been betrayed," said a furious Paul Brown, who headed the anti-abortion Life Amendment Political Action Committee. He and others argued that Reagan violated the Republican Party platform because it stated unambiguously that judges had to support "the sanctity of the innocent human life." Richard Viguerie, who had raised millions of dollars for conservative causes and Reagan's election, said angrily, "I see this as a slap in the face." He started a publication called *The O'Connor Report*, which tried to get her name withdrawn. He also filled it with charges of betrayal against Reagan. A woman who knew O'Connor well, Carolyn Gerster, a medical doctor from Scottsdale and a former head of the National Right to Life Committee, warned everyone who would listen that she was positive O'Connor was pro-abortion. The entire movement vowed to fight O'Connor's confirmation, and their views did not change when feminists weighed in with enthusiastic support for O'Connor. Patricia Ireland, who would later become president of the National Organization for Women, said O'Connor's selection was "a major victory for women's rights." She added, "Nine older men do not have the same perspective on issues like sex discrimination, reproductive rights or the issues that affect women's rights directly." Iris Mitgang, who headed the National Women's Political Caucus, exulted, "This nomination will be a major step toward equal justice in our land."

O'Connor's champion in the Senate would be fellow Arizonan Barry Goldwater, a conservative icon who ran for president in 1964 but who made no secret of his support for a woman to have a legal right to an abortion. Reagan, committed to getting O'Connor confirmed in the wake of his loss of many women voters to former President Jimmy Carter in 1980, told worried senators at the White House that they should not listen to the anti-abortion activists. Her record as a legislator in Arizona was definitely not as an active supporter of the Equal Rights Amendment to the Constitution or pro-choice on abortion, he assured them, letting them know his top aides in the Justice Department had combed through everything she had said or written, every judicial opinion, every bill she had introduced. One bill she introduced, which passed the Arizona Senate, gave doctors the right to refuse to participate in abortion procedures. And since some of "his people" did not want him to appoint a woman, Reagan suggested, they could be confident that no stone had been left unturned. Furthermore, he told wavering senators, O'Connor had personally assured him of her strong antipathy to abortion on a personal level. The White House quoted her as telling the president that abortion was "especially abhorrent" to her. And, he said, she believed abortion was a suitable subject for state regulation. Anti-abortion groups, increasingly worried they might never get a constitutional amendment passed and ratified outlawing abortion nationwide, intended to go state by state to fight abortion. Thus O'Connor's position, Reagan told the senators privately, should please them. Reagan even went so far as to write a letter to an Illinois anti-abortion leader, saying the opposition to O'Connor on the issue of abortion was being stirred up by a "vindictive" person in Arizona. The person Reagan was referring to was widely believed by conservatives to have been Carolyn Gerster.

As added insurance, the senators were told, several of Reagan's closest aides, Michael Deaver, Ed Meese, and James Baker, had spent ninety minutes trying to rattle O'Connor, testing her to see if she could be tricked into making a statement on abortion that could harm her chances of confirmation. She didn't fall for the ruse.

Finally, Reagan assured senators that O'Connor had the strong support of one of the most consistent conservatives in modern Supreme Court history—William Rehnquist, a former classmate of O'Connor's at Stanford University Law School.

During three days of intense hearings on O'Connor's confirmation in the Senate Judiciary Committee, the dominant issue was abortion. When

O'Connor refused to promise the Senate that she would vote to overrule *Roe v. Wade*, the anti-abortion movement demanded she not be confirmed. Bob Dole, then a Republican senator from Kansas, told fellow members of the Senate Judiciary Committee that while he personally had a strong pro-life record, "I'm not certain that we can just suggest that if, for any reason, a nominee does not totally repudiate *Roe v. Wade*, then we have to reject that nominee. I don't think we can subscribe to that." Howard Metzenbaum, a liberal Democratic senator from Ohio, said he found O'Connor too conservative for him on many issues but that he would vote to confirm her. He said that it was "un-American" to judge a nominee on just one issue such as abortion. Jeremiah Denton, a Republican from Alabama who said he believed that abortion "is the issue of the century, or perhaps the issue of our history," complained after getting an hour to cross-examine O'Connor, "I don't feel I have made any progress personally on the issue of where you stand on abortion." She was confirmed by a stunning vote of 99 to 0.

In O'Connor's first two years as a justice, the Supreme Court handed down no decisions on abortion, so all sides were eager to see where she stood when the Court voted 6–3 to uphold *Roe v. Wade* by ruling that the government cannot interfere with the "fundamental right" of a woman to abortion unless it is clearly justified by "accepted medical practice." O'Connor voted with the minority, joining Rehnquist and Byron White to challenge much of the 1973 abortion decision and arguing that states and localities should be permitted to set limits on abortion, including banning abortions at clinics, as opposed to hospitals, requiring waiting periods before abortions, and demanding elaborate informed-consent procedures. O'Connor's side lost on all of those issues and she wrote the dissent, arguing that the Court had a duty to correct "errors" of constitutional judgment in past decisions. In his decision for the majority, Lewis Powell wrote that such restrictions would make abortions more expensive and risky and allow legislators to make a judgment that should be left to doctors and their patients. Furthermore, he said, improved medical technology since 1973 meant abortions could safely be performed in clinics.

O'Connor's position infuriated women's groups. The National Abortion Federation expressed grave disappointment, saying, "It would have been nice to have a woman on the Supreme Court who was a strong advocate of a woman's right to abortion." The American Civil Liberties Union called her decision "unprincipled."

Yet an analysis of O'Connor's writing on the issue shows that it is not necessarily abortion itself that troubles her but usurpation of local and states rights. In true conservative spirit, she is adamant that the federal government not encroach on local rights to pass laws and ordinances. And O'Connor delighted abortion foes by upholding laws that require parental consent to an abortion for young women under the age of eighteen, with the right to appeal to a local court if they are unable to obtain parental permission. Further, she said in the 1983 decision, "The state's interest in protecting potential human life exists throughout the pregnancy," not just in the last trimester. But her dissent did not say she would vote to overrule *Roe v. Wade*.

"We must keep in mind," she wrote, citing a previous opinion, "that when we are concerned with extremely sensitive issues, such as the one involved here, the appropriate forum for their resolution in a democracy is the legislature. We should not forget that legislatures are the ultimate guardians of the liberties and welfare of the people in quite as great a degree as the courts."

After her third year on the Court, O'Connor was widely viewed as a strong ally of Rehnquist, having joined him in twenty-six of the twenty-nine cases the Court had decided by just one vote. But she also was increasingly viewed as a "swing" vote, a reputation that would anger her for the implication that she readily changed her positions. She preferred to think of herself as applying consistent doctrines year after year. Nonetheless, after her fifth year on the Court, she was universally viewed as a swing vote. Despite her staunch conservatism, she had moved to the floating center, which by then had shrunk to two justices: O'Connor and Lewis Powell. In the term that ended in the summer of 1986, she and Powell were on the winning side more than any other justices, each losing only fifteen times out of narrowly decided cases while Rehnquist lost thirty times.

In 1986, she had her second major opportunity to weigh in on the abortion debate and, once again, she was anything but a "swing" vote. She joined the minority in a 5 to 4 decision that struck down a Pennsylvania law, which the majority justices said aimed to "intimidate" women who wished to have an abortion. The Pennsylvania law required doctors to tell women of the "detrimental physical and psychological effects" of having an abortion, to discuss alternatives, and to discuss in detail what happened to the fetus, including showing the pregnant women pictures of fetuses in various stages of development. The law also required doctors to remind women that the father had a financial obligation to the unborn baby. Writing for the majority, Justice Harry Blackmun said the court was again affirming the 1973 decision. The states, in regulating abortion, Blackmun wrote, "are not free, under the guise of protecting maternal health or potential life, to intimidate women into continuing pregnancies."

In her dissension, O'Connor said that the issue in the Pennsylvania law was not really abortion but a procedural controversy over whether lower federal courts acted properly in striking down the disputed parts of the law. The true issue, she said, was that the appeals court overstepped its authority. "What is at issue here is a matter of legal principle," she said. "If this case did not involve state regulation of abortion, it may be doubted that the court would entertain, let alone adopt, such a departure from its precedents." Further, she said with some asperity, it was beginning to appear that the Court was adopting a new test that any state regulation "touching on abortion must be invalidated if it poses 'an unacceptable danger of deterring the exercise of that right.'"

Lawrence Tribe, the well-known Harvard Law School professor and an ardent supporter of *Roe v. Wade*, said that by no means was he convinced that O'Connor would ever vote to overturn the decision and thus outlaw abortions. It would be a "wholly unjustified leap," he told the *Washington Post*, "to say that Justice O'Connor would recognize no right to abortion." Indeed, O'Connor voted with the majority in a 7 to 2 ruling dismissing a Reagan administration appeal to the Court to overturn *Roe v. Wade*. Some wondered openly whether her refusal was a factor a few weeks later when she was considered but rejected by the White House for the post of chief justice to replace Warren Burger. White House aides said at the time that it was not the abortion issue but her relative newness on the Court, as well as Rehnquist's brilliance and consistency.

Irritated as O'Connor might be that abortion always came up in any discussion of her merits and opinions, she could not get away from it. In November 1986 the Court ruled 5 to 3 that Arizona acted improperly when it banned public funds to family planning groups that also offer abortions or abortion counseling. Not surprisingly, given the state and her family's past support for Planned Parenthood, a party in the case, O'Connor did not participate in the ruling. But she did work in a landmark 1989 decision—the most closely watched abortion case in fifteen years—involving a Missouri law that outlawed the use of public funds to encourage or counsel a woman to have an abortion, prohibited abortions in public clinics and hospitals, and required doctors to perform tests to determine whether a fetus older than nineteen weeks could live. If so, no abortion could be performed. The Missouri case was viewed as critical because in 1987, Lewis Powell, the "other" swing voter and a strong supporter of *Roe v. Wade*, had retired. The Missouri case would be the first abortion case that his replacement, Anthony Kennedy, helped decide. Kennedy was widely expected to vote in favor of the Missouri law, thus leaving O'Connor as the deciding vote. And while Reagan personally may not have done all he could to try to end abortion, his Justice Department vowed it was not going to lose another chance to overturn *Roe v. Wade*. It persuaded Missouri officials to ask the Court, flat out, to overturn the 1973 decision.

O'Connor, a disciplined woman of habit with a strong distaste for unreasoned discourse, could not go to work in the morning without seeing evidence of the passion on both sides. Demonstrations of hundreds of thousands of pro-abortion supporters and demonstrations of hundreds of thousands of abortion opponents took place on the steps of the Supreme Court. Everywhere she turned, the issue was front and center, with the question always being what she would decide. Toni House, spokeswoman for the Court that year, said that before the case was to be heard, the Court received about a thousand calls and letters a week. The week before the case was to be heard, more than forty thousand calls and letters were reaching the Court each day. More mail was being delivered to O'Connor's office than to any other justice. "While people have a right to write to the Court, I hope they do not expect that the enunciation of their opinion will have any effect on the justices," spokeswoman House said. She added that to the best of her knowledge, the justices did not read the mail. But later, several justices confessed that they did read some of the mail, curious to see what people were saying. And the Court was hearing from others as well as the general public. There were seventy friends-of-the-court briefs filed, twenty more than had ever been filed for a single case to that point.

The issues in the Missouri case were complex and emotional. The law required a medical doctor to conduct tests to see if the fetus was viable if a woman seeking an abortion seemed to be more than twenty weeks pregnant. The law barred abortions at public clinics or hospitals and prohibited the use of any public funds for abortion counseling. Supporters of the 1973 case were eager for the Supreme Court to reaffirm it completely by striking down all the tenets of the Missouri law. Opponents of *Roe v. Wade* were anxious for the Court to uphold the Missouri law completely. But many legal experts expected that the Court would narrow its approach, affirming *Roe v. Wade* in a broad sense but also giving states more authority. They noted that O'Connor had been growing more and more dissatisfied with the trimester approach to abortion, arguing that because of medical advances, it didn't make sense to permit abortion, with some restrictions, in the first six months but deny it in the last three months.

The legal briefs submitted by the National Abortion Rights Action League, the Women's Legal Defense Fund, and seventy-five other women's rights organizations argued that restrictions on abortion deny a woman her "constitutional promise of liberty" because such restrictions force a woman to have a child against her will. The brief argued that state restrictions on abortion violate the "principle of bodily integrity that underlies much of the Fourteenth Amendment's promise of liberty" and denies women "the capacity to control their own lives in the most basic of ways."

The brief submitted by the Knights of Columbus, a Catholic organization opposed to abortion, argued that the 1986 Missouri law was a perfect vehicle for overruling *Roe v. Wade*. And the Knights took heart in O'Connor's doubts that the viability of a fetus outside the womb was the proper way, given medical technology, to decide the issue of abortion. The Knights said, "More fundamentally, viability is an invalid benchmark for construing the meaning of 'person' in the Fourteenth Amendment because it has nothing to do with attributes of personhood, or a particularized state of being, but only the state of medical technology. Viability's true utility lies in its insight that a viable infant is certainly a person and that any limitations on technology prevent all unborn children from being viable. If a 'viable' unborn child is a person, then so are all unborn children."

The tension was ratcheted up on April 26, 1989, as *Webster v. Reproductive Health Services* came up for oral arguments. Outside the Court, two dozen protesters were arrested, amid shouts of "Two, four, six, eight. You can't make us procreate." Inside, four hundred journalists, lawyers, and spectators listened intently to Missouri Attorney General William Webster defend his state's restrictions on abortion and Frank Susman, a civil liberties lawyer, argue for the St. Louis clinic that sued to overturn the law. All eyes that morning kept swiveling to Sandra Day O'Connor. Since the 1987 departure of Justice Lewis Powell, the critical fifth vote defending *Roe v. Wade* was gone. Justices William Rehnquist, Byron White, Antonin Scalia, and Anthony Kennedy were all but certain to place limits on *Roe*. Justices Thurgood Marshall, Harry Blackmun, John Paul Stevens, and William Brennan were all but certain to vote to rein in the Missouri law. What would O'Connor, the first and, at that point, the only woman on the Court, do?

It was obvious from her first question that she was driving right to the heart of the issue. "Do you say," she asked Charles Fried, special assistant to the attorney general of the United States, arguing for the Missouri law, "there is no fundamental right to decide whether to have a child or not?" Fried answered hesitantly that the Court had never made such "sweeping generalities." O'Connor pressed further. "Do you think that the state has the right to, if in a future century we had a serious overpopulation problem, has a right to require women to have abortions after so many children?" Absolutely not, answered Fried, arguing that even if *Roe* were overruled and the states had broad power to regulate and even ban abortion, the Court would still have enough power to strike down regulations that did not permit abortion to save the life of the mother.

Frank Susman, on behalf of Reproductive Health Services, retorted that the Missouri law carried to the extreme could ban certain forms of contraception. "I think [Mr. Fried's] submission is somewhat disingenuous when he suggests to this court that he does not seek to unravel the whole cloth of procreational rights, but merely to pull a thread. It has always been my personal experience that when I pull a thread, my sleeve falls off. There is no stopping," said Susman.

Further, Susman argued, 30 percent of American pregnancies end in abortion because abortion is seventeen times safer than childbirth, one hundred times safer than appendectomy, "a safe procedure, minor surgery." And he added, "I suggest that there can be no ordered liberty for women without control over their education, their employment, their health, their childbearing, and their personal aspirations. There does, in fact, exist a deeply rooted tradition that the government steer clear of decisions affecting the bedroom, childbearing, and the doctor-patient relationship as it pertains to these concerns."

Pressed by Justice Antonin Scalia on whether women have a right to destroy "this thing that we don't know what it is," Susman insisted, "Women do not make these decisions lightly. They agonize over them. And they take what we see out front and what we see in the media and they personalize it and they go through it themselves and the very fact that it is so contested is one of those things that makes me believe that it must remain as a fundamental right with the individual and that the state legislatures have no business invading this decision."

By the end of the hour, the justices and lawyers were wrangling over whether to distinguish between abortion and contraception and whether restrictions on abortion could be extended to contraception. O'Connor said she thought "there should typically try to be [an interpretation] of the

Missouri law that would avoid constitutional difficulties, not encourage them." And she was clearly dubious that the Court could overturn the right to abortion without disturbing other rulings involving constitutional rights to privacy. But the oral arguments ended without any indications of what the Court would decide. Walter Dellinger, a Duke University Law School professor, put it succinctly: "If Justice O'Connor wants to continue protecting abortion rights, they will be protected. If she does not, they will not. It is her decision."

Everything she had ever uttered or done regarding abortion was national fodder for speculation. Yes, she had once voted as an Arizona legislator to decriminalize abortion. But she had assured President Reagan she found abortion personally "repugnant" and also strongly criticized *Roe v. Wade*, saying that life was just as viable early in a pregnancy as late in a pregnancy.

The Court did not rule until the last possible moment, the day it adjourned for the summer, July 3, 1989, as dozens of proponents and opponents camped outside. The justices did not support President George H. W. Bush's request that they overturn *Roe v. Wade*. But by a number of 5 to 4 votes, they upheld aspects of the Missouri law restricting abortions, including requiring a doctor whose patient is five months or more pregnant to determine if the fetus could live outside the womb. The Court also decided that states may ban public funds for abortions and require women to be counseled on the effects of abortion.

Anti-abortion forces rejoiced. Abortion rights activists were downhearted. "This is a very sad day for America," mourned Fay Wattleton, then president of Planned Parenthood of America. In a bitter, emotional editorial, the *New York Times* said the Supreme Court's "cold" and "ominous" decision disparaged "one of liberty's landmarks, the 1973 *Roe v. Wade* decision. Far from healing the deep national division over abortion, they invite the snarling battle to go on." But the *Times* editorial also said, "Only the relative restraint of Justice Sandra Day O'Connor slowed the assault on *Roe*. It will be time enough, she said, to revisit the case—'and to do so carefully'—when it unavoidably clashes with a state's abortion restriction. Time enough may come soon enough."

When Thurgood Marshall died and 173,700 of his papers were given to the Library of Congress, it became clear that three justices in the Missouri case had been ready to strike *Roe* down, with one draft opinion declaring, "*Roe* no longer survives." Just ten days before the decision, the Court documents showed, O'Connor refused to go along with Rehnquist's language attacking *Roe*. Thus while the restrictions in the Missouri law were upheld, O'Connor prevented the Court from making a sweeping new constitutional ruling.

Three months later, the Bush administration was back, demanding that the Supreme Court overturn *Roe v. Wade* in a decision on a Minnesota law requiring minors to notify their parents forty-eight hours in advance of having an abortion. Solicitor General Kenneth Starr, who would later come to prominence as the special prosecutor investigating President Clinton, urged the Court to agree with the Bush administration that *Roe v. Wade* "was wrongly decided and should be overruled." The Supreme Court also said it would rule on the constitutionality of an Ohio law that required notification of one parent or guardian at least twenty-four hours before an abortion. Nationwide, minors accounted for one-fourth of all the country's 1.6 million abortions each year.

O'Connor was again the swing vote, but this time she voted with the liberal wing, striking down Minnesota's requirement that all minors seeking abortion must notify both parents first. The problem with the law, she said, was that there was no provision for a judge to waive the rule. With many teens unable to find one parent or if a teen could be harmed if a parent was informed, the law was too restrictive, she argued, saying that minors had to have the opportunity to ask a judge to waive the notification requirement. The decision disheartened opponents of abortion. Gary Bauer, a conservative activist who would run for president in 2000, said disconsolately, "I don't think as of now there are five votes to overturn" the 1973 *Roe v. Wade* decision. Duke's Dellinger told reporters, however, that O'Connor still was straddling the issue. "She managed once again to say virtually nothing." As for the 1985 Ohio law, the justices voted 6 to 3 to uphold the requirement that a doctor notify one parent of a minor's intent to have an abortion.

After nine years on the Supreme Court, O'Connor was still refusing to answer the big questions: What limitations on abortion would she consider "unduly burdensome" on a pregnant woman and what limitations were not? Scalia, commenting on the 1989 *Webster v. Reproductive Health Services* case, openly ridiculed O'Connor's reasoning. He wrote that the *Webster* case "preserves a chaos that is evident to anyone who can read." Many wondered if O'Connor would ever vote to overturn *Roe v. Wade* completely, but whether she might continue to chip away at it out of a firm belief that states have a right to place restrictions on abortion without making it illegal. There were now only two firm votes on the Court for abortion rights, Justices Blackmun and John Paul Stevens. William Rehnquist, Clarence Thomas, Antonin Scalia, and Anthony Kennedy seemed more than ready to overturn *Roe*. That left David Souter and O'Connor as the big questions.

That ambiguity made it difficult for state legislatures to deal with hundreds of bills that had been introduced since the *Webster* decision. But abortion foes were clear in their strategy—pass restrictive laws at the state level, knowing that each time the Supreme Court had ruled in recent years, it had chipped away at *Roe v. Wade*. Idaho quickly passed one of the nation's sternest anti-abortion laws, but the governor vetoed it. Louisiana passed another restrictive law over the veto of its governor, sending the law to the courts. Utah, Guam, and Pennsylvania also passed restrictive laws, with everyone wondering which case would get to the top court first.

As it turned out, a Pennsylvania law was the vehicle that gave abortion foes one of their biggest victories, helped immensely by O'Connor. In an all-out gamble, abortion rights supporters decided that if American women were losing the right to an abortion, they should know about it. The strategy unfolded on the morning of April 22, 1982, when the Court heard legal arguments over the Pennsylvania law, which required a married woman to tell her husband if she planned to get an abortion, mandated a twenty-four-hour waiting period for any woman before she could get an abortion, and required doctors to give patients highly detailed information about the development of a fetus inside the womb and to give them information on alternatives to abortion. Abortion rights supporters saw that mandate as biased counseling. Abortion foes greeted it as informed consent.

Everybody most wanted to see if O'Connor's "undue burden" test would hold. That is, would the Court agree with her that restrictions on abortion constitute an unfair burden on a woman seeking an abortion. The Third Circuit Court of Appeals, sitting in Philadelphia, upheld most of the state law but not the provision that a woman notify her husband, citing O'Connor's undue burden theory. Many feared that a woman seeking an abortion against the wishes of her husband could face physical endangerment.

Friend-of-the-court briefs rained on the Court. Abortion rights supporters argued that precedent should not be overturned lightly and that precedent called for abortion rights to be upheld, a position supported in a brief filed by 250 historians. The American Psychological Association argued that women could be harmed psychologically by being warned in stark terms of the detrimental effects of abortion. Foes of abortion brought in their own experts, arguing vehemently that there was no undue burden on a woman to notify the husband of her interest in having an abortion. Ernest Preate Jr., the Pennsylvania attorney general, joined by U.S. Solicitor General Kenneth Starr, argued that the Court could decide in the case to ban abortion completely and still not find it constituted an undue burden on a woman because of a "compelling state interest in protecting potential human life." When the American Colleges of Obstetricians and Gynecologists filed a brief arguing against the Pennsylvania law, the American Association of Pro-Life Obstetricians and Gynecologists filed a rebuttal brief. It seemed, in fact, that just about every adult in America had an opinion on the Pennsylvania case. On this issue, neutrality had taken a holiday.

On the day of oral arguments, O'Connor raised a point many had not considered. "The state is compelling a woman to say something to her husband. I would have thought perhaps compelling speech would get us right into a First Amendment area." Preate answered that because 95 percent of married women in Pennsylvania already informed their husbands voluntarily, the spousal notice law would affect few women. That prompted Stevens, a pro-abortion-rights justice, to observe dryly that if "no one's affected by the statute, what is the state interest in upholding the statute?" As the morning wore on, however, abortion rights advocates grew alarmed when Starr, arguing for Pennsylvania, opened a door that had been closed when he said that fetuses might be considered persons under the Constitution, meaning that the states might have to outlaw abortion on grounds it could be considered murder. The government had never taken that position. The morning ended with Kennedy noting that such fundamental rights as the right of free speech have been abridged and that restrictions on *Roe* could fall under the same category.

The suspense was broken on June 29, 1992, when the Supreme Court voted 5 to 4 to uphold the 1973 *Roe* decision but 7 to 2 to say that Pennsylvania could require a woman seeking an abortion to get counseling on alternatives, to wait twenty-four hours before the procedure was performed, and could force doctors to tell state officials about all abortions and require minors to get parental consent. The Court said a woman did not have to inform her husband before getting an abortion.

Both sides recognized that an important principle had been established: abortion in the United States could be restricted by state law and, more to the point, would continue to be, but that the Court was not ready to overturn *Roe*. Kennedy, surprising many, decided that abortion is a personal choice and that the state under the Fourteenth Amendment can't prevent a woman from making that choice, although it can discourage the choice. Robert Casey, the sitting governor of Pennsylvania and an opponent of abortion, exulted that the decision "moves the country sharply away from abortion on demand and begins to reestablish in our law in a balanced and reasonable way the historic and traditional rights of members of the family, mothers, their unborn children, parents. The decision, while not overturning *Roe v. Wade*, clearly returns to the people the power to regulate abortion in a reasonable way so as to protect maternal health and reduce the number of abortions in our country." Likewise, the Center for Reproductive Rights' Kathryn Kolbert, who had argued against the law before the Court, said, "The Court has taken away the fundamental rights that women possessed prior to today. We decry that result." At the same time, she noted the

Court had stood up for battered women who now did not have to tell their husbands about a pending abortion or would be deprived of an abortion if they could not locate a husband. Bill Clinton, the governor of Arkansas, who would be elected president in less than five months, said it was "a very disturbing day. I regret it very much. You have four judges plainly committed to repeal *Roe v. Wade*, three others [including O'Connor] nibbling around the edges and a brave Justice Blackmun saying he doesn't know how much longer he can hang on."

O'Connor said in her opinion that while women do have a right to choose whether to have an abortion, the state has the power to regulate the practice of abortion and to encourage women to give birth rather than to have abortions as long as such regulation does not place "an undue burden" upon a woman seeking an abortion. That is not the widespread right conferred on women in *Roe v. Wade* and it makes abortion more difficult to obtain but does not outlaw abortion per se. She argued that disagreement about how to apply the undue-burden test was proper and inevitable because this is a complex issue. While others scoffed that the decision merely was a full-employment vehicle for reproductive-rights lawyers and that a twenty-four-hour waiting period for a woman who had to travel a long distance to get an abortion could be an undue burden, the Court said that a burden could be undue if it were designed to interfere with the legal right of a woman to have an abortion. Many said that, in fact, it was a tougher standard than O'Connor had advocated before, meaning she was liberalizing her position even though she, Kennedy, and Souter were now the middle-ground or centrist coalition on the Court. A sentence from their opinion is most telling: "The ability of women to participate equally in the economic and social life of the nation has been facilitated by their ability to control their reproductive lives."

As much as both sides awaited O'Connor's decision, it was Blackmun's words that rang throughout the country, inspiring both hope and fear. "I am 83 years old. I cannot remain on this Court forever, and when I do step down, the confirmation process for my successor may well focus on the issue before us today. I fear for the darkness as four justices anxiously await the single vote necessary to extinguish the light." The next appointment to the Court, replacing the conservative Byron White in 1993 as the 107th justice, would be the Court's second woman, Ruth Bader Ginsburg, a liberal vote in favor of abortion rights—the first Supreme Court nominee to acknowledge before her confirmation that she supported abortion rights—but a critic of how the 1973 *Roe* decision was arrived at, saying that grounding it in women's equality would have been more judicially proper than using the right of privacy—a distinct criticism of Blackmun's reasoning. Blackmun would step down from the Court two years later, leaving as his major legacy *Roe v. Wade*, which he had spent much of his career defending. Duke's Walter Dellinger, a strong advocate of abortion rights, said to the *New York Times* as Blackmun announced he was leaving: "*Roe v. Wade* is like an old Dick Tracy cartoon—it's shot full of holes but it's still standing. Blackmun had the instinct for the right result. It was picked apart by law professors, but it turns out that the reasoning of *Roe* appeared much more thin and brittle at the time than it does now. The more that women came to be seen as full moral agents, with rights against intrusion from the state, the more it has seemed to tap into a deep anti-totalitarian principle that's embedded in our notion of liberty." Blackmun, who died in 1999 at the age of ninety, would be replaced by Stephen Breyer, only the second Democratic appointment in thirty-six years.

But a Supreme Court of aging justices would continue to be a political issue in every future presidential race, with proponents and opponents of abortion convinced every four years that the overrule of *Roe* could be just one presidential appointment away.

O'Connor's "undue-burden" test restricting abortions has continued to dominate the Court's thinking. Waiting periods have been upheld in other states such as Mississippi. In a North Dakota case, the Court refused to block a waiting period for abortion while the case made its way up the court system. In that case O'Connor warned that each law would have to be judged on whether in "a large fraction of the cases in which the law is relevant, it will operate as a substantial obstacle to a woman's choice to undergo an abortion." A South Dakota law that required teens to notify a parent before getting an abortion was struck down and the Court declined to review it, letting stand an appeals court decision that such a law was unconstitutional because it posed an "undue burden" on a large number of young women. Seven months after the Pennsylvania decision, the Court decided, 6 to 3, that a federal civil rights law could not be used to prevent abortion protesters from blockading clinics. O'Connor dissented, saying that the law should protect women seeking an abortion. The case was not about abortion, she wrote. "This case is about whether a private conspiracy to deprive members of a protected class of legally protected interests gives rise to a federal cause of action." A few months later, on June 30, 1994, she joined in a 6 to 3 decision that upheld portions of an injunction against disruptive protests at a Florida abortion clinic, saying that a buffer zone of thirty-six feet around the Melbourne clinic and a ban on excessive noise by the protesters balanced the right of free speech with the right of patients and employees to unimpeded access. It was widely noted that Rehnquist, the staunch conservative, had on this abortion case, for the first time, joined with O'Connor, writing, "The First Amendment does not demand that patients at medical facilities undertake Herculean efforts to escape the cacophony of political protests," a sentence O'Connor herself might have written.

In April 2000, the Court heard arguments on what had become one of the nation's most divisive controversies, so-called partial birth abortion. While thirty-one states had adopted bans on the practice of delivering a fetus partially through the birth canal before collapsing its skull, the Court specifically addressed Nebraska's ban. O'Connor, the swing vote, noted that the Nebraska law appeared to prohibit not only partial birth abortion but also the most common form of second-trimester abortions, dilation and evacuation, in which the fetus is removed in pieces from the uterus. She also was concerned, she indicated through questioning, that there was no exemption in the law for the life or health of the mother if doctors agree it is the best operation for that purpose. In June 2000, the Court ruled 5 to 4 that the Nebraska law and thirty similar laws were unconstitutionally broad because they violated the "undue burden" test laid down in the Pennsylvania case in 1992 and failed to provide an exception to protect the health of the mother.

O'Connor was the swing vote, although she said that "a ban on partial birth abortion that only prescribed the [dilation and extraction] method of abortion and that included an exception to preserve the life and health of the mother would be constitutional." That same day O'Connor was the swing vote in upholding a Colorado law requiring protesters to stay at least eight feet away from people entering health care facilities such as abortion clinics.

There would be many more abortion decisions for O'Connor but none would be more important than the 1992 decision in the Pennsylvania case in which she, Kennedy, and Souter wrote, "It is settled now, as it was when the Court heard arguments in *Roe*, that the Constitution places limits on a state's right to interfere with a person's most basic decisions about family and parenthood, as well as bodily integrity." They continued that "the right to define one's own concept of existence, of meaning, of the universe, and of the mystery of human life" is at the heart of one's liberty and freedom. In explaining their decision in that case as to why they withstood immense pressure to overturn *Roe v. Wade*, O'Connor, Kennedy, and Souter said the Court maintains its public support by "making legally principled decisions under circumstances in which their principled character is sufficiently plausible to be accepted by the nation."

In later years, when she spoke of abortion, O'Connor looked grim. She said, "It is an issue on which people in the nation are deeply divided. They have been ever since I've been on the Court and, I think, still are. And it's an issue about which people feel passionately. And I'm very much aware of that when we have a case in that area."

CHAPTER EIGHT

Capital Controversy

If statistics are any indication, the system may well be allowing some innocent defendants to be executed.

—Sandra Day O'Connor, 2001

Nearly as controversial as abortion is the Court's evolving position on the death penalty, and capital punishment is one of the clearest examples of how O'Connor's views evolved. The longer she sat on the Supreme Court, the more O'Connor began dismaying her conservative friends and colleagues by her belief that the death penalty is flawed. In July 2001, she made headlines when she told a meeting of the Minnesota Women Lawyers in Minneapolis that she was becoming increasingly concerned that the death penalty is unfair. She noted that six death row inmates had been freed in the previous year and that in the past twenty-five years about ninety people facing execution had been freed because of new evidence. "If statistics are any indication, the system may well be allowing some innocent defendants to be executed," she said, in a remarkable statement that made headlines around the nation. She warned that even though the growing availability of DNA testing may help, most states that permit capital punishments have not yet passed laws addressing post-conviction testing. And she said she had concerns that the quality of defense lawyers for those in death penalty cases is often inadequate. "Perhaps it's time to look at minimum standards for appointed counsel in death cases and adequate compensation for appointed counsel when they are used," she suggested. She told the lawyers that they must "breathe a big sigh of relief every day" because Minnesota does not have the death penalty.

When the Court decided in a landmark case that it is unconstitutional to put to death convicted criminals who are mentally retarded, O'Connor sided with the majority in her zeal to have the Court fit in with the political will of America. It is a sea change in Court opinion and shows, above all, how interpreting the Constitution may change as America grows older.

Except for the emotional issue of abortion, there is no other area of the Court's jurisprudence that has a greater effect on life and death than the explosive issue of the death penalty. Chief Justice John Marshall wrote that a Supreme Court decision "comes home in its effect to every man's fireside; it passes on his property, his reputation, his life, his all." In no case is this truer than in decisions on whether the state may take a life. Since the landmark 1972 Supreme Court case *Furman v. Georgia*, which did away with then-existing death penalty laws, the death penalty issue has frequently come before the justices. The United States is alone among the major civilized nations in condoning the execution of prisoners who have been convicted of the most egregious crimes against humanity and the Court is final arbiter on who dies and who does not. When O'Connor was appointed to the Court many wondered if a woman justice would make a difference. Between 1967 and 1976, there was a moratorium on the death penalty in the United States. The Supreme Court ruled in 1976 in *Gregg v. Georgia* that the death penalty was not cruel and unusual punishment, and on January 17, 1977, Gary Gilmore was killed by a firing squad in Utah. Thus began a new rash of court challenges to the death penalty that would test the newest justice.

Opponents of the death penalty would soon learn the truth: O'Connor would not side with them, but she would consistently raise points that would give them some comfort about how the death penalty is meted out. But she also would vote to give governments more latitude in making errors in sentencing people to death, which prompted some to say that the Supreme Court had "deregulated death."

When O'Connor came to the Court, the last vestiges of the liberal Warren Court that had held sway for years on the dicey issue of capital punishment were giving way. Justices William Brennan and Thurgood Marshall, two of the most powerful voices for civil liberties ever heard at the Court, believed vehemently the death penalty was wrong—that it was often handed down against innocent people and that it was done in racist terms, with proportionately more black Americans than white Americans executed. Baldly put, the two justices distrusted state judges and, more importantly, the fairness of the state sentencing process to decide the life-or-death fate of many condemned to death. Whenever they had the chance, Brennan and Marshall overturned the death penalty. It didn't matter to them that they were ignoring the principle of stare decisis, the Court's habit of agreeing with past decisions.

But now O'Connor had replaced Potter Stewart. As would prove true again and again, she was adamant about the paramount importance of states' rights. O'Connor was firm: the federal government should keep its hands off on the issue of capital punishment. Was Texas permitted to shorten the appeal process for a death row inmate? Yes, said O'Connor, siding with the majority in a 5 to 4 decision. Was a man convicted of murdering three police officers permitted to raise new claims in subsequent eleventh-hour appeals? No, said O'Connor, again siding with the five-vote majority. Could a man fighting a death sentence be executed even while another pending case cast doubt on the constitutionality of his sentence? Yes, said O'Connor, again siding with a five-vote majority. The case electrified the nation, especially when the man, Alpha Stephens, lingered in agony for eight minutes because the state of Georgia didn't kill him properly. In one year, the nation had executed twice as many people as it had in the eight previous years, according to Edward Lazarus, a Supreme Court clerk from 1988 to 1989, in his book *Closed Chambers.*

To Lazarus and to many others, the series of 5 to 4 decisions on the death penalty dealt a death blow to a major component of how the Supreme Court had operated for a long time—the vital center that had given the Court's controversial rulings authority was gone. Americans are more likely to accept 6 to 3 decisions deciding major issues in American life than narrow 5 to 4 decisions. After a particularly divisive term in 1985, according to Lazarus, Justice Harry Blackmun, a liberal, said that the center might have held but "it had bled a lot."

The defining death penalty case of the 1980s came in 1986. In May 1978, during a robbery of a furniture store in Atlanta, a white police officer was killed at point-blank range. A black man, Warren McCleskey, was convicted of his death. At the same time, a study came out showing that murderers, black or white, were substantially more likely to receive the death penalty when they killed whites than when they killed blacks. When the McCleskey case was appealed to the Supreme Court by those who hoped to have the death penalty abolished, the study was a significant argument. But for O'Connor it raised different questions. Were more executions a solution to the indisputable fact that murders of whites in Georgia yielded harsher punishment than murders of blacks? Her implicit point was: Why not reform the system, but keep the death penalty? Her arguments were persuasive to others on the bench. But the complicated case dragged on, used as a basis for halting executions.

In the meantime, the Court got another death penalty case, *Tison v. Arizona*, that involved two brothers sentenced to death in a jailbreak in which they aided their father in an escape and he killed four people. Despite its own precedent that anyone who hadn't actually killed someone or intended to kill should not be executed, the Court upheld the death sentences of the Tisons. Assigned to write the opinion in that case, O'Connor skirted the precedent by saying that if someone showed "reckless indifference" for life, he or she could be executed. She was criticized by death penalty opponents for using what they claimed was faulty logic.

Her defenders cited Oliver Wendell Holmes: "The life of the law is not logic but experience."

When the McCleskey decision was announced, denying his appeal although there was some doubt about his guilt and without addressing the underlying racial discrimination inherent in the death penalty, it caused a national stir. When Justice Thurgood Marshall, the black civil rights leader, retired, O'Connor recalled that during the McCleskey deliberations, Marshall told about an innocent black man he had defended on a charge of raping a white woman. Marshall said the prosecution offered him life imprisonment instead of death if he would plead guilty. The man refused the deal, and Marshall said he knew then the man was innocent. When the judge sent the jury to deliberate, he said they could find the man not guilty, guilty, or guilty with mercy. When the jury had gone, the judge told everyone to stay in their seats until the defendant was taken away. Marshall said what if the man was found not guilty. "The judge looked at me and said, 'Are you kidding?' Just like that. And he was the judge." Marshall repeated his point: his client was innocent but the courts considered him of little consequence because he was "just a Negro." O'Connor said she had been "particularly moved" by the story. Nonetheless, she voted against *McCleskey*, a vote that effectively rejected claims that the death sentencing system in Georgia, indeed in the South as a whole, was riddled with racial bias.

The case caused many liberals to argue that conservative justices, with O'Connor's help, had used their majority to pare down the rights of people charged with capital offenses and minimize their representation in the courts while also shutting down the avenues by which prisoners condemned to death might challenge their sentences on constitutional grounds. Stephen Bright, then director of the Southern Center for Human Rights in Atlanta and a teacher on the death penalty at Harvard and Yale law schools, wrote an essay arguing that the Rehnquist Court, with O'Connor's help, had "made it easier for states to carry out executions no matter how incompetent the lawyer appointed to defend the accused, no matter how clear the racial discrimination in the infliction of the death penalty, and regardless of whether the condemned was a child at the time the crime was committed, mentally ill, or even innocent. A return to states' rights has taken precedence over the vindication of the Bill of Rights, and 'finality'—bringing proceedings to an end and carrying out executions—has taken precedence over fairness." For his part, Justice Harry Blackmun said at one point that the "death penalty experiment has failed." He added, "No combination of procedural rules or substantive regulations ever can save the death penalty from its constitutional deficiencies."

Although she was having increasing doubts about the death penalty's execution, O'Connor did not agree with Blackmun. In 1989, after *McCleskey*, the justices got another death penalty case involving a mentally retarded person. In that case Johnny Paul Penry, twenty-two, a paroled rapist, was convicted of beating, raping, and stabbing Pamela Carpenter. Prosecutors said that while he had limited mental capabilities, he knew right from wrong. His IQ was said to be 54, the equivalent of a child of six and a half years old. In a 9 to 0 decision, the Court upheld the sentence of death. In her opinion, O'Connor wrote: "We cannot conclude that the Eighth Amendment [which forbids cruel and unusual punishment] precludes the execution of any mentally retarded person convicted of a capital offense simply by virtue of his or her mental retardation alone."

In another case the Court held that federal courts could not review an issue argued by Roger Coleman, condemned to death in Virginia, who said he should have a right to appeal because his lawyers were late in filing his notice of appeal. O'Connor began her majority opinion, which denied his appeal, insisting, "This is a case about federalism." Blackmun expostulated, in his dissent, "Federalism; comity; state sovereignty; preservation of state resources; certainty: The majority methodically inventories these multifarious state interests . . . One searches the majority's opinion in vain, however, for any mention of petitioner Coleman's right to a criminal proceeding free from constitutional defect or his interest in finding a forum for his constitutional challenge to his conviction and sentence of death."

But O'Connor would eventually broaden her outlook. She wrote that Americans must realize that "constant change is part and parcel" of the writ of habeas corpus, meaning that prisoners have the right to ask judges to rule on whether they have been unlawfully imprisoned.

Proving her point, in 2002, the Court got one of those blockbuster cases that has reverberations for years. In *Atkins v. Virginia*, Daryl Renard Atkins, twenty-three, who had been on death row since 1998 for the 1996 abduction and murder of Eric Nesbitt (a U.S. airman assigned to Langley Air Force Base in Hampton, Virginia), argued that he had an IQ of 59, had never lived on his own or held a job, and should not be executed by the state by reason of mental incompetence. The Court in a 6 to 3 decision ruled that executing the mentally retarded would no longer be permitted because a national consensus against the death penalty for the mentally impaired had formed, meaning it constituted "cruel and unusual punishment." For the first time in sixteen years the Court had significantly limited the death penalty.

This time the difference was O'Connor, who found the fact that eighteen states had passed laws exempting the mentally retarded from capital punishment was the evidence she needed that the nation now considered killing the mentally infirm "cruel and unusual punishment." In 1958 Chief Justice Earl Warren had written that the Eighth Amendment, which forbids cruel and unusual punishment, draws its meaning from "evolving standards of decency that mark the progress of a maturing society." In the thirty-eight states permitting the death penalty in 2002, eighteen excluded the mentally retarded. In a speech to the American Law Institute, a group of judges and lawyers, just a few weeks before that decision was handed down, O'Connor warned that there was an international issue in deciding whether executing mentally retarded killers is cruel and unusual. A group of former U.S. ambassadors told the Court that America is the only democratic country that permitted such executions and that the practice was hurting international relations. The point of O'Connor's speech was that American judges have ignored international issues for too long.

In the majority opinion, written by Stevens and signed by O'Connor, Kennedy, Souter, Ginsburg, and Breyer—the Court's liberals—the justices said, "Those mentally retarded persons who meet the law's requirements for criminal responsibility should be tried and punished when they commit crimes. Because of their disabilities in areas of reasoning, judgment and control of their impulses, however, they do not act with the level of moral culpability that characterizes the most serious adult criminal conduct."

A few years earlier, in 1989, when O'Connor had voted with the majority to stay the death sentence of a convicted Texas killer with the mental age of seven because jurors had not been told that his retardation was a reason to spare him, she insisted the case did not affect other pending executions of the mentally retarded on death row. A few days later, O'Connor voted with the majority in a 7 to 2 decision that outlawed a law in Arizona that permitted judges to determine whether convicted murderers receive the death penalty. The justices said it violated the Sixth Amendment right to a trial by jury. In an earlier decision, the Supreme Court had said the Arizona sentencing process of letting judges set the death penalty was constitutional. O'Connor's trademark "case-by-case" approach to jurisprudence was showing itself fully.

But even her change of heart in 2002 on grounds that the prevailing national sentiment had changed and now made it unconstitutional for the state to take the life of a mentally incompetent criminal did not presage a change in her overall view that the death penalty is a legitimate tool society has to enforce the law and deter would-be criminals. She was becoming uncomfortable with the use of the death penalty in some forms, but not all. Michael Dorf, a former clerk to Justice Kennedy, told the *Los Angeles Times* that because O'Connor and Kennedy were inveterate globe trotters (in 2001, before the 2002 decision, O'Connor had lectured in Austria, Croatia, and England), they did not like to be perceived as extremists on the death penalty by judges in Europe, where the death penalty is universally regarded as outdated. But neither justice was ready to become an abolitionist on the issue of capital punishment. And it is an important footnote that the justices left it up to the states to decide who has a low-enough IQ to be excluded from execution. Supporters of capital punishment said the Court opened the door to a myriad of phony claims of retardation that would jam the court for years. Michael Rusford, president of the Criminal Justice Legal Foundation in California, told the *Washington Post*, "If you're still breathing and have been convicted and sentenced to death, now you need to get to a phone and call your lawyer to have a shrink come interview you, and tell him a square looks like a circle to you." Justices Rehnquist, Scalia, and Thomas agreed. But the *Washington Post* quoted James W. Ellis, a law professor at the University of New Mexico, a lawyer for those opposed to executing the mentally retarded, as disagreeing. Malingering, he said, "hasn't been a problem" in any of the states that abolished the death penalty for the mentally retarded.

Also in 2002, O'Connor was greatly dismayed when the Court overturned an Arizona case with which she was highly familiar. Timothy Ring and friends decided to rob and murder a Wells Fargo driver named John Magoch in 1994 in Maricopa County, Arizona. There were no witnesses to the murder or the robbery of $800,000 from the Wells Fargo truck, but informants led police to Ring. His phone was tapped and cryptic references he made led police to decide he was holding the money. On that basis police got a search warrant for Ring's home and found money and a gun. All the evidence was circumstantial and Ring did not confess. He was found guilty of murder after a friend of his testified against him, and sentenced to death by a judge. The issue was whether a judge alone without a jury could give a sentence of death. In 1990 the Supreme Court said Arizona could let a judge alone hand down a death sentence. Newer decisions were less clear.

At the end of the term in 2002, the Court decided that the Arizona law permitting judges alone to decide the death penalty without a jury hearing the arguments for why the death penalty was warranted was unconstitutional. The vote was a strong 7 to 2. Voting with the minority, O'Connor was clearly upset, saying the decision ignored "significant history in this country" that gives judges discretion in sentencing, She wrote in her dissent, "I fear that the prisoners on death row in Alabama, Delaware, Florida and Indiana, which the Court identified as having hybrid sentencing schemes in which the jury renders an advisory verdict but the judge makes the ultimate sentencing determination, may also seize on today's decision to challenge their sentences." There were 629 people on death row in the four states that had given judges the right to decide between life and death after hearing a jury's recommendation.

O'Connor's states-rights views were sanctioned by many. For example, Michael Mello, a specialist in capital punishment law at Vermont Law School, said, "This is the first time in 30 years the Court has issued a ruling that automatically invalidates a state's overall mechanism for imposing the death penalty." In 1972, the Supreme Court had nullified all state death penalty laws, but in 1976 reauthorized capital punishment on grounds each state had a constitutional right to use or abolish the death penalty.

Even though the country was clearly changing on the issue, O'Connor's increasingly conflicted views on the death penalty made her a target of the conservative right. Conservative critic Cal Thomas wrote in 2001 that O'Connor "lacks a unified legal and moral life ethic" because she wrote of a "possible" constitutional right to assisted suicide (*Washington v. Glucksberg*, 1997), while voting with the majority to uphold state laws that prohibit physician-assisted suicide. She made public her worries about the death penalty and yet said in *Planned Parenthood of Southeastern Pennsylvania v. Casey* in 1992 that a woman has a right to terminate an unwanted pregnancy. As much as anyone in America in the late 1990s and early years of the twenty-first century, O'Connor stood at a pivotal point on where life began, where it ended, and when, if ever, it should be terminated by the state.

CHAPTER NINE

Affirming America

While it is important to identify the causes of conflict in our society, regardless of the cause, we must find ways to mend the tears in our social fabric arising from these disputes.

—Sandra Day O'Connor, 1999

The normally staid Supreme Court was the locus of a buzz of excitement on April 1, 2003. After months of nationwide debate, the nine justices were holding a two-hour session for oral arguments, instead of the far more common one-hour debate, to hear the pros and cons of the University of Michigan's emotionally charged affirmative action programs in *Grutter v. Bollinger* and *Gratz v. Bollinger*. It would be the first time in twenty-five years that the Supreme Court had dealt square on with the prickly issue of affirmative action in higher education. The outcome would affect hundreds of institutions of higher learning in America and business practices as well. And in the more than two hundred questions and statements from the justices during the tense two hours, it was clear that what was at stake was the core of how more than two hundred years of racism is impacting modern America, a world where color of skin still matters, but where nuance in judicial decision-making about such key questions remains maddeningly vital.

With as many as five thousand protesters out in front of the building, guards were at every entrance, taut and ready for anything unusual. Busloads of demonstrators, many of them African Americans carrying signs supporting affirmative action, had begun arriving in Washington the night before. The lawyers' lounge was packed and about a hundred members of the press lined up to claim reserved seats behind the curtains in the courtroom. Celebrity spectators such as the Reverend Jesse Jackson and Democratic Senator Edward M. Kennedy of Massachusetts were escorted into the limited number of seats as were several spouses of the justices. The lucky few members of the general public who had seats had lined up a day early to get them. Those who hadn't been there before remarked both on the ornate, imposing features of the room and its relatively small size. Somehow many expected more spacious accommodations, possibly on the scale of ancient Rome or Greece. The nervous drone of conversation filled the room as everyone waited for the "hear ye, hear ye" that would precede the arrival of the two women and seven men making up the Court. And then in they filed, somber and black robed, striding purposefully to their seats, assigned by their seniority on the Court. In the middle, the place of honor, sat William Rehnquist, the chief justice. But most eyes were on the tall, white-haired woman to his right, Sandra Day O'Connor. Everyone knew that she would decide the case. With four votes likely to go against the University of Michigan and four likely to go with the university, her opinion would matter the most. As much as she tried to deny it and grimaced when the subject came up, O'Connor was the swing vote on the deeply divided Court. The twinned cases were so important that the Court took the unusual step of providing an audiotape (cameras remain forbidden in the Court) for the outside world, a step that hadn't been taken since the momentous decision in 2000 that gave the presidency to George W. Bush.

The facts of the two cases before them were not complicated. Jennifer Gratz and Patrick Hamacher had applied to be freshmen at the University of Michigan's Ann Arbor campus. Both alleged that the university's policy of giving 20 points out of a possible 150 points to minority students had in effect discriminated against them as white students. They sued university president Lee Bollinger on grounds the university's admissions policies violated their constitutional rights. Barbara Grutter, forty-nine at the time of the court hearing, argued that when she was rejected by the University of Michigan's law school at the age of forty-three, she was unfairly discriminated against, unconstitutionally discriminated against, because the law school had determined that it wanted a "critical mass" of minority students, which informally seemed to be about 12 percent to 17 percent. Without that policy, she contended, she would have been accepted at the university on the basis of good but not excellent credentials that were still better than some of the credentials of minority students who had been accepted. In both cases the plaintiffs argued that the university's policies amounted to a quota, which the Court had previously ruled illegal. In that case, decided in 1978, Alan Bakke had applied unsuccessfully to the medical school at the University of California at Davis and argued that its system of allotting sixteen slots to minorities had permitted students less qualified than he to get in. Universities could tailor admissions policies, said the Court, to help minorities get in but could not set quotas. In that landmark case, a divided Court had said that the goal of diversity was a good and legal one but the means to that end must fit within certain guidelines. The definitive arguments in the *Bakke* case were found in the separate opinion written by Justice Lewis F. Powell Jr., a justice greatly admired by O'Connor. In her book *The Majesty of the Law*, O'Connor wrote of Powell, "For those who seek a model of human kindness, decency, exemplary behavior and integrity, there will never be a better man."

In the *Bakke* opinion, Powell wrote that educational institutions had to be given leeway to use race in some manner—without fixed quotas—to achieve diversity because of their vital role in changing society and providing a better learning environment. That has been a guideline for universities ever since. And because any university that receives federal money in any form is bound by federal guidelines on race, a change in affirmative action would affect all such schools. That is one reason many universities sided with the University of Michigan in the record number of 120 briefs filed in the case.

Now, twenty-five years later, as the Court settled into stillness on a lovely spring morning, with sunshine streaming in the windows, tension was palpable—would O'Connor side against her beloved Powell and decide with the majority that race in admissions policies would no longer be tolerated or would she side with him, ruling against the Bush administration to see that in America in 2003 race was still too sensitive a matter to leave to chance.

Twenty-five years after *Bakke*, the University of Michigan was arguing that because it can take only 5,000 of the 25,000 people who apply each year for freshmen spots, it must use some sort of system to ensure that it has a mix of students. As for the law school, university lawyers said that a diverse student body is essential in the modern world to prepare the nation's leaders for a multiethnic society. Leaving admissions to chance would not ensure that, they said.

Lower courts ruled against all three white students; the Court said it would take the case to settle the issue of whether *Bakke v. the University of California* was moot or was still the law of the land.

Defending the university law school was a prominent Washington, D.C., lawyer, Maureen Mahoney of the firm of Latham & Watkins, a former law clerk for Chief Justice William Rehnquist and a deputy solicitor general when George H. W. Bush was in the White House. Defending the university's undergraduate program was John Payton of Wilmer, Cutler & Pickering.

Arguing for the plaintiffs was prominent Minnesota lawyer Kirk Kolbo of Maslon, Edelman, Borman, & Brand, who again and again would make the argument that the Equal Protection Clause of the Constitution gave his clients the right not to have their race count against them. At his side, arguing for the United States—and the Bush administration—was Theodore Olson, the solicitor general. As Olson got up to speak, the audience seemed to lean forward as one. But it wasn't just because of his position. Olson's wife, Barbara, had died aboard the hijacked plane that had been flown into the Pentagon on September 11, 2001 . She had left a note on their bed wishing him a happy birthday as she left early to head to the airport, bound for Los Angeles. As it became apparent that hijackers had taken control of the plane, she had called her husband. The passion and sadness of their last conversation had been widely reported in the press and compassion for Olson was nationwide.

Olson came to the argument knowing that Texas, the state of his boss, President Bush, forbids public universities by court order from using affirmative action. California public universities under Proposition 209 may not give preferential treatment to any student based on race or ethnicity. After the proposition took effect, minority enrollment at prestige public universities dropped dramatically but then started to climb. Voters have also acted to prevent race from being considered at the University of Washington in Seattle.

Sternly, Olson took the podium, arguing that the University of Michigan's policy was tantamount to "a thinly disguised quota." Repeatedly, Olson said that the university's admissions policy "fails every test this Court has articulated" on constitutionality. He said the school's policy of granting twenty points to minority students "might as well be an admissions ticket." But as he demanded the Court strike down the policies, justices sharply questioned him on whether he would rule out consideration of race in all programs. Reluctantly, it seemed, he could not do that, he said.

Justices David Souter and Ruth Bader Ginsburg and John Paul Stevens expressly pinned him down on a puzzling dilemma that had surfaced during the preargument phase of the debate. The nation's military academies, West Point, the Air Force Academy, and Annapolis, strongly endorse the use of race as a factor in admissions. Thus, despite the insistence of the commander-in-chief, President Bush, that race was an outmoded issue, military academies were siding with the University of Michigan. When pressed on the point, Olson dodged the issue, noting that the Coast Guard is prohibited by Congress from using race but otherwise saying obliquely that the government has not examined the issue and adding, "I don't accept the proposition that black soldiers will only fight for black officers." One of the briefs filed was from retired General Norman Schwarzkopf, who became a household name during the Persian Gulf War. He joined a number of retired military officers in arguing that the military depended on a multiethnic culture produced in part through affirmative action programs at the service academies.

Ginsburg pressed Kolbo, lead lawyer for the plaintiffs, on whether the military academies should never consider race even if it could be proved that without special consideration, minorities would not be represented fairly in the academies. Kolbo was adamant. "I believe race could not be used, your Honor. I think that other solutions could be looked at addressing the problem why there are not minorities in the military. I note that the United States has not taken a position. We have the brief as your honor has mentioned from several individuals, the United States has not taken a position in this case, the military academies have not taken a position."

"Yes, they have," shot back Stevens. "If the brief is accurate about the regulations, the academies have taken a position."

But Olson, aware that he was losing a key point, kept trying to stipulate that the government was not against him. The Coast Guard, he said, is prohibited by Congress from taking race into account in admitting students to its academy. But he had not studied the issue, he said, and did not have facts on how all the academies work.

Joining the military's line of reasoning were many large corporations, including Microsoft, General Motors, Boeing, and Procter & Gamble. All argued that they must have some legal way of keeping their work forces diverse and that well-educated minority students are essential to a diverse workplace environment.

Much of the debate as the two hours sped by was over the issue of what a quota is. Justice Antonin Scalia said that because the University of Michigan's policies were aimed at having the percentage of its student body range from 12 percent to 17 percent, on average, that essentially amounted to a quota. "Once you use the terms "critical mass," he said, "you're in Quota Land." He pushed the issue. What is a critical mass? Is it 2 percent? Eight percent? Ten percent? Not so, replied one of the university's lawyers, Maureen Mahoney. "Your Honor, what a quota is, under this Court's cases, is a fixed number. And there is no fixed number here."

Scalia also homed in on what to many was a major issue. The University of Michigan law school was one of the best in the country because of its high standards for admission. "It's done this by taking only the best students with the best grades and the best SATs or LSATs knowing that the result of this will be to exclude, to a large degree, minorities. It is not unconstitutional to do that, because that's not the purpose of what Michigan did, but it is the predictable result. . . . It then turns around and says, oh, we have a compelling state interest in eliminating this racial imbalance that we ourselves have created. Now, if Michigan really cares enough about that racial imbalance, why doesn't it do as many other state law schools do, lower the standards, not have a flagship elite law school, it solves the problem."

Mahoney was ready. "Your honor, I don't think there's anything in this Court's cases that suggests that the law school has to make an election between academic excellence and racial diversity." But Scalia was not willing to give up. "If it claims it's a compelling state interest, if it's important enough to override the Constitution's prohibition of racial distribution, it seems to me it's important enough to override Michigan's desire to have a super-duper law school." Mahoney couldn't resist. "Your honor, the question isn't whether it's important to override the prohibition on discrimination. It's whether this IS [emphasis added] discrimination."

Payton, arguing for the university's undergraduate program, said Michigan does not use a quota system. "The way it works, an application comes in, it is reviewed on the basis—every single application is read in its entirety by a counselor, every single application. It is in fact judged on the basis of the selection index, which has the 20 points for race and 20 points for athletics, but it also has all sorts of other things that it values, in underrepresented states, underrepresented counties within Michigan, socioeconomic status, what your school is like, what the curriculum that you took at your school is like."

Payton said that Michigan is "a very segregated state" and that its young people grow up having little exposure to other ethnicities and other races. A diverse student body, he argued, benefits every student, not just minorities.

That prompted Justice Clarence Thomas, known for taciturnity during oral arguments, to pick up on Scalia's point that if the standards were less selective at Michigan, wouldn't diversity automatically follow? Payton was firm in saying no, arguing that some of Michigan's "unselective schools" are "undiverse."

Even more the justices wanted to know when affirmative action could be expected to outlive its usefulness and end. Repeatedly, O'Connor pressed to know if affirmative action at the University of Michigan is open-ended. In the past, she said, the Court has decreed that affirmative action programs must have a fixed time period. "You could see an end to it," she said. The Michigan policies, she said with some uneasiness, seemed to be designed for perpetuity.

Once again Mahoney found herself trying to turn the Court. "I don't think the Court should conclude this is permanent," she insisted. When minorities catch up with whites in grades and test scores, she said, universities such as Michigan would conclude their affirmative action policies were no longer necessary. The real end would come, she said, when "we reach a point in society where the experience of being a minority no longer makes such a fundamental difference" in the lives of minorities.

O'Connor raised another argument she wanted debated. "How are we certain," she asked lawyers for Barbara Grutter, "that there is an injury to your client that she wouldn't have experienced for other reasons?" In other words, she wanted to deal with the possibility that rejection of students could be based on a myriad of factors, with race only a small part of the equation. Kolbo, arguing for the plaintiffs, responded, "Well, your Honor, first of all, race is impermissible because of the constitutional command of equality. The university is certainly free to make many different kinds of choices in selecting students. And to look for all kinds of different diversity, experiential diversity, prospective diversity without regard to race, but race because, your Honor, of the constitutional command of equality, must be beyond the bounds . . ."

O'Connor, in the habit of justices who feel the debate is getting out of the scope of their questions or that the answer has not homed in on the exact point the justice wished to have made, broke in. "You say that's not, it can't be a factor at all. Is that it? Is that your position that it cannot be one of many factors?"

Kolbo nodded. "Our view, your Honor, is that race itself should not be a factor among others in choosing students because of the Constitution."

O'Connor, seeming to nod to herself, pressed on. "Well, you have some, some precedents out there that you have to come to grips with because the Court obviously has upheld the use of race in making selections or choices in certain contexts for instance, to remedy prior discrimination in other contexts."

"Oh," said Kolbo, "Absolutely, your Honor."

"All right," O'Connor said in satisfaction. Interrupting as he started to explain, "Well, but you are speaking in absolutes, and it isn't quite that. I think we have given recognition to the use of race in a variety of settings."

Whenever she asked questions, the justices seemed to strain to listen. Tony Mauro, the Supreme Court correspondent for American Lawyer Media and *Legal Times*, wrote that "the justices seemed to give O'Connor wide berth whenever she asked questions, and at times seemed to be framing their own queries with O'Connor in mind." For example, Mauro noted, "After O'Connor had wondered about an ending point for affirmative action during the early part of the arguments, Scalia helpfully raised the issue again later on. 'Let me ask Justice O'Connor's question. When does all this come to an end?"

For justices, a crux of the issue was the Fourteenth Amendment to the Constitution, which is the famous Equal Protection Clause. Kolbo said that the clause makes race an impermissible factor in state university admissions policies. Americans have a "personal right" that their race not count against them, he argued. When universities give children of alumni an edge in admissions policies, he said, that is not a constitutional issue. The only kind of race-based preferences permitted, he said, are those to remedy direct past discrimination. Olson, arguing against affirmative action, refused to say that race must never be an issue. He noted that if the National Institutes of Health are studying an illness that affects races differently, race must be considered.

Justice Anthony Kennedy, a moderate who also is often a swing voter on the divided Court, was clear in saying he opposes quotas but also uncomfortable with the idea of always ruling out race as a factor. At one point he pressed Kolbo on the question of what happens if a major university has only 2 percent or 3 percent minority enrollment. "Is that a legitimate concern for the university officials?" he asked. Kolbo replied no. Even if it were, he said, it would not justify "racial preferences" in admissions policies.

O'Connor seemed to give aid and comfort to both sides at various points during the two hours, putting out question after question and trying to ferret out various ways to look at the issue. She seemed to have arrived at the bottom line that there are no absolutes in dealing with race in America. Scholars repeatedly have noted that she does not set formal legal rules if possible. When she noted in disapproval that Kolbo was "speaking in absolutes," she insisted, "it isn't like that." She noted that the Court in the past has approved of race as a factor in awarding benefits. But as a sign that the argument would live another day, Kolbo was not dissuaded from his arguments. Only in the case of "life and limb," he argued, was the government ever permitted to make race a dominant factor. Justice Breyer argued that some would say that student diversity is vital because without it the country might not function well at all. No, answered Kolbo, that was not more important than the constitutional rights at stake.

There was evidence of some frustration during the tense two hours of debate. Justice Stevens, in talking to Mahoney, who was arguing for the university, said, "We're all hoping someday race will be a totally irrelevant factor in all decisions. One of the arguments on the other side of your case, is these programs actually generate racial hostility, particularly on the part of the excluded members, and that in turn delays the ultimate day we are all hoping for. What is your comment about that?"

Mahoney responded, "The record does not support that inference under this program. . . . There is overwhelming support by the students at Harvard and Michigan law schools for maintaining the diversity programs because they regard it as so positive."

Scalia almost snorted. "Sure, they're in already. The people you want to talk to are the high school seniors who have seen people visibly less qualified than they are get into prestigious institutions where they are rejected. If you think that is not creating resentment, you are just wrong."

The final decision from the high court would not come down until June 23, when it became clear that affirmative action in America would survive and that colleges legally may continue to take race into account as a factor for admission. Given her pivotal role in the 5 to 4 *Grutter v. Bollinger* decision and the 6 to 3 *Gratz v. Bollinger* decision, which essentially upheld the University of Michigan's aim of affirmative action in both cases, O'Connor carefully noted that while quotas are and must forever be considered unconstitutional in America, the government has a compelling interest in diversity. She wrote, "The path to leadership must be visibly open to talented and qualified individuals of every race and ethnicity." But some day, she wrote, the path to leadership will no longer be blocked by racial barriers. Arbitrarily, she said, she hoped that time period might be the next quarter of a century. With what some called a "quixotic" belief, she wrote in her opinion, "We expect that 25 years from now, the use of racial preferences will no longer be necessary."

At a conference at Harvard University later that summer, university presidents decided that most schools would not have to make dramatic changes in their admissions practices but that some change was inevitable. Many presidents remain ambivalent about the legality of some race-targeted and race-exclusive programs, although Mary Sue Coleman, president of the University of Michigan, said that all summer college presidents told her that the Supreme Court ruling was a tremendous victory. Angeloa Ancheta, director of legal and policy advocacy programs at the Harvard Civil Rights Project, told the *Harvard Crimson*, "The leadership [college presidents] has to really go back to campuses, be very clear about what they want to do at their own institutions and really make some important decisions about how they're moving forward."

As for the University of Michigan, in August 2003 it released changes it had made in its admissions policies. Gone was the controversial practice of assigning points for minorities because, the Court ruled, for some students, it turns race into the decisive factor. Instead applicants must fill out a longer application, which asks about race but also requires more written essay-type answers to more probing questions. Many scholars said the university's changes could swerve over into the forbidden territory of quotas. Michigan's changes did not come cheaply, especially in a time of growing state budget deficits. Michigan officials provided estimates that the administrative cost of admissions would rise by about one-third to add about twenty more admissions counselors because the university will now look at each applicant more closely as an individual, not as a person who rates points for athletics, points for alumni connections, or points for race. The new policy did not satisfy critics, most notably the Center for Individual Rights, which argues that consideration of race should never be a factor, no matter how much evil America tolerated for two hundred years. The university's Coleman insisted, "Our fundamental values haven't changed. We believe that in order to create a dynamic learning environment for all our students, we must bring together students who are highly qualified academically and who represent a wide range of backgrounds and experiences."

Businesses, too, scurried to try to figure out what the pair of complex decisions would mean to them. No longer would businesses have to take race into account only as a way to remedy past discrimination—a difficult litmus test to apply. Now the Supreme Court had ruled that a diverse workforce in and of itself was a legitimate and legal goal, meaning that race could be a factor in hiring practices.

In the end, O'Connor's view held that in the touchy area of race in America, no absolutes may be applied. She had concluded the 2002–3 term of the Court in the majority of every one of the thirteen decisions that were 5 to 4. Perhaps her position resulted from her West-inspired, fierce belief in the sanctity of the individual coupled with her belief in fairness and devotion to pragmatism as a way to solve difficult decisions. Former acting solicitor general Walter Dellinger wrote in *Slate*, the online magazine, that what had become especially striking about O'Connor after twenty-two years on the Court was "the assurance with which this formerly obscure state court judge effectively decides many hugely important questions for a country of 275 million people."

It was a term of socially emotional decisions, including a decision to declare unconstitutional the Texas state law outlawing sodomy, a dramatic recognition of the rights of homosexuals in America. But it was affirmative action that would have the biggest impact on a generation. Christopher Edley Jr., a Harvard law professor who was special counsel to President Clinton's review of affirmative action, told the *New York Times* that the Supreme Court's decision on affirmative action was "a very visible symbol to cautious institutions that there is a way to stay the course and that they need not cower in the face of continuing litigation or political threats."

Ultimately, the 2002–3 term was O'Connor's. Noting the trepidation that accompanied the question of whether O'Connor would retire at the end of the term, Thomas Goldstein of Goldstein & Howe, a Washington, D.C., law firm, told Supreme Court analyst Tony Mauro that a retirement by O'Connor "would be thermonuclear war."

CHAPTER TEN

No Dearth of Opinions

> The courts of this country should not be the places where resolution of disputes begins. They should be the places where the disputes end after alternative methods of resolving disputes have been considered and tried.
>
> —Sandra Day O'Connor

No look at Sandra Day O'Connor's long and interesting life would be complete without an effort to understand the significance of her role in the lives of millions of Americans beyond her controversial decisions on abortion, the death penalty, and the election of George W. Bush. She not only has had a profound influence on the lives of Americans, but she has had an impact on the practice of law and future lawyers.

In examining the hundreds of cases in which she has expressed legal and judicial opinions, one is struck by the fact that virtually everything about life in modern America has been litigated at one point or another and that O'Connor has had a say in a remarkable number of those decisions. From the beginning, she has been slightly contemptuous of those who sue lightly.

Use any other means of compromise first, she has said right from the beginning of her legal experience. Her earliest opinions on the Court showed that after an early period of voting with Rehnquist 90 percent of the time, she developed herself as an independent vote, not the conservative Rehnquist clone many liberals feared. But by no means was she a liberal. She shrewdly staked out a position of independence that made her the swing vote, and thus a leader. From a few of her ironclad principles, she would not bend.

One of those principles is a reverence for law and order. Unlike some judges, Sandra Day O'Connor was never the criminal's best friend. She is clearly of the opinion that criminal cases must not be permitted to go on and on, but must come to an end. In an early case, *Engle v. Isaac*, decided in 1982, she wrote that in criminal cases the states have a more important and decisive role than the federal government. "The states possess primary authority for defining and enforcing the criminal law. In criminal trials they also hold the initial responsibility for vindicating constitutional rights. Federal intrusions into state criminal trials frustrate both the states' sovereign power to punish offenders and their good-faith attempts to honor constitutional rights." In twelve cases, one after another, she voted to deny petitions by prisoners seeking to be tried under federal rules of habeas corpus instead of by the state's.

Another principle that has guided O'Connor is a deep belief in the American concept of strength with fairness, especially when children are involved. She ruled that a one-year statute of limitations for paternity suits is unfair—children have a right to know their parents beyond one year. She said that no matter what kind of "social value" is claimed, the use of a minor depicted in explicit sexual conduct is not protected by the First Amendment right of free speech. "A 12-year-old child photographed while masturbating surely suffers the same psychological harm whether the community labels the photograph 'edifying' or 'tasteless.'" When the Court had to decide whether a six-year-old victim of child abuse must testify against the perpetrator face-to-face or by one-way closed-circuit television, she said that while there was a preference for a direct encounter, the Sixth Amendment was not absolute if other protections were available. Scalia accused her of yielding to popular opinion and denigrating the Constitution. But then in another case she argued (fruitlessly) that the courts have no right to tell school boards what books may be put in school libraries. In other words, a child's right to take out a certain book from a school library was not more important than the right of the school board to exercise its legislatively derived authority, even if the board decided the child's access to a certain book was to be restricted.

O'Connor's feminism, while more restricted than Ginsburg's, has shown itself repeatedly. In 1982 she wrote a narrowly decided opinion that a state-supported nursing school violated the Equal Protection Clause of the Constitution when it refused to admit a male student. Using logic new for many judges, she said that even though the school said it was addressing past wrongs to women by keeping men out, what the state really was doing was perpetuating the stereotype that some jobs are reserved for men and some for women. It was a decision that made many feminist groups decide they had been right to endorse her, instinctively deciding that a woman who was offered only a secretarial job after graduating third in her class at Stanford Law School might have strong views about the role of women.

In 1990, when the law firm that had offered her that secretarial job, Gibson, Dunn and Crutcher, celebrated its centennial, she observed, "I have calculated from looking at Martindale-Hubbell that had this firm offered me a job in 1952 as a lawyer, and had I accepted it, remained in the firm and progressed at the usual rate, I would now be at least the tenth ranking lawyer in the firm, which today numbers 709 attorneys."

She went on, "I want to thank Bill [William French] Smith. I can remember as if it were yesterday when he [then attorney general under Ronald Reagan] telephoned me on June 26, 1981, to ask if I could go to Washington, D.C., to talk about a position there. Knowing his former association with your firm, I immediately guessed he was planning to offer me a secretarial position—but would it be as a Secretary of Labor or Secretary of Commerce? Of course, it was not. He had something else in mind."

O'Connor prefers rulings that narrowly apply. She broke with Rehnquist and Powell and Burger to rule that Title IX sex discrimination bans be extended to employees of educational institutions as well as to students. But then she turned around and said that Title IX applied only to programs that got direct aid. And she refused to let the Court take a broader step by deciding whether Title VII outlaws any sex-based retirement payment plan even if voluntary. And, again, she strenuously rejected any concept of a "new feminism," and tended to view any gender differences, at least those incorporated into the law, as the same old stereotypes in new dress. Scholars Alan Freeman and Elizabeth Mensch theorize that, as O'Connor herself has speculated, the western roundup was an activity where every hand was essential and that it didn't matter whether one was male or female.

In her first year on the bench, she cast a key vote in ruling that Richard Nixon, who had resigned in disgrace after the Watergate scandal, was immune from damage suits for his actions in office. The year before the justices had split 4 to 4 on the question of presidential immunity, unable to resolve an issue that O'Connor decided was imperative to the proper conduct of the presidency. Thus her vote decided the issue, for the moment, until President William Jefferson Clinton was sued in office by Paula Jones for alleged sexual harassment while he was in the office of governor of Arkansas.

O'Connor's role in separation of church and state became increasingly significant. She single-handedly pushed the Court to use the endorsement test for governing interrelations between the state and religious organizations—government may not endorse any religion but also may not prevent individuals from practicing their religion. This has been a tricky arena for the Court for two hundred years. On the one hand, the Establishment Clause of the Constitution warns that the federal government may make no law establishing or favoring any religion. On the other hand, the Constitution gives every citizen the right to worship freely. O'Connor argued the issue was more a question of whether the community is sending signals, along with ostensible freedom of religion, that outsiders are unwelcome. "Endorsement sends a message to non-adherents that they are outsiders, not full members of the political community, and an accompanying message to adherents that they are insiders." Suddenly the reserved justice was sounding almost touchy-feely.

Dominating much of her tenure on the bench was the issue of religious displays on public property. Her vote made the difference in a case that decided that a display of a single crèche with an angel declaring "Glory to God in the Highest" was an endorsement of religion when it appeared on public property and thus illegal. But then her vote made the difference in a decision that a menorah next to a Christmas tree under a sign saluting liberty was permissible because they could be taken together as declaring that both Christmas and Chanukah are part of the same winter holiday, which has achieved secular status in America, and thus was legal as a message of a pluralistic society.

She scoffed frequently at the idea of political correctness, refusing to believe that a moment of silence is a bad idea. According to O'Connor, a state-mandated "voluntary moment of silence" for school children was unconstitutional because its stated purpose was to encourage prayer. But it would have been legal had it not favored "the child who chooses to pray . . . over the child who chooses to meditate or reflect." During oral arguments, she said, "It is difficult to discern a serious threat to religious liberty from a room of silent, thoughtful schoolchildren. A moment of silence is not inherently religious."

She was adamant that someone's religion or lack of it must never be used in any official government proceeding. "The Establishment Clause [of the Constitution] prohibits government from making adherence to a religion relevant in any way to a person's standing in the political community," she wrote in a 1984 opinion, clearly worried that a government-established church would disenfranchise those who did not choose to become members. In another support of the famous clause, not popular with many, she prevailed in insisting that if government support for religious organizations is transformed into support for religious missions and proselytizing, that is contrary to the Constitution.

Legal scholars attempting to analyze O'Connor's rulings inevitably come back to the realization that they tend to be pragmatic rather than all-encompassing or rigidly formulaic. While this tendency sometimes drove her more conservative colleagues to distraction, it gave her the swing vote and thus ensured her power. In *O'Connor v. Ortega* (no relation), she insisted in 1987 that when public employees expect privacy in the workplace, there is no hard and fast rule. She said that while there was a reasonable expectation of privacy, it depended on the relationship in the specific office. Scalia was new to the Court and lost no time in calling her insistence on a case-by-case approach "a standard so devoid of content that it produces rather than eliminates uncertainty." He said that whether an employer is public or private, that employer has the right to conduct reasonable searches. It would not be the last time Scalia went after her with verbal venom. It would not be the last time his doctrinaire certitude conflicted with her case-by-case approach.

Decades from now, O'Connor's chief legal legacy may be her insistence on federalism—that the states have unique autonomy that the federal government must not usurp. That belief, above all of her principles, is defended again and again in her decisions through the years. When she was confirmed she said that her experience on the state courts and in the state legislature gave her a perspective different from other justices and one that she would continue to pursue. She said repeatedly that the framers of the Constitution saw a national government capable of solving national problems but also a "republic whose vitality was assured by the diffusion of power not only among the branches of the federal government but also between the federal government and the states." If there is any principle that guides O'Connor's opinions more than that, it would be difficult to find it. In a complicated case on disposal of radioactive material, she said that the federal government may regulate directly in some circumstances but may not force states to regulate.

Nancy Maveety, a political science professor at Tulane University and author of *Justice Sandra Day O'Connor: Strategist on the Supreme Court*, said in an interview aired on C-Span in 2000 that "one thing that stands out about O'Connor is that she's a moderate conservative." Maveety said she calls O'Connor's jurisprudence "accommodationist" in that it is based more on fact-finding than on the doctrinaire opinions of other justices. Maveety said O'Connor tried to build coalitions on the Court and was a leader behind the scenes.

Maveety said O'Connor's comments at that time show how interested she is in collegiality. "She is meticulously well prepared, thoughtful, and always oriented to compromise." Maveety strongly rejects the thesis that women judge differently than men. "It certainly does not apply to O'Connor," she said.

Sooner or later, everyone who meets the first woman justice is struck by her pragmatism and down-to-earth views on government and public service. And nobody but her family has come to know her better than her law clerks, who all have opinions on what her impact has been on America and the Court.

Viet Dinh, a former law clerk to O'Connor who went on to become an influential official in the Justice Department during George W. Bush's presidency before becoming a constitutional law professor at Georgetown University Law School, said on C-Span that he first met her when she interviewed him for the clerk job.

"I stayed up a couple of nights reading everything, researching all her opinions, reading the entire transcript of her confirmation hearing, reading the record and the books and biographies of her," he recalled.

> I came in and expected to have a deep philosophical, jurisprudential discussion, and we had that. We had a very deep and very long discussion about the law and my work habits and how I see my work as a law student and where I'm going as a lawyer. But something surprised me. Justice O'Connor smiled very warmly and asked me, the first thing out of her mouth, was "I see you were an intern for the city of Yorba Linda in California." It was my first summer out of college. I thought, "this is an interesting way to start off an interview." I thought it was just a pleasantry. But it wasn't. She was trying to see what my experience working for Yorba Linda was, because she saw some parallels with my experience working for the city manager of Yorba Linda with her experience in state and local government and how government affects people's lives.
>
> She is a very warm person, a person who cares a lot about people and cares a lot about the decisions the Court makes and how they

> affect people's lives. Not just about the concrete or high-faluting rules of law but at a practical level how it affects primary conduct of citizens in a democratic society.

He said he saw O'Connor's job as very difficult. "It starts early and it ends late. And we are there simply to provide her the research and the sounding board for her decisions. Quite often we would meet on Saturday morning in a chamber with the four law clerks and Justice O'Connor and she would bring in lunch. She's a great gourmet cook and would bring in lunch and we would have meetings all morning, talking about the cases . . . so she could do her job in the best way she can."

O'Connor saw her law clerks as the future and enjoyed discussing the facts of cases and the points of law with them, with the understanding that those discussions remain private until the end of time. In August 2000, she told federal judges,

> One of the real joys of the position is the privilege of working with these marvelous law clerks. We're just so blessed at that Court with having applications from the most talented young lawyers in the country. It's just such a luxury to be able to pick up these applications and to select from many qualified, wonderful young people you think will fit the bill for that year. I see so much of my law clerks because I do like to work at the office rather than at home. Some of my colleagues find it more satisfactory to work at home. I'm down there, and I like to see them and we have lunch together on days when I'm not having lunch with my colleagues. I'm talking to them all the time. They become like part of my family. They really do. I get to know them so well, and I'm so fond of them. And it's just a very close relationship, as you know. And there's something about a relationship that forms with a law clerk when you're privileged during that year to talk intimately about the details of the issues before us and with total frankness on both sides and to really work on these issues together. It brings you very close to these people, and

it gives me probably a very inaccurate picture of youth in America because those I see are fabulous.

Once a year she took her law clerks on an outing either white-water rafting or fly-fishing or hiking in the Blue Ridge Mountains. There were frequent picnics or jaunts to the botanical gardens on Capitol Hill to look at the plants. Sometimes she played tennis and golf with her law clerks, who always remarked on her low handicap. "I have made most of my close friends in life through tennis," she said. When she came to Washington, one of her first outings was a tennis date with several other women. Decades later, she was still playing with them. When a former law clerk becomes a parent, O'Connor, feeling a family connection, sends a red T-shirt that says "grandclerk." Her clerks say they respect her for her concern about their lives, her hard work and dedication to public service, and they all mention, as an avid outdoorswoman who sees being outside a kind of freedom from the constant work and a connection with the people whose lives are often directly and significantly impacted by the decisions she makes in the office.

"She is a woman of many talents," Dinh said.

Another key to O'Connor, say those who know her best, is that she doesn't look back or second-guess herself. She is self-confident enough to believe that before she decides a case, she has done her homework and has thought long and hard enough about it that she doesn't have to ever wonder "shoulda, coulda, woulda." Yet it sometimes has pained her to know that much of the criticism she receives comes from emotion or ideology.

But she takes solace in knowing that those who excoriate her in one decision applaud her in another. For example, in another painful area of human life, most notably abortion, those who applauded her decision in *Bush v. Gore* denounced her decision in *Planned Parenthood v. Pennsylvania*. Even though she refused to "enter the discussion as to whether or not *Roe* should be overruled, saying there would be 'time enough to reexamine *Roe*' when a state passed a law, presumably one prohibiting abortion, whose constitutionality actually turned on *Roe*," as John McKenzie, a former Supreme

Court reporter for the *Washington Post*, wrote in an essay, she passed up chance after chance to outlaw *Roe v. Wade*.

Likewise, in the many cases involving business that come before the Court, she was not always predictable. Despite her western love for the little guy, the entrepreneur who wins out against the big guys, she was often a stalwart vote for big business. When Eastman Kodak entered the market for medical imaging machinery, it helped small independent businesses by supplying repair parts. But when the repair business became lucrative, according to Eleanor M. Fox, an antitrust specialist at the New York University Law School, Kodak stopped supplying repair parts and then raised its prices, causing the service industry to sue it. In a 6 to 3 decision, the Court denied Kodak's argument that its behavior was not anticompetitive and ruled that the case must go to trial in lower courts. O'Connor joined with Scalia and Thomas to argue that the marketplace will punish anticompetitive behavior and that Kodak was not enough of a "monopoly power" to justify having the "sledgehammer" of antitrust law brought down upon it.

Her thinking dismayed opponents of vouchers as a government tool to fund private schools; on the last day of the 2001–2 term, the Supreme Court, in a 5 to 4 decision, upheld the Cleveland school voucher program. Since the Court had a history of invalidating direct financial assistance to religious schools, O'Connor agreed with the majority in arguing that the voucher program was not the same as financial grants and said it was similar to other programs of direct financial assistance, including those to religious schools, even though the Constitution says the government may not establish any religion. Norman Redlich, dean emeritus of New York University Law School, wrote, "Thus, the most eagerly anticipated Establishment Clause case [in years] was treated by the chief justice and by Justice O'Connor as a case that added nothing to Establishment Clause jurisprudence and, indeed, was compelled by precedents." The *National Law Journal* said that even though O'Connor argued the decision was not a "dramatic break" from the Court's previous rulings, it was because of O'Connor that Rehnquist had his way on the controversial decision. In that term, the 2001–2 term, O'Connor appeared in the majority in 17 of 21 split decisions.

she leaned over and said, "Learn to read and read fast. We read 1,500 pages a day, on average." But she's a little intimidated by new technology. She revealed that she didn't know what a blog (a Web site diary) was. "Don't tell me, I don't have time," she said.

O'Connor believed firmly that every Court changes when a new member comes on. She noted that every term she learned something new, which she loved, but that every time a new member comes on and an old one goes off, the dynamics of the Court completely change, and that a decision made in one term might not be made in another term, with different members. And she stressed that ideology has little impact on how the members feel toward one another. Even though she frequently disagreed with Thurgood Marshall before he resigned and subsequently died, she said, "I haven't known too many true heroes in my life, but Thurgood Marshall certainly was one. He felt the law had not worked well for black people. He was a storyteller. [And his stories] usually were relevant to the case we were discussing. Beneath his wit and charm and rambunctiousness, he was shy. He was a quiet man, and his stories were touching. He told me once that he was in Shreveport waiting for a train when he went to get a sandwich. He said, 'A white man with a pistol told me to be on the next train because niggers ain't welcome after dark. Guess what? I was on that train.'"

Influenced by Marshall, in one of her early decisions on the high bench, she joined with six other justices to overturn a decision by a federal appeals court requiring that a state exhaust its administrative remedies before a plaintiff could bring a suit in federal court under the Civil Rights Act of 1871, one of the most powerful and widely used federal civil rights laws, even though she had once written an article in favor of making a state exhaust such administrative remedies.

Possibly yearning to be a legend, as Marshall has become, she continued to insist that her reputation as the "swing vote" on the Court is wrong. In her National Press Club remarks, she said, "Frankly, I think the press just likes to find things to write about. They said let's call her 'the swing vote.' I don't relate to that discussion very well. I just do the best I can and hope my vote is the same as the others' [votes]." But then she said, "The only thing you get from sitting on the fence is a sore crotch, whether you're a cowhand or a judge."

When she was inducted into the Cowgirl Hall of Fame in June 2002, she invoked another image of her childhood, "I now find myself riding herd on lower court judges rather than cattle." She also revealed that whether she is on one side or another she believes she has a duty to enforce her opinions.

In 2001, Jeffrey Rosen, associate professor at George Washington University Law School, wrote in the *New York Times*, "We are all living now in Sandra Day O'Connor's America. Take almost any of the most divisive questions of American life, and Justice O'Connor either has decided it or is about to decide it on our behalf." He concluded that without question, O'Connor had become "the most powerful woman in America." He said her power came from writing narrow opinions that "have the effect of preserving her ability to change her mind in future cases."

It is not that O'Connor was easily swayed by the lobbying of her fellow justices, he said. "It is that she approaches her job less like a typical justice than the state legislator she once was. O'Connor, who prefers vague standards to clear rules, does not derive her opinions from consistent principles that guide her from case to case. Her pragmatic approach allows her to remain not only at the center of the Court but also at the center of American politics."

The longer O'Connor served on the Court, the more comfortable she was in speaking her mind about various aspects of the law in America. And despite her glowing comments about the high quality of law clerks she sees, O'Connor has grown increasingly concerned and vocal about what she regards as the drop in professionalism in the legal community. In a speech in 1994, she said,

> I've been really concerned over the years with what I see as a decline in the professionalism, if you will, in the bar as a whole. A lot of us look back and see the good old days. I'm guilty of that. I look back and the situation then when law firms were not looking at putting in 2,200 billable hours a year and insisting every young lawyer do that. They were more concerned with the development

> of a lawyer and getting involved in the community as a whole. I don't know how a young lawyer today would ever have that chance because there's so much pressure on them to put in the billable hours. Now in terms of constant dollars, when my husband and I started practicing law, lawyers, young lawyers, were paid far less in constant dollars than they are today. Today a young lawyer is paid far more in constant dollars than we were. But the consequence of that is the law firms have to make the money to pay those salaries, and that puts more pressure on lawyers to have more billable hours than ever before. As a consequence of that and discovery practices, that increases tension in lawyers and behavior in lawyers that we shouldn't see. When we practice law in smaller communities, I think lawyers tend to conduct themselves better than they do in a larger city where they aren't likely to encounter the same lawyers over and over again. And that contributes to a lack of professional standards.

In 2004, she said in a speech in Laramie, Wyoming, that lawyers had become "an unhappy lot," with many of them wishing they had gone into another line of work. "Job dissatisfaction among lawyers is widespread, profound, and growing worse," she said, pointing out that lawyers are three times more likely than those in other professions to suffer depression and that drug dependency, divorce, and suicide are more significantly common among them. She said that at the thirtieth reunion of her Stanford Law School class, the "vast majority" said in a response to a survey that they would not become lawyers if they had the choice to make again.

She argued that a decline in professionalism was the culprit. "Lawyers have to do more than know the law and the arts of practicing it. A great lawyer always remembers the moral and social aspects of an attorney's power and position. It has been said that a nation's laws are an expression of its highest ideals, while the conduct of some lawyers in the United States has sometimes been an expression of its lowest." She added, "A win-at-all-costs mentality sometimes prevails. Many attorneys believe that zealously representing their client means pushing all the rules of ethics and decency to the limit."

This most civil of women went on to deplore the "brutality" of some in her chosen profession, worrying that "civility is not a virtue that the majority of lawyers today choose to advertise."

There now is a national award, the Sandra Day O'Connor Award, to honor high professional standards in the practice of law.

CHAPTER ELEVEN

And the Winner Is . . .

We don't always have a choice about what comes up here.

—Sandra Day O'Connor

For many Americans, their first conscious thoughts of the Supreme Court in a long time came in the aftermath of the 2000 presidential election. For weeks, the country didn't know who the winner was—Al Gore, who had won the popular vote, or George W. Bush, who seemed to have won the electoral vote in Florida and thus the election. Or had he? It was finally resolved in the Supreme Court, but the dispute left a bad taste in many mouths, and for the first time, millions of Americans started looking at the nation's highest court with skepticism. Was it really roiled with politics? Did O'Connor—the deciding vote—do what she thought best for the country? Or was she acting as a Republican?

At a $150-a-person benefit dinner for Washington's Shakespeare Theater in the summer of 2001, O'Connor and Anthony Kennedy took part in a mock trial of Shakespeare's King Lear. As O'Connor was announcing the verdict, that Lear was not mad when he disinherited his daughter Cordelia, she joked that "it was suggested that we remand the case to the Florida

Supreme Court." It was another reminder of how deeply the Supreme Court remained affected by the divisive 5 to 4 decision.

Decades from now, the debate is likely to rage on. Was the Supreme Court correct in stepping in to rule on the 2000 "cliffhanger" presidential election? Did the Court's ruling decide the outcome? And what was the role of Sandra Day O'Connor in the process? Did she and Anthony Kennedy, the other "swing" vote on the nation's highest court, put George W. Bush into the White House?

As the long election cycle of 2000 came down to the wire, pollsters were perplexed. They couldn't say definitively who was ahead. Democrat Al Gore, the sitting vice president and heir to eight years of a booming economy, nonetheless had made many mistakes. In trying to run from President Bill Clinton's impeachment scandal, he had put too much distance between himself and his predecessor's accomplishments, according to many worried Democrats. He often seemed stiff and wooden on the campaign trail. He wasn't doing well in his home state of Tennessee. Meanwhile, dogging Gore all along the road to defeat was Ralph Nader, who had far more in common with Gore than with Bush but would be blamed by many bitter Democrats for Gore's defeat because he siphoned off votes that would have gone to Gore, they said, and because of what happened in Florida.

But to many voters, Republican George W. Bush, a two-term governor of Texas, was no prize either. He was derided by some in his own party as "frat boy." He could not remember having a favorite book while growing up. In January 2000, he said in Florence, South Carolina, "Rarely is the question asked: Is our children learning?" He had no foreign policy experience, although his father had been president of the United States. He was doing poorly with African American voters. He was not perceived as introspective: "I'm not really the type to wander off and sit down and go through a deep wresting with my soul," he once told reporters.

The puzzlement of the results of the election confounded historians and analysts. Gore beat Bush by half a million popular votes, five times the margin of John F. Kennedy's victory over Richard Nixon in 1960. But Bush won the presidency because he won five votes more than Gore did in the

Electoral College, one more than Rutherford B. Hayes had in 1876. In that election Hayes, the Republican governor of Ohio, battled Democrat Samuel J. Tilden, the Democratic governor of New York. Tilden thought he had won the popular vote and had squeaked by in the Electoral College to win that too. But Hayes, using political operatives in such states as Florida, was given enough electors to win despite alleged voting irregularities. The votes of two competing slates of electors were sent to Congress to resolve. Democrats controlled the House and Republicans controlled the Senate. The lawmakers set up a bipartisan electoral commission that included lawmakers and five justices of the Supreme Court to mediate. The result was a strict party-line vote, eight to seven for Hayes. Democrats agreed to let Hayes becomepresident in exchange for concessions involving the post–Civil War Reconstruction.

In the chaotic aftermath to election night 2000, when the television networks calling the results bounced back and forth like tennis balls in play, all eyes shifted to Florida, where significantly, Bush's brother Jeb was governor. Jeb had said just a few months before, in August, "I would never live it down if my brother didn't carry Florida. Imagine all the family gatherings for the next twenty years when he looked at me every time and said, 'What happened in Florida?'" Even the most optimistic Bush supporter knew he had to win Florida to win the White House. Some Republicans privately thought Jeb Bush had not campaigned hard enough for his brother.

By Election Day, November 7, it was clear that Florida was a tossup. Both campaigns had poured money ($20 million just for TV ads) into the Sunshine State, and both candidates had been in and out repeatedly for months. In a traditionally Republican state, Bush had the politically active Cuban American community on his side and his brother Jeb, but Gore had his running mate, Joe Lieberman, the first Jewish American on a major party ticket, and there were many Jews in Florida and most of them took pride in voting. Gore was also courting African Americans in Florida, where he would win an astonishing 93 percent of their votes.

About 8 P.M. eastern time on the night of the election, the major television networks, citing exit polls, said that Gore had won Florida. A few hours later they took back their early call on Florida, saying the race was too close to declare a victor. About 2:15 A.M. on November 8, 2000, the networks declared that Bush had won the Sunshine State by about fifty thousand votes and thus had won the presidency. By the morning after the election, Gore had won the popular vote nationwide and he was leading in the electoral vote, 267 to 246. But nobody was certain what was happening in Florida, a state with 25 crucial electoral votes—and a state that once adopted the tourism slogan "The rules are different here!" In Florida, the election was simply too close to call. A recount was going to be inevitable, said Gore, confident it would turn out in his favor. For the next thirty-six days, the nation would not know who the president would be.

The Bush campaign went into hyper speed. James Baker, who had been secretary of state for Bush's father as well as his campaign manager, was dispatched to Florida to gauge the legal lay of the land. He was optimistic that Katherine Harris, the secretary of state for Florida and thus the overseer of the state's election process, would help. And in fact the *New York Times* would report that every decision she made was in Bush's favor. She became such a lightning rod she had round-the-clock bodyguards. A registered Republican and wealthy citrus heiress, she would go on to parlay her fame into a new political career as she was elected a member of Congress. The Gore team was convinced their man would win a recount and took the process less seriously.

The basic problem in Florida was that after ballots were run through punch card voting machines, some ballots were not counted because the chad on the ballot had not been pushed completely through and on some ballots two votes had been marked for president. The confusion for vote counters grew worse when the butterfly ballots came to light—confusing paper ballots on which voters colored in ovals that resulted in some voters who favored Gore mistakenly voting for Pat Buchanan.

The Gore campaign said that every ballot should be looked at manually and counted if the intent of the voter seemed clear, for example, if Gore's name had been written in. Florida law said that a candidate may seek a hand count in any county if he or she can demonstrate that a preliminary hand count of at least 1 percent of the votes in three precincts "indicates an error in the voter tabulation which could affect the outcome of the election."

But the Bush campaign said no, a manual count was not a good way to go—the machine count was fine and that was fine with the Bush people, because the first count went their way. In the meantime, the Bush campaign made it clear that Bush was going to act as the winner, preparing to govern, talking with prospective nominees for his Cabinet, and acting as though Al Gore was trying to "steal" Florida, which he wanted the public to think was rightfully his. After all, as the public had gone to bed Tuesday night, network television had declared Florida for Bush instead of saying it was just too close to call. And on that basis, to his undying regret, Gore had conceded in a call to Bush although his own people thought the margin was only one thousand votes out of nearly six million cast in Florida. During the messy recount process, he never expressed the confidence he had won the state as Bush kept doing. Gore's strategy was basically to keep his fingers crossed, and, to most political analysts, it was a public relations disaster. Gore was vice president, but to the networks, Bush was now "president-elect." Meanwhile, thousands of African Americans in Florida were claiming that they had been "disenfranchised" because their votes were being discounted in greater proportion and because they had in some precincts not been permitted to vote. In one county, Gadsden, Florida's only majority black county, one out of eight ballots was thrown out. Kweisi Mfume, a former member of Congress who would later become president of the NAACP, said, "We received scores of calls from Florida complaining about irregularities, intimidation, and the inability to vote." The rest of the world was thunderstruck—was this how the world's greatest democracy elected its presidents?

Now the courts were where the action was. The Leon County Circuit Court in Florida ruled that Harris, as secretary of state, could certify that Bush had won. But then on November 17 the Florida Supreme Court issued a two-sentence ruling in an unequivocal 7–0 decision that Harris was not to certify the election. Four days later the Florida Supreme Court ordered Dade County, where Miami is located, and other counties where recounts were being conducted, to finish by the next Sunday and submit the results to

Harris. Republicans called this "judicial aggression." Baker was apoplectic and said the court ruling was unfair and unacceptable. "It is a sad day for America and the Constitution when a court decides the outcome of an election," he said. The next step, Baker complained, was to take the matter out of the hands of the judiciary to the Republican-controlled state legislature. That could make the entire issue a constitutional crisis—one branch of government refusing to abide by the decision of another branch. As protesters and legal analysts and even sports commentators got into the fray, the vote-counters were buffeted by all sides. The public was riveted on Florida, wondering what would happen next. Legally, it seemed, the election could go either way. If there was any lesson the public had learned so far, it was that every vote counts, a concept that had not been popular for a very long time.

It was not looking good for Bush. He had lost before the Florida Supreme Court. He had been turned down in his request to block all hand recounts on grounds they were unconstitutional. The Eleventh U.S. Circuit Court of Appeals in Atlanta said the federal courts must stay out of the state election process at that stage.

But then the Miami–Dade County election canvassing board stopped counting votes, saying it could not finish by the Sunday deadline, denying that the "coat-and-tie" Republican brigade from Washington had influenced the decision. On November 26 Harris certified the final vote in Florida, giving Bush 537 votes more than Gore had in the entire state. Bush's brother Jeb signed the certification. Bush claimed victory; Gore went to court. Just in case, both sides filed briefs with the U.S. Supreme Court. Then Gore won at the Florida Supreme Court level once again when it ordered the recount to continue.

Bush appealed to the U.S. Supreme Court. And now, all eyes were on the Court, which has the power to decide which cases it will and will not take. Technically, there was no legal impediment to its reviewing the Florida Supreme Court decision. Politically, stepping into an election process before it was concluded was risky for the nine justices, who try to guard above all the perception that they are not partisan. David Boies, the super-sharp lawyer who was now representing Gore, argued that there was "no basis" for the Supreme Court to get involved at this point. What Boies feared was that the justices might be tempted to pick a president because they thought they had the power to do so. Even James Baker was dubious that Bush's chances would be good at getting the justices to intercede, at one point telling Bush that there was a 50–50 possibility the Court would, in effect, tell the Bush campaign to get lost.

On a Saturday, two days after Bush's lawyers went to the Supreme Court demanding intervention in Florida, five justices said that they would hold a hearing on the Florida situation on the following Monday, a dazzling rate of speed for the normally turtle-like pace at which the Court proceeds. The justices said they would not discuss Bush's claim that the recount violated the Equal Protection Clause of the Constitution but would delve into whether the Florida Supreme Court had the authority to extend the time-frame for extending the certification of the election winner in Florida. Gore told his people not to worry. The Supreme Court would rule 5 to 4 in his favor, with Justice Sandra Day O'Connor acting in her traditional role as the swing vote, he predicted. The Supreme Court would not go against the will of the American people, he said confidently.

O'Connor was the only Supreme Court justice serving on the bench who had ever held federal office. Surely, the Gore people tried to conclude optimistically, she would be most reluctant to get involved in an election. Possibly more important, core to her judicial decision-making, she stood for states' rights.

The Bush legal team argued that the Court had the authority and duty to decide any legal issue that arose in the United States. They argued that the chaos in Florida was a circus and must be stopped. The process of trying to "divine" the intent of the voters had become a ludicrous spectacle and was undermining the entire process of democracy, the Bush lawyers argued. All that stood in the way of a return to sanity was the Florida Supreme Court, they said.

The Gore team said that federalism, much beloved by the Rehnquist Court, must mean that deference to the state in an election process was paramount. Gore's lawyers decried the Bush team's constitutional histrionics and said there was no crisis. Bush had lost in a Florida state court, and who was better to decide the next move than the Florida Supreme Court, final arbiter of Florida state law? Gore was counting on the Supreme Court's ultimately handing the decision on recounts to the Florida Supreme Court, which already had shown a preference for "counting all the votes."

On December 1, a Friday, the electricity of a historic day was in the air at the Supreme Court. In the audience were the elite of the political world and Gore's family and Bush's family. More than two-dozen members of Congress were there. The 122 seats reserved for the press were snatched up immediately. Members of the public eager to attend waited all night in line. At 10 A.M. precisely, the familiar "Oyez! Oyez! Oyez!" rang out. The justices took their seats and settled in for ninety minutes of some of the most impassioned arguments they had heard. They aimed seventy-five questions at the lawyers, led by Ted Olson, arguing for Bush, and constitutional lawyer Laurence Tribe, arguing for Gore although he would be replaced at the eleventh hour. Why, the justices wanted to know, was this a federal case? Why should the Supreme Court get involved in a state matter? Was the Florida Supreme Court wrong in its decision-making when the state legislature had the power to decide electors under the federal Constitution?

There was intense interest in O'Connor's questions, which seemed to go up the mountain and down. In some questions she seemed to be on the side of the Florida Supreme Court, and thus Gore's side. In other questions, she seemed to be admonishing the lower court, thus supporting Bush. After the ninety tension-filled minutes, nobody seemed certain enough to second-guess what the Court would do, at least not for public consumption. Meanwhile, the country did not know who the next president would be.

On December 4, a clerk at the Supreme Court was horrified to find that the Court's pending ruling in the presidential election had been posted on the Internet for law schools and subscribers to the Court's opinion-delivery service before the justices had delivered the ruling. So, abruptly, in mid-morning Rehnquist ordered the decision released to the public. The Court had sent the case back to the Florida Supreme Court for clarification, thus giving the lower court a second chance at deciding what to do.

Unanimously, the nine justices said they were "unclear" about the extent to which the Florida Supreme Court had decided the state constitution limited the state legislature's role in picking electors for the Electoral College. In a blow for Gore, a judge in Tallahassee decided about five hours later that further recounts were unlikely to place in doubt the results of the election—that Bush had won Florida. The judge in the state court decided that although all the other courts had dodged the issue—to date—any recount would have to include all ballots under the Equal Protection Clause of the U.S. Constitution. So, once again, it all went back to the Florida Supreme Court. And this time in a forty-page opinion the state court ruled for Gore, but on a 4 to 3 decision, that the recount of votes deemed undercounted begin immediately, statewide, regardless of what voting system had been used—punch card or optical-scan, which means voters make marks in lottery-card-type ovals or connect the ends of arrows. In a stunning development, the state court set no deadline for the recount. The state court all but pretended that it had not just been severely admonished by the Supreme Court for lackadaisical decision-making.

Mere minutes passed before the Bush lawyers were preparing another appeal to the Supreme Court. Around the country there now was dire speculation that the 2000 election would go to the Congress, setting up a constitutional mess that might take generations to sort out. Fingers crossed, many on both sides of the political aisle hoped that this would not happen. At one point, it was (sarcastically) suggested that one Florida judge, who kept getting the case no matter how he tried to dodge it, count all the ballots himself, which would have taken more than six years. "What is Plan B?" Judge Terry Lewis asked dryly.

And then, suddenly, the U.S. Supreme Court was back in the picture. The justices ordered the recounts in Florida to stop immediately and said they had jurisdiction in the case. The major voice, suddenly, was Sandra Day O'Connor, who believed that the Florida Supreme Court had vastly overstated its bounds. The vote, not surprisingly, was 5 to 4. The "unanimity" of the Court was gone. Justices Souter, Stevens, Breyer, and Ginsburg dissented, making clear they were for Gore. And the other five—all appointed by Republicans, including Gore's last best hope, O'Connor—were for Bush. The Gore campaign went into a tailspin of despair.

As the justices met for a final hearing, O'Connor's line of questioning made clear what she was thinking. Didn't the U.S. Constitution and the Electoral Count Act require the state court to give "special deference" to the state legislature when an election dispute arose? Her fellow "swing vote" on the Court, Justice Kennedy, wanted to know why there shouldn't be a "uniform standard" for counting the ballots. It would be a pivotal point. "You're not just reading a person's mind," Kennedy said. "You are looking at a piece of paper." Ergo, there should be an objective standard. The Gore team pretended that wasn't the issue.

At 10 P.M. on December 12, 2000, it was nail-biting time as the final Supreme Court ruling came down. It was a sixty-five-page decision so convoluted that at first everyone was struggling to figure out what the verdict was. Essentially the Court ruled that there were constitutional problems with the Florida Supreme Court decision ordering the recount to continue and that there was no time to remedy them. Basically, the Court said, the system was a mess, but there was no time to clean it up. The Court claimed that the different ways of figuring a legitimate vote in Florida amounted to a violation of the Equal Protection Clause of the Constitution. But, the Court continued with baffling logic, its decision in the Florida case had no relevance for the rest of the country. The power of the Supreme Court to declare unconstitutional the actions of other branches of government is not explicitly found in the Constitution but was asserted by the justices in the 1803 decision *Marbury v. Madison*.

Justice John Paul Stevens, the Court's senior associate justice, said the true winner of the 2000 election might never be known. "But the identity of the loser is perfectly clear. It is the nation's confidence in the judge as impartial guardian of the rule of law."

Justice David Souter said that the recount was a monumental task but it was one the courts of Florida had committed to trying to get done until the Supreme Court weighed in and stopped it without justification.

Justice Stephen Breyer's dissent said, "In this highly politicized manner, the appearance of a split decision runs the risk of undermining the public's confidence in the Court itself. That confidence is a public treasure."

Constitutional scholars weighed in on all sides. Alan Dershowitz, a liberal Democrat and supporter of Al Gore who had clerked for Justice Arthur Goldberg and went on to become the youngest full professor ever appointed at Harvard Law School, said, "The five justices who ended election 2000 by stopping the Florida hand recount have damaged the credibility of the U.S. Supreme Court, and their lawless decision in *Bush v. Gore* promises to have a more enduring impact on Americans than the outcome of the election itself [and] threatens to undermine the moral authority of the high Court for generations to come."

Shaken to the core and convinced the Supreme Court's decision was legally wrong, Gore decided that with the Electoral College meeting in a week, with the unity of the country at stake, he would not continue the fight in Florida. He conceded, having won more popular votes than any other candidate in U.S. history except for Ronald Reagan. There were 100 million votes cast for president in 2000, and 537 of them in Florida decided the election.

It was curious that the five justices expressed great consternation that people were upset. O'Connor told her friends she didn't understand why the justices were getting such vitriolic mail and e-mail from American voters. Some wondered why, if the Court wanted to stay out of the fray, it didn't let the Florida legislature decide who won, or the Congress, both of which were dominated by Republicans and presumably would have chosen Bush.

The issue for the Court was how to convince future generations that there had been nothing political about its controversial decision to intervene, or rather that there had been nothing political in its unprecedented decision to choose the president of the United States.

There was bitter speculation that O'Connor did not want Gore to win because she wanted to retire and wanted her successor to be named by a Republican president. The night of the election, at a party, watching the chaotic returns in Florida, she exclaimed, "This is terrible." When her comment was reported in news accounts, many interpreted it to mean she thought it terrible that the networks were projecting Gore the winner. But four years later, with Bush in office, she had not announced her retirement. And her comment is open to interpretation. Her husband said he thought she meant she wanted to go home to Arizona and could not do that if Gore won, but she might have just been reflecting the general dismay of the country at large that the outcome was so unclear.

It is interesting that in her book *Majesty of the Law*, published two years after the disputed election of 2000, O'Connor made only one reference to the Florida case. It is probably "unsurprising" that the Court sometimes finds itself the center of public controversy, she wrote. "In 2000 the Court again set off widespread criticism when it held unconstitutional Florida's presidential election-recount procedures, and thereby determined the outcome of the election." She went on to say that the Court "and its power of judicial review" survived controversy through the years and is, she insisted, "quite likely to survive current and future controversies as well."

Many have spoken out on the justices and the election of 2000 and on whether the justices had a conflict of interest. Judge Richard Posner, who went to the University of Chicago with Scalia, possibly the most ideological and opinionated justice on the bench, said that many accusations of conflicts of interest and improper ideology on the part of justices are false. "The real conflict of interest," he was quoted as saying in *Harper's* magazine in May 2001, "is that justices are not indifferent to their colleagues and successors, and the president appoints them. That's an inherent serious conflict, because even if the justices play it straight and each says to himself or herself, 'I'm not going to think about the effect of this decision on my legacy as a Supreme Court justice,' you can't exclude the possibility of an unconscious influence."

His point was that if the Supreme Court justices had not had their own innate interest in the outcome, they might have intentionally overlooked some of the mistakes of the Florida Supreme Court. In other words, he said, they were looking for points they could use to justify what they wanted to be the outcome, even subconsciously.

For better or worse, the election of 2000 was decided by the U.S. Supreme Court for the first time in 212 years. And without O'Connor's vote, that would not have happened.

In 1887, when Congress was debating the establishment of the Electoral College, Senator John Sherman said that whatever happened the Supreme Court must stay out of the electoral process. "There is a feeling in this country," he said, "that we ought not to mingle our great judicial tribunal with political questions.... It would be a very grave fault indeed and a very serious objection to refer a political question in which the people of the country were aroused, about which their feelings were excited, to this great tribunal, which after all has to sit upon the life and property of all the people of the United States. It would tend to bring that Court into public odium of one or the other of the two great parties."

The Court, in its 2000 session, issued a number of momentous decisions. It said the Food and Drug Administration could not regulate cigarettes unless Congress gave it specific authority. It ruled that states could not overrule the wishes of parents by giving grandparents visiting rights for their grandchildren. It said public schools could not countenance student-led prayers at football games. It upheld the validity of the *Miranda* decision, that police must read suspects their rights at the risk of the case's being thrown out of court. The Court said that in general Congress must defer to states on a number of thorny issues.

Yet for most Americans, many of whom had never given the Court much thought, the Court was suddenly praised or maligned for its decision that had the effect of giving Bush the election. Earlier, in 1997, the Court had ruled that President Clinton was wrong in arguing that proceedings in a personal lawsuit against him (the Paula Jones case, in which she alleged sexual harassment by him while he was governor of Arkansas, a charge he emphatically denied) should be delayed until he was out of office. In 1988 the Court had ruled that an independent counsel could investigate the executive branch without violating the Constitution. That led to Kenneth Starr's investigation of Clinton, which Clinton, in his book *My Life*, derided as part of a conspiracy against him. (He did not use the words of his wife, Hillary

Clinton, "vast-right-wing conspiracy," but he agreed with his wife's assessment.) Thus by the end of George W. Bush's first term in office, many Democrats were arguing that the Court had become a political tool. While the justices strain to remain "nonpartisan," mainly because partisanship is deemed unseemly, Americans were coming to realize that the Court—and Sandra Day O'Connor—are innately political creatures. As Lawrence Baum wrote in his book *The Supreme Court*, the Court is political chiefly because "it makes important decisions on major issues; people care about those decisions and want to influence them. As a result, appointments to the Court are frequently the subject of political battles."

Certainly, presidents who think they will leave a major legacy on the Supreme Court are often doomed to be disappointed. And often justices who may privately think they are doing the right thing politically are surprised. Court watcher Lita Epstein noted that after the Court's ruling that stopped the counting of ballots in Florida, many legal experts who also are Bush supporters were appalled. For example, Robert Bork, a constitutional scholar who did not win confirmation to the Supreme Court when Reagan appointed him, said the decision "endorsed a new and possibly damaging rationale." Richard Epstein of the University of Chicago Law School said the decision was weird and that the theory that the Court was protecting the Equal Protection Clause of the Constitution was a dog that would bark only once.

Some have speculated that the decision may go down in history as among the Court's most egregious errors, along the lines of the *Dred Scott v. Sandford* case, which hastened the Civil War by the ruling that blacks could not be citizens, even if free and not slaves. The decision said that even if slaves moved to a free territory that outlawed slavery, they were not free and could be subjugated again and that Congress did not have authority to deprive citizens of their "property" by freeing slaves.

O'Connor grows still and wary and slightly tense whenever critics lambaste her decision in *Bush v. Gore* that way. Herman Schwartz, professor of law at American University's Washington College of Law, said the decision ranks "with history's worst. No, *Bush v. Gore* is not *Dred Scott* and it's not *Plessy v. Ferguson*. It didn't consign black Americans to unendable slavery or render the Fourteenth Amendment moot by sanctioning racial apartheid in America. But it shares a salient characteristic with the *Dred Scott* decision of 1857. In reaching these decisions, both Courts decided matters beyond those necessary to resolving the case, cloaking themselves in the mantle of statesmanship, national savior, and crisis averter."

Scholars, lawyers, and politicians will continue to debate the Court's wisdom in 2000 and O'Connor's role. But many think that for Sandra Day O'Connor the real issue was not the perfidy of state election officials or politics at all. It was voter stupidity. She had no sympathy for those who couldn't follow directions in this most sacred of civic obligations. If they couldn't follow directions on how to punch out the chads on their ballots, maybe they didn't deserve to have their votes counted. "Why isn't the standard the one that voters are instructed to follow, for goodness sakes?" she said out of exasperation. "I mean, it couldn't be clearer."

Pressed in an interview about her vote to stop the Florida recount, thus delivering the White House to Bush, she seemed almost irritated. "There was a great deal of criticism. It was a difficult case. It's too bad it ever came up. We don't enjoy being thrust into the middle of political controversy. We don't always have a choice about what comes up here."

But later, in a speech at the National Press Club in April 2003, O'Connor revealed that she loved sitting on big, controversial cases, even when the outcome is not always popular. She said that if she had to leave the Court, she would most miss "the fascination of seeing up close the power to help decide big social challenges in the United States. Who would have thought that I would end up deciding the election in a presidential election year? How strange is that?"

CHAPTER TWELVE

Icon

> Despite the encouraging and wonderful gains and the changes for women which have occurred in my lifetime, there is still room to advance and to promote correction of the remaining deficiencies and imbalances.
>
> —Sandra Day O'Connor

Throughout her long tenure on the Court, O'Connor has been a beacon of inspiration to millions of women, a trailblazer honored by young and old, whether because of her bout with breast cancer in 1988 or curiosity about how she does her job. Her name is consistently on lists of the most admired American women. When rumors sprang up in the early 1990s that she was thinking of retiring, she quickly batted them down, somewhat irritated that others might be trying to push her out and determined to go when she was ready, when she thought it best for the country. For example, she decided not to retire in the 2004 presidential election year, partly because she was not ready and partly because she feared the debate over her successor might be too political during an election year. When rumors sprang up that she might be the next chief justice, she smiled enigmatically. She was believed eager for the job but not eager to look eager. She was also shrewd enough to realize that she was not conservative enough for Bush's most conservative supporters. After her first term on the Supreme Court, in July 1982, she gave the commencement address at her alma mater, Stanford University. She quoted a passage from the Talmud: "In every age, there comes a time when leadership suddenly comes forth to meet the needs of the hour. And so there is no man who does not find his time, and there is no hour that does not have its leader." She said for her, the ancient saying means that "each of us, in our own individual lives and the crises we face, will have a time to lead. Whether we will lead only a family, or a handful of friends, and where and how we will lead, is up to us, our views and our talents. But the hour will come for each of us, and because we know this, we surely must also know that the very nature of humanity and society, regardless of its size or complexity, will always turn on the act of the individual and, therefore, on the quality of that individual."

In an unusual plea at a commencement, she urged the graduates to resolve disputes in their lives "someplace other than in the courtroom." For those going into business, she urged, consider putting in their contracts "that any dispute arising between the parties will be resolved by arbitration." And the second piece of advice she gave was to remember the Golden Rule: do unto others what you would have them do unto you. "That might make you a little more generous, save you a lot of time and money and make my job a lot easier."

A recurring theme that took on increasing passion for her while on the Supreme Court was the state of the law and the importance of turning out better, more ethical lawyers. In a speech at the dedication of the Alyne Queener Massey Library at Vanderbilt Law School as early in her tenure on the bench as 1982, she said law schools must not only teach students to be competent lawyers but also imbue them with a sense of professional responsibility. She was particularly worried that 77 percent of students said their law schools provided little or no training in negotiation skills and nearly 69 percent said their schools provided little or no training in counseling clients. "When lawyers are licensed to practice law, the public has a right to assume and does assume that the person licensed has received training in how to perform the basic functions of a lawyer," she said. Despite the increase in the disciplining of lawyers by state and federal courts, she said, more lawyers need training in "moral and social responsibility."

In a speech at the University of Toledo, she said that she became aware of the law early on in life. She said she heard of a cook who was elected a justice of the peace but refused to perform weddings. "He said he knew the Constitution, and it prohibited cruel and unusual punishments."

In addition to her dry wit, which she loves to use, O'Connor also cherishes her privacy. The Court and its traditions helped preserve it, but she also, somewhat reluctantly, recognized that she had a duty to travel around the country to encourage the next generation. While she sometimes is slightly disdainful of her celebrity, even annoyed by it, she also is aware of her responsibility. She is considered exceptionally thoughtful about accepting dozens of awards that clearly are designed to promote fund-raising and get an audience to show up. When the Freedoms Foundation at Valley Forge, a conservative, nonprofit organization, presented its public service awards in 1982, O'Connor was there to receive her award. But Beverly Sills, Pearl Bailey, Arthur Ashe, Roger Staubach, and Rod McKuen didn't show. "Where's Beverly Sills?" complained the chairman of the Securities and Exchange Commission. "That's why I came. I can't believe they're not here."

But sometimes for the busy justice it took an added incentive to get her attendance. When tiny Centre College in Danville, Kentucky, with 1,050 students, invited O'Connor to be a commencement speaker, she said yes. The reason, according to a *New York Times* interview with the college president, John Roush, was that a retired federal judge who was an alumnus of the college asked her, and that another alumnus, a chief executive of a Fortune 100 company, offered to fly her to Danville in a private jet. For a sitting Supreme Court justice, recognized everywhere she goes, flying commercial can be a pain.

For a wealthy woman, who by necessity spends much of her time locked up with books and briefs and deferential clerks, O'Connor impresses many as surprisingly down to earth. In 1981, O'Connor told the American Bar Association's *ABA Journal*, published by the nation's largest lawyers' association, "I am not a person who carries a lot of tension around. I try to do the best job I can and then never look back." She also said she worked a seventy-two-hour week, putting in twelve hours daily plus working at home and on Saturdays.

O'Connor was one of the most mild-mannered of the justices. Scalia is often acerbic, ridiculing even his Republican brothers if they disagree with him, almost gleeful when tearing apart their arguments. He does not hesitate to use such words as "silly" and "incomprehensible" when skewering opinions he holds in contempt. David Souter, who strikes most people as likely to cross the street rather than step on an ant, can be almost vituperative when reading a dissent in open Court.

For all her honors and awards, she never got over the awe of being on the nation's highest court or stopped being grateful to the fortieth president of the United States for putting her in what she considers the best job in the country. On June 5, 2004, Reagan died after a ten-year struggle with Alzheimer's disease, which robbed him of his memory. His wife of fifty-two years, Nancy Reagan, said that he no longer knew her but that throughout the "long goodbye" he remained sweet and gentle. Before he lost his memory, he and his wife worked out the details of what would be a weeklong national tribute to the former president, who was ninety-three, the longest-living ex-president in U.S. history. And among the three hundred pages of instruction was the wish that Sandra Day O'Connor, the first woman ever appointed to the Supreme Court, would be a reader at the state funeral, to be held at the magnificent National Cathedral in Washington, atop the highest point in the city.

O'Connor was immensely pleased. And there was no dispute about what she would read: a passage written in 1630 by Puritan John Winthrop on his way from England to the Massachusetts Bay Colony. It referred to the city on the hill that Reagan loved to cite in his speeches as the "shining city on a hill," which he always equated with America. And it quoted the Bible's Book of Micah: "What does the Lord require of you but to do justly, love mercy and to walk humbly with your God."

Wearing her trademark ruffled neckpiece, O'Connor read her passage firmly and with dignity. It meant a lot to her to be included among fewer than ten people who spoke at the hour-and-a-half service, attended by nearly four thousand of the most politically powerful people in the United States and abroad. It meant a lot because Ronald Reagan, an icon for his age, meant a lot to her. And few knew her own husband, John, was in the early stages of Alzheimer's.

Reagan's choosing of her, she said at the time of the funeral, was so important "because a woman had never held a position of that level in our government, and it was a signal that women could be in such positions and that they could do well. So opportunities for women opened all over the country. It was wonderful. I see the appointment of a woman to this court as a door opener for women across this land. And I think that's a wonderful legacy for President Reagan." Indeed, the year after Reagan nominated O'Connor to the Supreme Court, Canada put its first woman on the Canadian Supreme Court, Bertha Wilson, who was then fifty-eight and had been on the Ontario Court of Appeals for seven years.

After Reagan died, CBS News asked O'Connor what she thought Reagan would think of her today. Eighty percent of the time she voted with conservatives, as he would have wanted. But on many key issues, including abortion and affirmative action, her votes would have disappointed the former president, according to Charles Cooper, a former Reagan aide who helped screen judicial nominees. "I don't know," she said candidly. "I wish I did. He was a remarkable president. He understood the presidency. I'd like to think he would have understood this [her decisions] as well."

In 1994, speaking to an audience in Newport Beach, California, O'Connor said that a president's legacy is shaped to a great extent by his appointment of federal judges. She noted that years after Reagan left office, his impact was still being felt, partly because he was the first to name a woman to the Supreme Court. Yet Reagan was not known for the number of women he appointed to the federal bench. Numerically, Jimmy Carter appointed far more (about 20 percent of his judicial appointments were women). The Carter administration had trouble early with the American Bar Association committee, which gave a thumb's up or thumb's down on judicial appointments, supposedly based on qualifications. The ABA was troubled over some of Carter's female and minority candidates, until the ABA added the following experience criterion: "In evaluating experience, the committee recognizes that women and members of certain minority groups have entered the profession in large numbers only in recent years and that their opportunities for advancement in the profession may have been limited."

O'Connor, according to the Supreme Court's public relations office, received more requests to speak than any other single justice. And she relished speeches where women or young lawyers are honored for their service to others as well as for the quality of their work. Shortly after she was appointed to the Supreme Court in 1982, she proudly swore in Carol Los Mansmann, then thirty-nine, as the first woman to serve on the federal bench in Pittsburgh. From the U.S. District Court Mansmann was appointed to the Third U.S. Circuit Court of Appeals three years later. A tireless trailblazer, she was one of only two women graduates in Duquesne University Law School's class of 1967. Like O'Connor, she could not find one private law firm that would hire her. Like O'Connor, she went to work for a district attorney's office. In 1970 she became the youngest woman to argue before the Supreme Court. She maintained a law practice, served as an associate professor of law at Duquesne; she married and had two sons. O'Connor took an instant liking to her and followed her career with interest. When Mansmann died of breast cancer in 2002, O'Connor publicly expressed her sadness. O'Connor received the first Carol Los Mansmann Award given by Pittsburgh lawyers for distinguished public service, describing her friend as one of a "distinguished class of jurists."

Another sad day for O'Connor came when Judge Judith J. Jamison, who served on the bench in Philadelphia Court of Common Pleas and the Philadelphia Orphans' Court and was a well-known mentor to women lawyers, died of breast cancer in August 2001. She was posthumously given the Sandra Day O'Connor Award of the Philadelphia Bar Association, established in 1993 and given to a female attorney who has demonstrated superior legal talent, achieved significant legal accomplishments, and furthered the advancement of women in both the profession and the community.

O'Connor was in especially high demand for graduations, which she liked to do when she could because she said she had a deep responsibility for the young women who follow her. She said that as much as she tells her granddaughter, Courtney, born in 1989, about the need to appreciate how fortunate she is to live in an era when the world is becoming more democratic, she is certain that such a concept is almost impossible to grasp.

She was asked in an interview with *USA Today* in 2002 if she was sorry that Courtney, who was featured as a nine-year-old in a thirty-two-page photo-picture children's book, *Meet My Grandmother: She's a Supreme Court Justice*, has no memories of visiting O'Connor's beloved Lazy B ranch as a baby. O'Connor said she was extremely sad that her grandchildren will never know what it was like to experience the way of life that molded herself, her brother, her sister, her three sons, and her nieces and nephews. As a working mother, O'Connor said, the ranch was invaluable because her sons spent their summers there. Slyly, perhaps, she recalled that the Navajo Native Americans believe that discipline of children should be carried out by the mother's brother, the children's uncle. She said, "The day after school got out," her sons were gleefully running around the ranch, under the tutelage of her brother, Alan Day, and her parents. The first thing he did, she said, was to get their hair cut before he put them to work. At her son Brian's bachelor party, Brian described his uncle "Big Al" as the perfect uncle.

As O'Connor settled into her seventh decade, the honors came faster than she could accept them. One that made her especially proud, in 2000, was becoming an honorary alumna of The Citadel, the South Carolina military college that did not graduate its first female cadet until 1999. "I'm one of the very few alumna of The Citadel," she said. "It's going to be a growing number, so watch out. We're a small group now, but just you wait." She might have recalled that she was on the Supreme Court when it ruled four years earlier that Virginia Military Institute's all-male admissions policy was unconstitutional, prompting The Citadel to revoke its ban on female students.

In 2002, when Arizona celebrated its ninetieth year of statehood, six prominent historians in the state drafted a list of the ten most important people in Arizona history. First was Carl Hayden, a politician who saw that

Arizona would need water to thrive and pushed his vision of the Central Arizona Project, bringing Colorado River water to Phoenix and Tucson. The second was Barry Goldwater, the senator and 1964 conservative presidential candidate. The only woman on the list of politicians, missionaries, environmentalists, and scientists was Sandra Day O'Connor, ranked number eight. One reader, Irene Tseng, a former elementary school teacher in Phoenix, told the *Arizona Republic* that she admired O'Connor because "she embodies all that is best in Arizona—the drive to achieve and the persistence in the face of great odds."

In 2002, a nine-foot-tall bronze statue of O'Connor was unveiled at the Sandra Day O'Connor United States Courthouse in Phoenix, an $84.7-million soaring glass structure with a misting system that air-cools the building and its magnificent atrium. It's rare, early in the twenty-first century, that anyone in his or her own lifetime unveils a statue of himself or herself. The artist, Susan Henningsen, who was an elementary school art teacher, used a drawing based on an Internet photo of O'Connor to win the commission and worked in her dining room on the project. She said she had complete cooperation from the busy justice, who even called to make certain the artist had everything she needed. When Henningsen suggested she would like to come to Washington to see O'Connor in person, the justice said that if she came she would be the O'Connors' houseguest. When she arrived in Washington, Henningsen said, O'Connor fixed her dinner, posed for photos, and took her to a luncheon. "She's very sweet to be around," the sculptor said. The bronze statue, weighing one thousand pounds, is on a granite pedestal inside the courthouse atrium on the second floor. The hem of O'Connor's judicial robe is inscribed with the names of her family members. She is carrying a copy of *U.S. Reports* to indicate her love for the law.

Most people who have followed O'Connor's career are particularly struck by her vigorous work ethic. In a review of O'Connor's book about growing up on a cattle ranch, writer Susan Salter Reynolds said she was struck that O'Connor's book reminds her of those "no-nonsense New England memoirs that conceal a disdain for the seduction of beauty over hardiness. The moral is: Hard work builds integrity. Don't expect anyone else to do yours for you. Do the best you can or don't bother."

In 1988, shortly after her appendix was removed, O'Connor was diagnosed with breast cancer. She said nothing publicly about it. Few people, including friends and family, even knew about it until it was all over and she was back on the bench. The day before she was to undergo a mastectomy for breast cancer, she was supposed to deliver a speech at Washington and Lee University two hundred miles from Washington. She made the seven-hour round trip by car, gave the speech, had the surgery the next day, and, was back at work ten days later. Through a long period of recovery and treatment, she did not miss a single day of work. She had chemotherapy on Friday afternoons and, somehow, went to work on Monday morning. Not until after the surgery did she tell her brother and sister of her cancer, and when she did, she did not shed a tear or admit to any serious concerns that she wouldn't make it. Her brother, Alan, has told interviewers, "She never once cried on my shoulder." For O'Connor, who values stoicism and self-containment as well as intellectual skills above all else, cancer was just a small setback—she was used to seeing cowhands on her father's ranch lasso and brand calves despite having broken ribs. O'Connor's sister, Ann Day, who shared her older sister's political ambitions and became a senator in the Arizona legislature, once said, "You keep your problems to yourself, you don't lose control—that's the way we were raised."

Finally, after six years, O'Connor began talking about her bout with cancer publicly. She said, "I did what I do at the Court. As much research as I possibly can and then I make my decision and don't look back." At a meeting of the National Coalition for Cancer Survivorship, the nation's most prominent jurist talked not about jurisprudence but about her ordeal with cancer, confirming for the first time that she had a mastectomy.

In that speech in 1994, she said,

> My own experience and observations, as I've said, are like those of others. When you're dealing with things as basic as life and death and a disease like cancer there's a universality to the experience. We

> began with the anxiety of going through the testing. Something is seen in a mammogram or an X-ray. Or there's some little spot on your back, whatever it is. And then you start this round of testing, X-rays, cat scans, whatever. The initial impact for me was one of general disbelief. I felt fine, just fine. But I was told you better go have these tests and find out. And then after the usual biopsies and other tests that are made, I was told I had a potentially fatal disease. Now that gets your attention. The Big C. The word cancer overwhelms the psyche, just the word. I couldn't believe it. I was unprepared for the enormous emotional jolt I received from the diagnosis. All of a sudden my face, my hands, my whole body tingled. It couldn't be true. I was too busy. I feel fine. You can't be serious.

She talked about what every woman undergoing cancer treatment worries about—her hair. She said that she had a hairdresser who helped her find wigs that were similar to her own then blondish-gray hairstyle. The worst part of the ordeal, she confided, was her public visibility. "There was constant media coverage: 'How does she look?' 'When is she going to step down?' 'She looks pale to me.' 'I don't give her six months.' This was awful."

But with her usual burst of optimism after a setback, she said to her fellow survivors, "Is there an upside to all of this? Yes. It made me value each and every day of life more than ever before." Another time she said she thinks the lesson she learned was to "appreciate and treasure each day because you don't know how many more you'll be given, so make those that you have count." She also said another lesson she learned was to keep busy with something else, to keep her mind off her troubles.

In February 2002, O'Connor traveled to Los Angeles, despite her dislike of taking on speaking engagements while the Court is sitting, to rename the downtown Criminal Courts Building after California's first female lawyer, Clara Shortridge Foltz. Foltz was a woman she could identify with: the first woman admitted to the state's first law school, the first woman to practice law in California, the first female notary public in the state, the first woman to serve as deputy district attorney in Los Angeles County, and the founder of the public defender system in the United States. And O'Connor particularly liked a phrase that Clara used in her speeches: "Did God fail in his last crowning work when he made woman, that she is not the equal of man? Genius, talent, hard labor know no sex." O'Connor's sentiments, exactly.

But Foltz did something that O'Connor did not—she sacrificed her personal life. She was relentless in her pursuit of women's rights from the time she was a young girl through her motherhood into her late years. At the age of eighty-one she ran for governor of California on a women's rights ticket and lost. Before she died in 1934, she wrote, "I have lost more for myself than I have gained for all women. All the pleasure of my young motherhood, I sacrificed for woman's cause." O'Connor did not do that. She followed her husband overseas, she had three children. Only when they were well launched did she fully immerse herself in the world of politics and the law. She was a quiet feminist, leading by example and hard work rather than by marches in the street or hot rhetoric.

In any list of the most powerful people—men or women—in the United States, O'Connor was prominently there. But her technical boss for years, Chief Justice Rehnquist, is usually not on "popular" hot lists. For one thing, until 2000, the Supreme Court was not particularly prominent. In a typical term, fewer than half of the cases decided are so-called "hot button" issues. Also, the Court is considered the pinnacle of a career, not a stepping-stone to political office. So justices tend to stay quiet, content to do their work out of the public spotlight.

A key to understanding O'Connor is that she truly never spent much time on clearing emotional hurdles. Perhaps it was a result of her hardscrabble early life on the ranch when making ends meet was far more important than any discussion of how someone felt about his or her lot in life. Even if a young girl wanted to have such a discussion about her parents' choices in life, her taciturn father would have ridiculed it. Certainly, despite her remarkable memory, she never dwells for long on the conflicted adolescent emotions she undoubtedly must have felt, nor does she ever psychoanalyze her parents or their relationship or the most serious of the personal problems of the cowboys she knew as a child.

Perhaps it is ironic, then, that in 2002 a $40 million new high school for two thousand students opened in Deer Valley, Arizona, named the Sandra Day O'Connor High School, with the guiding principle that it would be dedicated to making children "feel connected," in the words of its principal, Jack Dillard. One goal was for teachers to find out why a student didn't turn in a paper, not just mark down that the paper wasn't handed in. Upperclassmen are asked to be a buddy, mentor, and tutor to younger students. At O'Connor High School, the aim was to make students feel they were in a small group, not a mammoth one. Dillard said, "People have begun to recognize that how people think and feel really determines how they act." O'Connor, advocate of taking responsibility for what one does, would never have put it that way. (Another O'Connor High School named for her opened in 1998 in San Antonio, Texas, which had a more pragmatic goal possibly more to her liking: it features an agricultural center, including animal pens and a show barn.)

O'Connor's star dimmed, for many, after the election of 2000, when her swing vote helped decide the election and gave it to her fellow Republican George W. Bush, instead of to Al Gore, who won the popular vote. It was, many thought, a strange decision for O'Connor. She had twice come under fire from judicial ethicists for agreeing to conduct a 1987 private briefing for Republicans who had contributed at least $10,000 for GOPAC, which was trying to gain Republican control of Congress. After an initial uproar, she begged off, but not until her name had been used in fundraising efforts, pointed out one of her harshest critics, Harvard University constitutional lawyer Alan M. Dershowitz. She also wrote a letter in support of a proposed Republican Party resolution declaring the United States to be a "Christian Nation" based on the absolute law of the Bible. The Court said that she did not know the letter would be used to benefit the Arizona Republican Party. And many of her liberal critics argue that her strong belief in states' rights ignores the Constitution's stipulation that the federal government does have supreme rights over states in a number of matters; thus, they say, the question should be why some rights were reserved for the states and others for the federal government.

Whenever lawyers gather, sooner or later O'Connor's name comes up, far more than any other justice, except possibly the iconoclastic Scalia. She and her fellow justices had been on the Supreme Court as an unchanged team for eleven years, longer than any other team in U.S. history. Some conservatives began worrying after 2000 that she was becoming too "incremental," meaning they thought she tended to view each case along narrow legal lines and that more and more she was "tentative" and "cautious." Others complained that her decisions showed that she was power-hungry. Others said she was just "pragmatic."

Others wondered whether, as O'Connor entered her mid seventies, she had become more liberal. In the 2004 term, for example, she voted to let disabled Americans sue states for access to courthouses. Then she joined the liberal branch of the Court to rule that crucial parts of the highly controversial campaign finance law restricting donations to national political parties were constitutional. She said the government had the power to enforce the Clean Air Act even when that placed a burden on the states. She said taxpayers could sue their states to challenge tax credits that benefit religious schools.

One of her former law clerks, Marci Hamilton, a Cardozo Law School professor, once told *USA Today* that because O'Connor had actually been in public office, raising money for reelection campaigns, she understood politics more than some of her fellow justices, who, indisputably, were more insular in their experiences. "She is the anti-ideologue. She will never let theory trump reality," said the admiring Hamilton.

O'Connor, despite her insistence that life on the Court is that of an academic, was not a legal scholar or a flashy, in-your-face intellectual such as Scalia. She was not a brilliant legal strategist and thinker such as John Marshall or Benjamin Cardozo, who reshaped common law inherited from England into a body of laws fit for the modern age, or an Oliver Wendell Holmes, who once described the Supreme Court as nine scorpions in a bottle. Nor would she fit in with the other spectrum of justices, such as the notoriously lazy and despotic Chief Justice Fred Vinson, elevated beyond his capability or brainpower by the death of Harlan Stone in 1946, or the scandalous James Wilson, imprisoned for debt.

Yet while lawyers and scholars probably will debate for centuries her contributions to jurisprudence and American society, there is no doubt about her impact on the Court and American life. She molded a generation of clerks into caring, hard-working legal advocates. She did it with high expectations and kindness. She humanized the Court by instituting 8 A.M. exercise classes (for women in the Court who came when it was dark and left when it was dark and had no other way to exercise). And she was known for her true love of social events. Yet she rarely "let her hair down." She was known for being a perfectionist, a disciplined woman dedicated to a strict work ethic, yet cheerfully optimistic and loyal. When she wrote *Majesty of the Law*, she dedicated it to her law clerks, past, present, and future. Since the book came during a period of intense speculation she was about to retire, the dedication was a cheerful tweak at the conventional wisdom in Washington.

O'Connor, as do the other justices, considered that one of her most important duties was choosing law clerks, who serve for one year. Each justice hires three out of four each year. These clerks work hard but get invaluable experience, and most go on to successful legal careers. Most of the clerks rank in the top 10 percent of the top ten law schools in the country—Columbia, Duke, Harvard, New York University, Stanford, University of California at Berkeley, University of Chicago, University of Michigan, University of Pennsylvania, and Yale. (They are listed in alphabetical order here, not by ranking.) As late as 1998, in a study by the NAACP, 24.3 percent of clerks hired by then-sitting justices during their tenures so far were women, 4.5 percent were Asian American, 1.8 percent were black, 1 percent were Hispanic, and all the rest were white males. Four out of ten came from either Harvard or Yale. Rehnquist responded, "We select clerks who have very strong academic backgrounds and have previously successful law clerk experience, most often in the federal courts. As the demographic makeup of this pool changes, it seems entirely likely that the under-representation of minorities . . . will also change."

After the terrorist attacks of September 11, 2001, Congress passed the Patriot Act, which gave police and prosecutors broad new powers in dealing with suspected terrorists. O'Connor visited Ground Zero, site of the twin towers of the World Trade Center destroyed by two planes hijacked by al-Qaeda terrorists. She said, "We're likely to experience more restrictions on personal freedom than has ever been the case in this country." She, Scalia, and Breyer were traveling out of the country at the time of the attacks and were brought back to the United States with the help of federal officials.

The attacks prompted O'Connor to warn American judges, including those on the nation's highest courts, that they must stop ignoring international issues. Speaking at the American Law Institute, a group of judges and lawyers, in May 2002, she said American courts get high marks for handling domestic matters, but when it comes to international issues, "the jury is still out. No institution of government can now afford to ignore the rest of the world." She said she was disappointed that the Supreme Court had refused to review a case in the fall of 2001 involving a child custody fight between a New York mother and a father in Hong Kong. She said this refusal was wrong because justices were passing up a chance to consider for the first time how American authorities handle the Hague Convention on child abduction, a treaty that has as signatories sixty countries, including the United States. The treaty is aimed at stopping parents from taking children to other countries to bypass child custody orders. "The fates of nations are more closely intertwined than ever before," O'Connor said. "We're more acutely aware of the connections. As we learned from September eleventh, these connections can sometimes be devastating."

In a speech a month and a half after the 9/11 attacks, she told students at Principia College in Elsah, Illinois, that the terrorist threat was one of three new developments that concerned her. "Our legal system abhors punishment without due process, but no single approach is appropriate to all situations," she said. The other two legal developments that worried her, she said, were the increasing "rigidity" of the law such as zero-tolerance policies in schools and the "commercialization" of the law, forcing lawyers to run up "billable hours" that clients must pay.

And yet in a surprise decision, in the 2004 term, O'Connor sided with the majority in another 5 to 4 decision that the Bush administration was wrong to deny lawyers and access to the court to enemy combatants held at

Guantanamo Bay. It was an enormous setback to the administration's efforts to fight the war on terrorism, administration lawyers said.

A visit to the Supreme Court to watch O'Connor in action showed that she was more interested in getting the facts of the case straightened out than in engaging in philosophical debate. When the emotional issue of the Pledge of Allegiance came before the Court in 2004, brought by Michael Newdow, who argued that the phrase "under God" does not belong in the pledge because of the separation of church and state, it was O'Connor who refused to get into a philosophical debate. Even though no child can be forced to say the pledge (a Supreme Court decision that goes back decades), Newdow, an atheist with both medical and legal degrees, argued the case himself, saying his daughter risked ostracism if she refused to say the pledge in the classroom. O'Connor asked skeptically, "It's all right for her to have [coins which say 'In God We Trust'] and use them and read them, but it's the problem of being asked to say the pledge, which she doesn't have to say?" In handing down its decision, the Court did a Sandra O'Connor–type thing. It said that Newdow had no standing to bring the case because he didn't have legal custody of his daughter. The constitutional rightness or wrongness of the wording of the pledge would have to wait for another day.

O'Connor voted with Rehnquist, her old Stanford Law School buddy, about 90 percent of the time, differing with him mainly on women's rights, affirmative action, and First Amendment issues. Despite worries by conservatives as she entered her third decade on the Court that she was "turning liberal," the bulk of her decisions places her solidly with the conservative-to-moderate bloc, not the liberal side. She was without doubt one of the hardest-working judges. It was not unusual to see the lights at her home or in her chambers burning late into the evening and on weekends. An early riser, she was always disciplined in her personal habits, eating right, and exercising, and urging those around her to do the same. But she remained a Republican loyalist, and when she agreed to appear before GOPAC, a conservative political action campaign fundraising group, and wrote a letter supporting a Republican Party resolution declaring the United States to be a "Christian nation based on the absolute law of the Bible, not a democracy," liberal critics were outraged. They did not buy her explanations that both actions were inadvertent mistakes.

One such liberal critic, Martin Garbus, a trial lawyer who appears regularly before the Supreme Court, often on First Amendment cases, wrote in *Courting Disaster: The Supreme Court and the Unmaking of American Law*, "She [O'Connor] rarely writes broadly and while she contributes to the revisionist tide, she is circumspect by often refusing to join in the broad sweeps of Rehnquist, Scalia and Thomas. Clearly, the Court would change even more radically if O'Connor stepped down and Bush got the kind of justice he wants—someone in the Thomas and Scalia mold. The Court could take cases it does not hear now. The decisions that would come from the Court could be broad, sweeping decisions that Scalia favors, not the narrow ones O'Connor crafts."

A conservative critic, Kenneth Starr, took umbrage at what he considered O'Connor's swing toward the left in the 1990s as she "teamed up with someone new—an appointee of President Clinton" instead of Anthony Kennedy. Starr said disapprovingly, "On several large issues (with federalism a notable exception), Justice O'Connor and Justice Stephen Breyer were solidly together. Their growing judicial kinship was evidenced most provocatively on partial-birth abortion." She and Breyer agreed that Nebraska's ban on the procedure was unconstitutional, a position Starr roundly opposed.

To Starr, O'Connor was "the most influential and powerful woman in America." And he was not happy with her influence and power. He argued that O'Connor came up with "highly creative" interpretations of the separation of church and state doctrine in the Constitution. "She created a new concept or principle in the law—the idea of 'endorsement.' That is, in her view, a violation of the Establishment Clause (the government shall establish no religion) occurs when government 'endorses' religion or religious practice. What did this mean? O'Connor states the idea at a high level of generality. Government could not make one's religious beliefs, or lack thereof, relevant to one's standing in the political community. To do so would effect an 'endorsement' of religion (or conversely irreligion)."

Thus, said Starr, "a centrist, common-law constitutionalist from Arizona, with little prior judicial experience before arriving in Washington, became the Court's most powerful member. Her path to power was simple. Step one: positioning herself at the Court's center—avoiding strict doctrines or rigid . . . principles and thus leaving some running room for later cases. That meant, necessarily, rejecting textualism. Step two: being ready and willing to create new law. She was, in short, farther along the common-law constitutionalism spectrum than Justice Kennedy."

O'Connor refused to engage in debate of that nature. She sometimes thought that if the far left and the far right both criticize her vituperatively, she must be doing something right. She might have admitted that Starr's analysis of her is that she is subjective, but she would say that she was bending the Court's decision-making to the popular culture, not that "she herself is the reasoned arbiter of competing interests," as Starr said disdainfully.

When history judges O'Connor, it will find a strikingly disciplined, well-organized, modern woman of the twentieth century who decided at an early age she wanted it all. She wanted a family. She wanted to work. She wanted power. She wanted to see the world. She wanted to make a difference. She wanted to grow old gracefully. And few would disagree that she got what she sought. She inspired thousands of young women, convincing them they could do whatever they put their hearts and minds into achieving.

One of the ten worst decisions ever made by the Court, according to historian Lisa Paddock, was *Bradwell v. Illinois*. In 1873 the Court ruled that Myra Bradwell, an ambitious woman who studied law before founding the *Chicago Legal News*, did not have to be admitted into the Illinois bar because she was a woman. The Court's opinion said: "The paramount destiny and mission of woman are to fulfill the noble and benign offices of wife and mother. This is the law of the Creator." Certainly, little more than a hundred years later, O'Connor would never have gone along with that determination.

O'Connor is perhaps most notable for striking down laws that she thought restricted the authority of the states. Thus she shocked many by knocking down a law that would have made it a federal crime to carry a gun within one thousand yards of a school. She struck down a provision of the

Americans with Disabilities Act that gave disabled state government employees the right to sue for discrimination. She struck down a provision of the Violence Against Women Act that would have encouraged victims to sue attackers in federal court. Yet she was not always predictable, as the *Washington Post*'s Charles Lane frequently pointed out. He noted she let state employees sue on grounds their rights have been violated under the Family and Medical Leave Act. Then she said that states may be sued if they fail to make their courthouses accessible to the handicapped. She refused to overturn *Roe v. Wade* but ruled that states may restrict abortion as long as they don't impose an "undue burden" on the right of a woman to have an abortion, whatever "undue burden" means.

Former Supreme Court Justice Harry Blackmun, who regarded *Roe v. Wade* as his crowning achievement, would write of O'Connor: "She is a believer in states' rights in the sense that she feels an issue of this general nature should be left to the state legislatures and not be federally constitutionalized. [Also] she is a woman and may fear somewhat any accusation of being a traitor to her sex."

On affirmative action, she repeatedly said that it must get the same "strict scrutiny" that minorities get when they claim they have been discriminated against. But when she had a chance to outlaw affirmative action in the University of Michigan case, she did not do it, saying that diversity in higher education is a worthy goal as long as all applicants are given equal consideration. Once again she infuriated the conservative base of the Republican Party because she listened to the military and universities, which said they could not come up with any other way to address racial inequality.

Summing up what he thinks the Constitution is like after more than two decades with O'Connor on the Court, reporter Charles Lane of the *Washington Post* said it is a Constitution that protects the state from too much federal power, unless Congress wants to make a point of defending the equality of women. It is a Constitution that guarantees the right of abortion but permits states to put restrictions on that right as they see fit. It is a Constitution that protects the rights of whites and blacks unless universities say racial preference of minorities is good for society.

In effect, it is a Constitution that tries to make living in a polarized, modern American society possible for everyone. It is a pragmatic, changing, commonsense Constitution that O'Connor made possible, sometimes angering the left, sometimes angering the right.

When O'Connor ponders her legacy, after decades of dealing not just with the best and brightest but much of the time with the problems of some of the sorriest specimens the human species has to offer, she is sometimes surprised to find that she is still an optimist. As she looks at her granddaughter, Courtney, she wrote in *Majesty of the Law*, she is struck by the need to preserve democracy by educating its citizens. "Establishing the right to vote is essential, but as we have discovered in the United States, citizens may not participate in the political process unless they understand it and believe they have a stake in the community." Democracy, she said more fervently as she grew older, takes time and effort and vigilance. "Liberty requires us to place ourselves in another's shoes, to see that things may not be as fair or as equitable as they appear from our own vantage points. Justice compels us to understand the rage, to feel the pain, to respond to the cries."

David Broder, the esteemed political reporter for the *Washington Post*, wrote in 2003 that O'Connor used "skill and tact" to fortify her position on the Court. "O'Connor is a great one for finding the center, not just of legal disputes but of the political spectrum." He noted that she cannot safely be put in the liberal bloc or its opposition. In two 5 to 4 decisions, he noted, she upheld California's tough three-strikes-and-you're-out law. She upheld the life-in-prison sentence, with no possibility of parole, for a defendant convicted of stealing $253 worth of videotapes from a Kmart. She did it because she believes California has a right to insist that a pattern of criminal behavior justified the punishment and because the Constitution permits a state to do that. Yet she has been in the majority of some of the Court's most liberal rulings as well. Broder concluded, "No one else in America has more authority in more areas of domestic policy than she does. And no one calculates her use of power more carefully."

At the age of seventy-four, when O'Connor received the first Role Model of the Year Award from a group called Jobs for America's Graduates, a nonpartisan group dedicated to finding jobs for at-risk high school graduates, she told the audience her favorite story: how she couldn't get a job offer from a law firm as a lawyer when she first left law school. "You can start at the bottom and make something of it," she told the group. And then, lifting the huge plaque she had been given, she exulted, "Look at this marvelous thing!"

When O'Connor was undergoing the Senate confirmation process, she was asked what she would like her epitaph to be. "Ah," she said. "The tombstone question. I hope it says, 'Here lies a good judge.'"

But, she said, she also takes enormous pride in the fact that she didn't have to give up "life" to be a judge, to be the first woman on the U.S. Supreme Court, to be a lawyer among lawyers. She had a happy marriage. She produced three children who grew up to be successful, independent, caring adults. She was a doting grandmother. She had two homes that she loved and which gave her peace and contentment and great kitchens. She filled her chambers with evidence of her passions: with Zuni drums; a Carl Oscar Borg landscape of the Grand Canyon and George Catlin paintings of a buffalo hunt in the Rocky Mountains; books by her favorite author, Wallace Stegner, the chronicler of the West who taught her creative writing at Stanford; and an embroidered pillow with the motto "Maybe in error but never in doubt." She was a good cook. She hiked and fished and traveled and climbed and golfed and played tennis and exercised and beat cancer. She had good friends. She had peace of mind. She had adulation and respect. She wrote books. She had the satisfaction of living a life of hard, productive, well-rewarded work.

In short, she had it all.

Perhaps of all the accolades in O'Connor's life, the best came from her brother, Alan: "The essence of Sandra is that if you're around her very much, the bar is raised in your life. You just feel like doing better things and being a better person."

Epilogue

On Thursday, June 30, 2005, the White House counsel, Harriet Miers, received a phone call from the Supreme Court's head marshal, Pamela Talkin, saying that a letter would be hand-delivered to President George W. Bush the following morning. Miers rushed to tell Bush and Vice President Cheney, who were having their usual Thursday lunch together. Speculation buzzed around the West Wing—Chief Justice William Rehnquist, frail at eighty and battling throat cancer, was certain to resign, confirming rumors that had swirled about Washington for weeks.

But shortly before 9 A.M. the next morning, Miers got a call from the marshal's office that the letter was coming from the office of Sandra Day O'Connor, the swing vote on the Court. Miers quickly called the president. This was a far greater development than if Rehnquist had retired that day. For twenty-four years O'Connor often had been the deciding vote in many of the Court's most controversial, 5 to 4 decisions, holding the balance of power in her hands. Rehnquist's looming resignation would presumably mean another conservative would go on the Court. But O'Connor's resignation would undoubtedly mean that Bush would have the opportunity to appoint a more conservative justice, with the prospect for a far greater impact on society. From separation of church and state to abortion, affirmative action, the death penalty and government regulations, O'Connor's decisions had affected nearly every aspect of human life for nearly a quarter of a century. With four staunch conservatives and four moderates or liberals, she was repeatedly the justice who often decided the outcome. Without her moderating influence and decisive vote, *Roe v. Wade* might be overturned. Minorities might not get special treatment in applying to colleges and universities in an effort to provide diversity. The lines between church and state might become more blurred.

Bush immediately told Cheney; Karl Rove, his senior adviser and deputy chief of staff; and Dan Bartlett, his communications adviser, that they had to get to work at once to provide him with a short list of potential nominees. Bush then called O'Connor shortly after ten o'clock Friday morning to accept her resignation, thank her for her service, and wish her well. He told her, "For an old ranching girl, you turned out pretty good."

O'Connor's letter was, typically, short—just three sentences—and to the point—no unnecessary words, no rhetorical flourishes. "This is to inform you of my decision to retire from my position as an associate justice of the Supreme Court of the United States effective upon the nomination and confirmation of my successor. It has been a great privilege, indeed, to have served as a member of the Court for 24 terms. I will leave it with enormous respect for the integrity of the Court and its role under our constitutional structure."

She did not offer the reason for her resignation. At seventy-five, while still full of energy and intellectual curiosity and her legendary passion for her work, she was leaving to take care of her husband, John, in the early but clearly progressing stages of Alzheimer's Disease. He would be facing loss of memory, and she wanted to cherish their time together before he was lost to the mental fog of the dreaded disease. Also, they both yearned to spend more time in Arizona, where their children and grandchildren were living. They sold their elegant Washington home, a block from the Chevy Chase Country Club, immediately trading it for apartment living. Now there would be more time for tennis and golf and cooking and trips back to Arizona. And she was about to agree to take on the advisory post of chancellor of the College of William and Mary, following in the footsteps of such notables as Henry Kissinger, Margaret Thatcher, and Warren Burger.

At a dinner party the month before her resignation letter was sent, John O'Connor had mentioned that while his wife had been the most powerful woman in Washington, that time was coming to an end. "We're out of here," he said. It had been at another dinner party four and a half years earlier, that he had titillated guests by saying that his wife was ready to resign. Then she was forced to deny the rumor. This time, there was no denial. She was ready to leave, ready to work on a possible memoir and finish a children's book about her favorite childhood horse, Chico, and to lecture about the need for civility in the law and, at last, eager to enjoy a day without reading thousands of words in mountains of legal briefs.

The accolades that poured in for her were astonishing, from her point of view. She was again on the cover of the news magazines. *Newsweek*, devoting its cover to her official photo, dubbed her "queen of the center" and said, "She was a deep believer in the sensible center, in humane compromise, in finding ways to defuse quarrels and sand down bitter edges. It is typical of O'Connor that when conservative ideologues began ranting on the floor of the House of Representatives about 'mass impeachments' for liberal judges, she quietly invited them to her chambers for lunch as a lesson in civility."

Thousands and thousands of words were written about her legacy. Television stations paid homage to her morning, noon, and night. There was no other major national topic of conversation for a week. She had become one of the best-known women in America with a reputation in legal circles as a centrist. She had become regarded not as a legal theoretician but as a pragmatist, searching for practical, workable solutions in nearly every aspect of human life.

In various decisions, she upheld the right of a woman to have an abortion without government putting "undue burdens" on her; cast doubt on the justice of the death penalty; fretted that the government was becoming too intrusive in religion, voting against permitting a moment of silence in schools; voted to give Bush the election in 2000; and most recently sided with the minority when she said state and local governments should not take private property to enhance their tax base. In the previous five years, she voted that the partial birth abortion ban was illegal because it had no exception for the life of the mother, upheld the controversial McCain-Feingold campaign finance reform law that was loathed by conservatives, permitted some affirmative action at the University of Michigan, and ruled against new installations of the Ten Commandments in government buildings.

While he did not agree with a number of her decisions, Bush went before TV cameras in the Rose Garden to praise her as a "discerning and conscientious judge and a public servant of complete integrity." Referring to the fact that President Reagan's choice of O'Connor in 1981 made her the first woman on the Court after 191 years and 101 male justices, Bush said, "Americans had high expectations of her, and she has surpassed those expectations in the performance of her duties. This great lady, born in El Paso, Texas, rose above the obstacles of an earlier time and became one of the most admired Americans of our time. She leaves an outstanding record of service to the United States, and our nation is deeply grateful."

With liberals and conservatives braced for a bruising battle over O'Connor's successor, Bush promised to consult with members of the Senate. He said he would select someone who would make America proud and who would meet "a high standard of legal ability, judgment, and integrity, and who will faithfully interpret the Constitution and laws of our country."

Not everyone praised O'Connor. Robert Bork, the outspoken and bitter conservative judge whose nomination to the Court by Ronald Reagan was shot down by the Senate in 1987, said O'Connor had been what he found unconscionable: an activist judge. She didn't have "a firm judicial philosophy," he scoffed, and said that for a reported conservative, she far too often "lined up with the liberal side" on social issues. Asked if he thought she was a moderate, he told Cable News Network, "There are judges who depart from the actual Constitution and those who stick with it. She departed from the actual Constitution. I wouldn't call that moderate. I call it unfortunate."

A former law clerk of O'Connor's, Nelson Lund, who had become a law professor at George Mason University, said that while she did not have as theoretical an approach to the law as Bork, she was "extraordinarily influential during her time on the Court." But ultimately her legacy would depend on other possible retirements and what the Court does in the future, he said.

Ken Gormley, a law professor at Duquesne University who had become friendly with O'Connor while arranging for her to lecture at the university, said that what always struck him was that she remained, basically, "very much a western girl." He said he thought O'Connor never felt at home in Washington and despite her full country club life, considered herself something of an outsider on the East Coast.

"She has a strong personality and she's physically imposing. She's fun, and she's been everywhere. And she always said it like it was," Gormley said. "I once gave a lecture at Chautauqua [in New York] saying that *Bush v. Gore* [the 2000 decision in which the Supreme Court gave the election to George Bush] was constitutional but politically naïve. Afterwards she came up to me and I said I didn't know she had been in the audience. 'Yes,' she said. 'I was naïvely sitting there.' Ten days after September 11, 2001, she was supposed to give a lecture in Pittsburgh and called to ask if she should still come. I told her many people would be disappointed if she didn't. Ronald Reagan Washington National Airport was still closed. So she and John got in a car and drove to Baltimore where they could catch a plane."

There is "no question she did have it all" in life, Gormley agreed. "She felt lucky she had her family early and took five years off from practicing law to do that. She was always grateful. She was really proud she managed to walk this tightrope."

Gormley once made a twenty-minute documentary of her life and didn't tell her before hand, nervous that she would forbid it. Her former law clerks warned him she might see it as an invasion of her privacy. But when she saw it, she loved it, delighted at stories and images she'd long forgotten. "My sense is that thought she has a big following in Washington, she still doesn't feel at home there, even after all these years. Her home is in Arizona and she likes the idea of having some time off again," Gormley said.

As once again O'Connor shone in the national limelight, she spent it mostly out of sight. She gave no in-depth interviews. She simply slipped on the mantle of being a private person. Senator Arlen Specter, the moderate Pennsylvania Republican, also seventy-five and battling Hodgkin's disease, would have the onerous job of conducting confirmation hearings for her successor. He mused publicly that his job would be a lot easier if Bush had simply nominated O'Connor to be chief justice in the event of Rehnquist's resignation. There had been so much adulation pouring out for her, Specter suggested, that her confirmation (any new chief justice, even one who has been on the Court, must be confirmed again) would be "more like a coronation."

It was not to be. She was adamant. It was time for her to leave the Court.

But there was more drama yet to come. To replace her, Bush chose a little-known jurist, John G. Roberts, Jr., from the U.S. Circuit Court of Appeals for the District of Columbia, a brilliant conservative with impeccable credentials. O'Connor, on a fly-fishing trip out West, said Roberts was "confirmable," but she also told friends she was disappointed that Bush did not choose a woman to replace her. With her usual dry wit, she said Roberts's confirmation would cut the female population on the high court by 50 percent.

But before Roberts's confirmation hearings could start on September 3, 2005, O'Connor's longtime friend and mentor, Chief Justice William Rehnquist, died from complications of thyroid cancer. Bush quickly renominated John Roberts to be the chief justice, meaning O'Connor would have to stay on the Court until another nominee was named and confirmed. At Rehnquist's funeral, she was the only justice asked to speak. "I met Bill Rehnquist when I was a freshman at Stanford University in 1946. He was serving as a 'hasher' at my dormitory during the evening meal. He amazed all the young women by carrying such heavy loads of dishes on his tray. I guess that is how he learned to carry all those heavy loads in all the years that followed."

She said that as chief justice, Rehnquist frowned on long-winded speeches but was gracious in making certain each justice was able to express his or her opinion. When tensions rose, she said, he would invariably inject humor. She said that even as he lay dying, when emergency room physicians asked Rehnquist the name of his primary doctor, he could not resist a joke. "My dentist," he wheezed.

"Thanks to him, relations among the Court have been remarkably harmonious despite our different viewpoints," she said.

It was the end of an era, and everyone who had watched O'Connor shakily raise her handkerchief to wipe away tears as she stood at the top of the steps of the Supreme Court as Rehnquist's coffin carried into the rotunda knew it.

To replace O'Connor, Bush next selected his own general counsel, former personal attorney and longtime friend, Harriet Miers, who had been in charge of selecting Roberts. There were many similarities between the two women. Like O'Connor, Miers was from the Southwest, born and reared in Dallas. She had been a pioneer and trailblazer, in Bush's words, the first woman managing partner in a big Dallas law firm, the first woman president of the Dallas Bar Association, and the first woman president of the Texas Bar Association. And, as happened to O'Connor, there was consternation among conservatives—would Miers be conservative enough to change the Court? What were her personal views on abortion? How had she, in charge of picking the next justice, become the one chosen? Never married, Miers was fiercely devoted to her work. Like O'Connor, she, too, was athletic, a vigorous tennis player, often joining the president as he jogged or cleared brush from his ranch. Inevitably, her selection raised the charge of "cronyism," which had not happened to O'Connor, who had briefly met Reagan once before he interviewed her to be on the Supreme Court, and he didn't remember meeting her. Miers was an evangelical Christian, completely loyal to the president. He told conservatives, in effect, to trust him—he knew she would not change (become more moderate) over the years.

As the debate raged, O'Connor stoically again took her seat on the nation's highest bench for more arguments. True to form, her old zest was back as she plunged into questioning during arguments on Oregon's law permitting doctor-assisted suicide, twice endorsed by Oregon voters but under attack by the U.S. government as violating federal drug laws. O'Connor at once challenged Solicitor General Paul Clement, asking if federal drug laws also prevented doctors from participating in the execution of murderers. She seemed ready to let Oregonians decide whether to permit dying patients to obtain lethal doses of medication from their doctors.

But it was time for someone else to make life-and-death decisions for the nation. She was ready for her successor to take over. The trailblazing modern-day pioneer who had nervously stormed the East twenty-four years earlier was ready to venture back to the West. She had mastered the art of balancing children, husband and, in her no-nonsense but ever civil way, the pursuit of justice. Now, at long last, she looked forward to some Miller time, eager to plunge into the next chapter in her full and remarkable life.

Bibliography

Abraham, Henry J. *Justices and Presidents: A Political History of Appointments to the Supreme Court.* New York: Oxford University Press, 1985.

Baum, Lawrence. *The Supreme Court.* 7th ed. Washington, D.C.: CQ Press, 2001.

Biskupic, Joan, and Elder Witt. *The Supreme Court and the Powers of American Government.* Washington, D.C.: Congressional Quarterly Books, 1997.

———. *The Supreme Court at Work.* 2nd ed. Washington, D.C.: Congressional Quarterly Books, 1997.

Cooper, Philip J. *Battles on the Bench: Conflict Inside the Supreme Court.* Lawrence: University Press of Kansas, 1995.

Cushman, Clare, ed. *The Supreme Court Justices: Illustrated Biographies, 1789–1993.* Washington, D.C.: Congressional Quarterly Books, 1993.

Dean, John W. *The Rehnquist Choice: The Untold Story of the Nixon Appointment That Redefined the Supreme Court.* New York: The Free Press, 2001.

Dershowitz, Alan M. *Supreme Injustice: How the High Court Hijacked Election 2000.* New York: Oxford University Press, 2001.

Dover, Edwin D. *The Disputed Presidential Election of 2000.* Westport, CT: Greenwood Press, 2003.

Epstein, Lee, and Jack Knight. *The Choices Justices Make.* Washington, D.C.: Congressional Quarterly Books, 1998.

Epstein, Lita. *The Complete Idiot's Guide to the Supreme Court.* Indianapolis, IN: J. D. Alpha, 2004.

Friedman, Lawrence M. *American Law in the Twentieth Century.* New Haven: Yale University Press, 2002.

Friedman, Leon, and Fred L. Israel, eds. *The Justices of the U.S. Supreme Court: Their Lives and Major Opinions.* Vol. 5. New York: Chelsea House Publishers, 1997.

Garbus, Martin. *Courting Disaster: The Supreme Court and the Unmaking of American Law.* New York: Henry Holt and Company, 2002.
Gillman, Howard. *The Votes That Counted: How the Court Decided the 2000 Presidential Election.* Chicago: University of Chicago Press, 2001.
Gottfried, Ted. *Capital Punishment: The Death Penalty Debate.* Berkeley Heights, NJ: Enslow Publishers, 1997.
Greenfield, Jeff. *Oh, Waiter! One Order of Crow! Inside the Strangest Presidential Election Finish in American History.* New York: G. P. Putnam's Sons, 2001.
Hall, Kermit L., ed. *The Oxford Guide to United States Supreme Court Decisions.* New York: Oxford University Press, 1999.
Harrison, Maureen, and Steve Gilbert, eds. *Death Penalty Decisions of the United States Supreme Court.* Carlsbad, CA: Excellent Books, 2003.
Herda, D. J. *Furman v. Georgia: The Death Penalty Case.* Hillside, NJ: Enslow Publishers, 1994.
Kaplan, David A. *The Accidental President: How 413 Lawyers, 9 Supreme Court Justices and 5,963,110 Floridians (Give or Take a Few) Landed George W. Bush in the White House.* New York: William Morrow, 2001.
Lazarus, Edward. *Closed Chambers: The First Eyewitness Account of the Epic Struggle Inside the Supreme Court.* New York: Random House, 1998.
Maveety, Nancy. *Justice Sandra Day O'Connor: Strategist on the Supreme Court.* Lanham, MD: Rowman and Littlefield, 1996.
Merzer, Martin, and the staff of the *Miami Herald. The* Miami Herald *Report: Democracy Held Hostage.* New York: St. Martin's Press, 2001.
Murdoch, Joyce, and Deb Price. *Courting Justice: Gay Men and Lesbians v. the Supreme Court.* New York: Basic Books, 2001.
O'Connor, Sandra Day. *The Majesty of the Law: Reflections of a Supreme Court Justice.* New York: Random House, 2003.
O'Connor, Sandra Day, and H. Alan Day. *Lazy B: Growing Up on a Cattle Ranch in the American Southwest.* New York: Random House, 2002.
Paddock, Lisa. *Supreme Court for Dummies.* Indianapolis, IN: Wiley Publishing, 2002.
Political staff of the *Washington Post. Deadlock: The Inside Story of America's Closest Election.* New York: Public Affairs, 2001.
Rehnquist, William H. *The Supreme Court.* Rev. ed. New York: Knopf, 2001.
Rimm, Sylvia. *How Jane Won: Fifty-five Successful Women Share How They Grew from Ordinary Girls to Extraordinary Women.* New York: Crown, 2001.
Scalia, Antonin. *A Matter of Interpretation: Federal Courts and the Law.* Princeton, NJ: Princeton University Press, 1997.
Schwartz, Herman, ed. *The Rehnquist Court: Judicial Activism on the Right.* New York: Hill and Wang, 2002.
Simon, Roger. *Divided We Stand: How Al Gore Beat George Bush and Lost the Presidency.* New York: Crown Publishers, 2001.
Starr, Kenneth W. *First Among Equals: The Supreme Court in American Life.* New York: Warner Books, 2002.

Index